# Farming and the Law

# Farming and the Law

By

**Karen Walsh**

B.Comm, Dip. TEP, Commissioner for Oaths

**Published by**
Clarus Press Ltd,
Griffith Campus,
South Circular Road,
Dublin 8.

Reprinted 2022.

**Typeset by**
Datapage International,
Dublin 3

**Printed by**
SprintPrint
Dublin
Ireland

**ISBN**
978-1-905536-86-3

Disclaimer
Whilst every effort has been made to ensure that the contents of this book are accurate, neither the publisher nor author can accept responsibility for any errors or omissions or loss occasioned to any person acting or refraining from acting as result of any material in this publication.

For my parents and my dear friend Michael.

# Foreword

The August Bank Holiday weekend brought the usual mix of weather to the Uíbh Ráthach Peninsula, driving rain, and Coomakista enveloped in rolling sea mist and fog. While in this holiday idyll I heard the "Morning Ireland" segment on the proposed change to the start of the hedge cutting season, from 1 September to 1 August. Contributors from the IFA and BirdWatch Ireland argued the pros and cons. Any such extension required Ministerial supervision, a two-year pilot programme and an end-of-extension audit! The topic had particular resonance here, where bye roads are often challenged with flowers of fuschia and ditches of hanging fern and hogweed. It just goes to show that farming and the law has a far reaching scope.

To move to a more serious topic of farm safety, 18 people died in farm accidents in 2015. Imagine the devastation and heartache behind that statistic. I am aware that there are many different events involved, everything from driving machinery, working with loads, management of stock and, indeed, storage of chemical and bio-chemical products. All of these increasingly demanding tasks are usually being undertaken by sole practitioners under time constraints.

While there is no doubt that a great deal of awareness has been raised on farm safety to date, I do not believe that we have a properly developed safety culture on farms. If health and safety is viewed as just a legal obligation, then health and safety becomes about compliance, rather than a conscious decision to do things in the best way to protect everyone's well-being. More work has yet to be done to ensure that people view farm safety as an investment rather than a cost, and an ongoing process that can always be improved.

Since 2008 there have been a worrying number of animal welfare cases before the courts. The recession, together with a number of harsh winters, may contribute to, but not entirely explain, this phenomenon. Very often, those involved are socially isolated persons with mental health challenges, but trying to resolve these cases in a fair and just way is not easy.

All of the foregoing brings me to Karen Walsh's welcome publication, dealing as it does with the legal framework to farming endeavours. This book *will* provide an ideal handbook for the legal practitioner and the general public alike. Ms. Walsh writes in an authoritative, yet informative way. The information is professional, well researched, and her writing style clear.

The range of topics covered is prodigious. Chapters include, Wills, Administering an Estate and Enduring Powers of Attorney, Planning, Land Leasing, Collaborative Farming, Solar Farms and Wind Farms and Transferring the Family Farm. Each topic has a definite relevance to farming and should be fully understood by the farmer. Within these covers there is a comprehensive reference point for the multitude of questions which arise at various stages in the farming endeavour.

This book should prove an invaluable reference point for farming organisations. The perennial discussions on public liability and occupier's liability can be informed by reference to the legal framework pertaining, and which is so well covered here.

Karen Walsh puts her own farming background, together with her experience of working in a busy solicitor's office, to very good effect in the writing of this book.

Guím gach ráth ar a saothar.

Judge Seán Ó Donnabháin
August 2016

# Preface

I commenced the journey of writing this book as someone from a farming background with an interest in law, not as a lawyer with an interest in farming. I became interested in this area of law as farming has become increasingly complex. Farmers now work in a highly-regulated environment. Farming is, and always has been, crucial to Ireland's economy and has changed significantly over the years. It is constantly evolving and farmers are continually challenged to keep up with developments that alter an already bewildering variety of laws and requirements. In a short space of time, farming has become much more bureaucratic and legalistic. I believe that if farmers and landowners are fully informed of all the laws and regulations that are relevant to them, they will be in a much stronger position to make well-informed, effective decisions regarding their businesses.

As I learned the principles of law in college, and became familiar with headline making issues in relation to farming, I considered how those principles could apply to farmers. I began to make notes, identifying the issues and areas of the law relevant to farmers in the twenty first century. When I commenced writing for various weekly publications it became very clear to me that there was a huge need and appetite among farmers in Ireland to become more aware of the legal issues involved in their day to day farming lives. I also felt it was necessary that farmers and landowners should have access to a legal service that would be tailored to suit their particular needs, requirements and farming businesses. This book is the result of my original notes, my own experiences and dealings with farmers and landowners over the years, as well as much additional hard work and research carried out over many years. The law can be an intimidating topic, and farmers make no secret of feeling overwhelmed and increasingly encumbered by legal requirements. The primary purpose of this book is to better inform farmers and landowners for decisions they make every day. I have tried to explain what the law requires of farmers, and not to comment on how well it does so.

A number of people helped me in the writing of this book, some directly, others indirectly, but all significantly. I am especially indebted to Daniel V Sheehan, Solicitor, of Walsh and Partners, for his valuable discussion, opinions and boundless generosity. His assistance made the task so much easier. I am especially thankful to all my staff at Walsh and Partners Solicitors for their support.

I would like to thank my friend and colleague Fachtna McCarthy, a retired solicitor from Clonakilty and my friend and colleague Harold Brooks BL for their invaluable assistance and advices. I also wish to acknowledge my colleague Michael McGrath BL, MCI Arb. for his invaluable expertise and contribution, in particular in relation to planning law. I am extremely grateful to Denis Collins BL, who brought together some of the background material, who was immeasurably helpful.

I would also like to thank a number of people who assisted me by reading the drafts of the book and for their invaluable feedback; Cian Cotter BL, Thomas Curran Farm Structures Specialist Teagasc, Denise Fitzgerald, Gary Hayes BL, Siobhan Lankford BL, Donnchadh McCarthy BL, Deirdre O'Callaghan BL, David O' Dwyer BL, Patrick O'Riordan BL, Roger Pope BL and Cara Jane Walsh BL.

I would like to thank Judge Seán Ó Donnabháin for writing the foreword.

Last, but not least, I would also like to express my gratitude to the team at Clarus Press, led by David McCartney, for the support and guidance I received.

Finally, the law relating to farming in Ireland is constantly changing. One should never rely on the contents of this book without referring to up-to-date legislation, including tax legislation, which changes on a regular basis. I have strived to present the law in Ireland as it stood on the 20 September 2016. This book does not claim to exhaustively discuss all topics or to be a substitute for specific legal advice, hence, every reader should always consult a solicitor in relation to his/her particular set of circumstances.

Karen Walsh
20 September 2016

# About the Author

Karen Walsh is from a farming background in Grenagh, Co. Cork. She was raised on a farm that has been in her family for generations. She is the principal of Walsh & Partners, with offices in Dublin and Cork.

She takes an active interest in farming related issues. She is a popular newspaper columnist and television and radio guest.

Walsh and Partners practice in all areas of law including:

- Civil Litigation
- Solar Farms and Wind Farms
- Medical Negligence
- Agricultural Law
- Conveyancing
- Family Law & Child Law
- Wills and Probate
- Land Law
- Debt Collection
- Commercial Law
- Personal Injuries/ Compensation Claims
- Employment Law
- Professional Negligence
- Property Disputes
- Landlord and Tenant Law

If you would like to contact Karen Walsh she can be contacted at her offices in Dublin or Cork.

Dublin
Walsh & Partners
Unit 7A Block E, Nutgrove Office Park,
Rathfarnham, Dublin 14
Tel: (01) 291 0300
Email: info@walshandpartners.ie

Cork
Walsh & Partners
17 South Mall, Cork
Tel: (021) 427 0200
Email: info@walshandpartners.ie

Please also see www.walshandpartners.ie for further information.

# Table of Content

# CHAPTER ONE

# Property Law

Irish people have a greater attachment to the land than most other nationalities. Our long affection for, and obsession with land, and involvement with boundary and other land disputes, have been regularly depicted over the years in literature, theatre and film, most famously in the 1990 film based on John B. Keane's play, *The Field*.[1] Recent anecdotal evidence has shown that property boundary disputes have increased over the past number of years.[2] Irish people value land for a variety of reasons, most notably, social, economic and spiritual reasons. Land constitutes more than just a source of livelihood to many people. Rather, it forms part of a person's identity, culture, values and standing in the community.

This chapter examines the different land registration systems in Ireland. It also discusses adverse possession (more commonly known as squatting), and it provides an overview of the complex law on easements, such as rights of way. It emphasises the areas that farmers need to be aware of when buying agricultural land, and, in particular, when doing so at auction. The chapter also provides an overview of the complicated area of compulsory purchase orders (CPOs). It concludes by discussing boundary disputes.

## Registration of Title

The Property Registration Authority (PRA) is an independent statutory body now responsible for the control and management of both the Land Registry and the Registry of Deeds, discussed in detail below. These two systems, which deal respectively with the registration of title and the registration of deeds, are now governed by the Registration of Deeds and Title

---

[1] "The Field" John B. Keane (1965).

[2] O'Brien, D., Prendergast, W.: Why are Property Boundary Disputes increasing in Ireland? International Postgraduate Research Conference, University of Salford, Manchester, April 8th–10th, 2013.

Acts 1964 and 2006, the Registration of Title Rules 2012 to 2013, and the Registration of Deeds Rules 2008 to 2013.[3]

## Land Registry[4]

Land Registry is a registration of title system[5] that provides State-guaranteed title to property.[6] The title is registered in the Land Registry, with each registered property allocated its own separate folio number. Lands registered in the Land Registry are referred to as 'registered land'. It is a public system, and members of the public have an absolute right to inspect any title registered in the Land Registry office.[7]

In 2005, the Land Registry announced that all existing paper-based maps would be converted into electronic format over a five-year period, as part of the Digital Mapping Project. In 2010, the project was completed, with maps for all 26 counties fully digitised. The Digital Mapping Project now provides easy access to data. However, the maps must still be checked on the ground by a competent engineer or surveyor to verify their accuracy, as no guarantee of accuracy is offered by the Land Registry.

Subject to what has just been noted about the accuracy of maps, the title shown on the folio is guaranteed by the State,[8] which is bound to indemnify any person who suffers loss through a mistake made by the Land Registry.[9] Again, it is important to note that the Land Registry map identifies properties, not boundaries, and it is specifically provided that "the description of land in a register nor its identification by reference to a registry map is conclusive as to its boundaries or extent".[10]

---

[3] Registration of Deeds Rules 2008, SI No 52 of 2008; Registration of Deeds Rules 2009, SI No 350 of 2009; Registration of Deeds (No. 2) Rules 2009, SI No 457 of 2009; and Registration of Deeds Rules 2013, SI No 387 of 2013.

[4] For more information, see Property Registration Authority, 'Land Registry Services' <www.prai.ie/land-registry-services/> accessed 30 July 2016.

[5] Registration of Title Act 1964, s 8.

[6] ibid, s 31.

[7] http://www.prai.ie/land-registry-services/.

[8] Registration of Title Act 1964, s 31.

[9] http://www.prai.ie/land-registry-services/.

[10] Registration of Title Act 1964 s 85 as amended by Registration of Deeds and Title Act 2006, s 62.

A folio and filed plan (or map) is the title document issued by the Land Registry in respect of every registered property. Any person can inspect a folio and filed plan on payment of a prescribed fee to the Land Registry. The filed plan shows the area of the land attached to the folio.

## Registry of Deeds

There is still a considerable amount of property in Ireland that is not registered in the Land Registry. Such property is generally then registered in the alternative system, known as the Registry of Deeds[11]. Land registered in the Registry of Deeds is referred to as 'unregistered land'. The Registry of Deeds system records the priority of registered deeds not recorded in the Land Registry. The Registry of Deeds gives priority to a registered deed over unregistered and subsequent deeds.[12] The Registry of Deeds does not record official ownership of property. It records the existence of a deed in relation to particular land and a particular transaction.[13] The Registry of Deeds does not guarantee title. Even defective deeds can be registered in the Registry of Deeds. Thus, it is very limited in its usefulness.

## Compulsory First Registration

Some 93% of the total land mass of the State, and almost 90% of the legal titles in Ireland, are now registered in the Land Registry.[14] It is now compulsory to register Registry of Deeds titles in the Land Registry in Ireland.[15] The requirement to register arises upon sale, with the obligation to register being placed on the purchaser.

---

[11] Registration of Deeds and Title Act 2006, s 33.

[12] ibid, s 38.

[13] ibid, s 35(1).

[14] Property Registration Authority, 'Land Registry Services' (<www.prai.ie/land-registry-services/> accessed 30 July 2016.

[15] SI No 87 of 1969 – Compulsory Registration of Ownership (Carlow, Laois, Meath) Order 1969, SI No 605 of 2005 – Registration of Title Act 1964 (Compulsory Registration of Ownership) (Longford, Roscommon and Westmeath) Order 2005, S.I. 81 of 2008 Registration of Title Act, 1964 (Compulsory Registration of Ownership) (Clare, Kilkenny, Louth, Sligo, Wexford, and Wicklow) Order 2008, SI No 176 of 2009 Registration of Title Act 1964 (Compulsory Registration of Ownership) (Cavan, Donegal, Galway, Kerry, Kildare, Leitrim, Limerick, Mayo, Monaghan, North Tipperary, Offaly, South Tipperary and Waterford) Order 2009 and SI No 516 of 2010 Registration of Title Act 1964 (Compulsory Registration of Ownership) (Cork and Dublin) Order 2010.

## Adverse Possession

Adverse possession, or, as it is more commonly known, squatting, allows a third party to claim a right over land which is owned by another person, on the basis that he or she has occupied the land continuously for a specific period of time, with the intention of excluding all others, including the true owner. This procedure has often been used to rectify potential or actual defects on title. Essentially, a squatter is someone in possession of land inconsistent with the title of the true owner.

The traditional view of a squatter is that of a land thief who sees an opportunity to occupy unused lands. In reality, however, the most common form of squatting arises where encroachers, often inadvertently, assume ownership of parts of neighbouring land because there are no clear physical boundaries, or the maps on title are inadequate or inaccurate. In Ireland, there has always been a high incidence of adverse possession in the case of intestate deaths (where there was no valid will) of property owners, especially farmers.

### Requirements for Adverse Possession

Each case is examined on its own facts and circumstances. The onus is on the claimant to show that he or she has established adverse possession:

- The claimant making the claim must be in sole and exclusive occupation and possession of the land for 12 years or more. Section 13(2)(a) of the Statute of Limitations 1957 lays down the 12-year rule. The 12-year rule relates to an adverse possession claim against privately owned land. However, the period is extended to 30 years for land owned by a State authority.[16] Because claims in respect of State property are very rare, for the purposes of this chapter, the time period referred to will be 12 years i.e. an adverse possession claim against privately owned land;
- The person making the claim must exclude all others, including the owner, from the land for a minimum of 12 years. The claim must be established by physically occupying the land continuously in a manner that is inconsistent with the title of the owner. There must be an intention to dispossess the true owner. This is known as 'animus possidendi'. If the owner still uses the land occasionally, the claimant is not using it exclusively, and the claim will fail. The question of

---

[16] Statute of Limitations 1957, s 13(1)(a).

what acts constitute physical and continuous occupation depends on the circumstances, the nature of the land and the manner in which that land is commonly enjoyed or used;

• The acts relied upon by the squatter must be so definite and positive that they leave no doubt in the mind of the landowner that occupation adverse to his or her title is taking place. Small acts or acts that take place now and again will not be sufficient to oust the original owner, for example, the occasional grazing of cattle owned by the claimant on the land. Examples of actual and exclusive use of land would be the construction of a house or the erection of a fence.

## Case

In a High Court case of *Dunne v Iarnrod Éireann*,[17] the court took the view that the following two matters should be examined in particular when determining if adverse possession existed:

• Whether or not there is a continuous period of twelve years in which the squatter is in exclusive possession of the property to the extent sufficient to establish an intention to possess; and
• Whether or not the period of possession was broken by any act of possession by the owner of the land.

The court held that the latter point allowed a low threshold for the landowner to establish possession and stop the clock from running on the adverse possession. Certain acts of possession by the landowner would break a claimant's possession. In that particular case, the owner carried out works to part of the property being claimed by the squatter.

If the claimant is successful, the claimant is entitled to become the owner of the land in question. The previous owner is ousted and the claimant gains the title to the land. Again, whether a person is successful in a claim for adverse possession depends on the facts and circumstances of each individual case. All conditions must be satisfied.

## Protecting Against a Claim for Adverse Possession

As can be seen from the decision in the *Dunne* case,[18] the threshold of proof for a landowner who seeks to regain possession of his or her lands

---

[17] *Dunne v Iarnród Éireann* [2007] IEHC 314.
[18] [2007] IEHC 314.

is relatively low. However, it is important that a landowner is not careless, and that he or she makes it known to whom the property belongs.

In the case of farmland, it is advisable that a farmer inspects his or her land regularly. If the owner is away for long periods of time, he or she should appoint someone to inspect the lands to ensure that no third party is in occupation. It is prudent to look for signs of entry or use, such as new fences having been erected, animals grazing, or crops planted. If there is such evidence, the identity of the person must be ascertained immediately and legal advice sought as to how to remove him or her from the property. Instituting legal proceedings against the trespasser will "stop the clock running" on the adverse possession. The landowner should also exercise some act of ownership over the property in the interim, for example, erecting fences or buildings, or placing animals on the land. Another potential option available to the farmer is to procure, from the person in possession (squatting), an agreement, signed by him or her, to rent the land at a certain figure (which could be nominal) and for a certain period, or alternatively, simply acknowledging that he or she is present on the land with the owner's permission. If such an agreement is signed, then the person in possession cannot bring a successful adverse possession claim.

It must be emphasised that a landowner cannot afford to be complacent, and must act promptly. The adverse possession clock only stops when legal proceedings are instituted, not when a call is made to a solicitor for legal advice.

### Claiming of Adverse Possession

The procedure for making an adverse possession claim is governed by the Registration of Title Act 1964 (hereafter 'the 1964 Act'). An application is made under s 49 of the 1964 Act, and the applicant must swear an affidavit setting out all the facts regarding the taking of possession and the precise use to which the property has been put since possession commenced. The application is lodged in the Land Registry.

It is worth reiterating that the applicant making the claim must have been in sole and exclusive occupation and possession of the land for 12 years or more to the exclusion of all others, including the owner.

A lengthy and detailed affidavit[19] must be prepared, setting out the history of the squatting and showing indisputable evidence that the squatter is now entitled to the property. The affidavit should be comprehensive and should include details of when the applicant entered into possession, the uses made of the property, and it should set out fully the acts of possession. In addition, it should trace the title to the property from the registered owner against whom title is being claimed up to the date of swearing the affidavit. It should state the names and addresses of all persons whom the claimant claims to have barred. All available evidence of the claim must be lodged in the Land Registry. In addition, a map of the property must be lodged if the claim relates to part only of a folio, or where the property is not already registered in the Land Registry.

When an application for ownership by a squatter is filed in the Land Registry, notices are usually then served on the following persons:

- Current registered owner(s);
- Personal representative of a deceased registered owner, and immediate next of kin if the registered owner died intestate (without leaving a valid will); and
- Adjoining landowners and/or occupiers.

The service of these notices by the Land Registry puts those likely to have grounds for objection on notice of the application, giving them the opportunity to object. Objections, whether or not they are merited, will delay the application. A successful objection will result in the claim being rejected.

All applications must be accompanied by a clearance certificate under s 62 of the Capital Acquisitions Tax Consolidation Act 2003. This is a statutory requirement. The application to the Revenue Commissioners for this certificate puts the Revenue Commissioners on notice of the application and affords them the opportunity to investigate the facts in order to ascertain if the process is being used in such a manner as to avoid payment of any taxes. This might arise if there was collusion between the registered owner and the applicant, and the application was being used as a means of avoiding the taxes which might otherwise be payable on a standard transfer of ownership.

---

[19] Land Registry Form 5 or Form 6.

Each application for title based on adverse possession will be considered on its own merits. No two cases are the same.

Where the Property Registration Authority is not satisfied that the claimant has acquired title, an order refusing registration will be made. This may arise because of a flaw in the application or proofs presented. However, refusals usually occur when there is an objection, and conflicting claims are made to the property. Where conflicting claims are made, it is not the function of the Property Registration Authority to make a determination. The matter must be determined by the Circuit Court. An order of refusal may be appealed to the courts under s 19(1) of the 1964 Act. However, in practice, applicants usually do not appeal these decisions. Instead, they bring equity proceedings in court, seeking declarations in relation to the title of the property.

## Easements

The law relating to easements is very complicated, and has changed significantly in recent years. This section is designed to provide the reader with a solid grasp of the basics, so as to allow him or her to be aware of the issues. It is critical that legal advice is sought in relation to the individual circumstances and title.

An easement is a right which accrues to an individual by reason of his ownership of land and it permits that individual to perform some act on the land of a neighbouring landowner which, in other circumstances, would amount to trespass.

A good example of an easement is a private right of way. Other common examples of easements are a right to light or a right of support.

It should be noted that an easement attaches to land. This means that, when the land is passed on to a successor in title, the easement passes with the land. An easement cannot be sold without the land attaching to it.

An easement exists for the benefit of one property (the 'dominant lands') over another property (the 'servient lands'). In the case of a right of way, the servient lands are the route or the 'way', often a track, lane or roadway.

An express easement is an easement documented by way of express grant in writing.

## Profits à Prendre

'Profit à prendre'[20] means 'right of taking'. It refers to non-possessory interests in land, similar to an easement, which gives the holder the right to take natural resources, such as minerals, timber, and wild game, from the land of another. It is, in essence, a right to take from another's land, something that is part of the soil, or is on the soil, and is the property of the landowner. A common example of a profit à prendre in rural Ireland is that of turbary, which is a right to cut and take turf off the land of another, though many of these rights are now restricted by EU Habitat Directives.[21] Another common example is that of fishing rights, which are frequently a cause of difficulty and litigation.

An essential element of a profit à prendre is an implied easement to enter on to another's land for the purposes of taking the resources permitted by the particular prendre.

## Characteristics of a Profit à Prendre

To be classified as a profit à prendre, it must satisfy the following:

1. It can be attached to land;
2. It must be connected to land and improve its amenity, utility or convenience;
3. It involves at least two plots of land;
4. The plots of land must be owned by different landowners; and
5. Unlike an easement, a profit à prendre can exist as a right in gross.[22]

## Prescription

The passing into law of the Land and Conveyancing Law Reform Act 2009 (hereafter 'the 2009 Act') has introduced a number of significant reforms in the area of land law, and one of them has been an attempt to simplify the law of prescription, which is fundamental to the law of easements. The new rules are dealt with in more detail later in this chapter. Previously, the acquisition of an easement through prescription arose in one of three ways, namely, prescription by common law, prescription under the doctrine of lost modern

---

[20] The term originates in Middle French, a historical division of the French language that covers the period from the 14th to the early 17th centuries.

[21] Council Directive 92/43/EEC.

[22] Meaning it need not be attached to land.

grant and prescription under the Prescription Act 1832 (hereafter 'the 1832 Act'), which was introduced into Ireland under the Prescription (Ireland) Act 1858 (hereafter 'the 1858 Act'). However, many of the established easements we see today were obtained under the 1832 Act.

It is very common to find, especially in the case of rural land, that, although a right of way has been used for a very long time, it may never have been registered as a burden on the folio containing the servient lands, nor been granted under a deed or document. In most cases it may simply have arisen as a result of long user of the right in question over many years. If a dispute arose, a court order might have been sought, and granted, declaring that such right of way existed, based on the provisions of the 1832 Act. The 1832 Act provided for two periods of user for a right of way — a minimum of 20 years and the longer period of 40 years. Enjoyment of the right of way for the shorter period of 20 years could not be defeated by proof that user commenced after 1189 (the date fixed as the limit of legal memory), but could be defeated by reason of the fact that the owner of the servient land had given oral or written permission. Enjoyment for the longer period was deemed "absolute and indefeasible"[23] unless that user could be attributed to a written consent or agreement. The 1832 Act required that the user must be as of right, and it must also be *nec vi, nec clam* and *nec precario*, i.e. not by force, nor stealth, nor licence.

### The New Position

The 2009 Act changed the law in relation to prescription and, very importantly, abolished prescription at common law, prescription under the doctrine of lost modern grant and under the 1832 Act and the 1858 Act.[24] The introduction of the 2009 Act provided for a universal user period of just 12 years, thus reducing the statutory prescriptive periods of 20 and 40 years, for the establishment of an easement.

The 2009 Act introduced a transitional period of three years in order to phase out the old methods of claiming prescriptive rights, and allowing the introduction of the new method of acquisition under the 2009 Act by 1 December 2012. Unfortunately, the introduction of this transitional

---

[23] Prescription Act 1832, s 2.
[24] Land and Conveyancing Law Reform Act 2009, s 8(1).

period created a lacuna (gap or missing part) in the law, as a person was not able to rely on either the old method or the new method of acquiring prescriptive easements in the period between 2012 and 2021. However, this unintended gap in the law was rectified by the passing of the Civil Law (Miscellaneous Provisions) Act 2011, specifically s 38, which extended the application of the former methods of prescription to 30 November 2021.

The question that has caused difficulty is whether the Prescription Act 1832 has continued application during the 12-year transition (1 December 2009 to 30 November 2021). One view is that, if the old statutory user period of 20 years, under the 1832 Act, ends during the transitional period, then the easement is claimable during the transition period.[25] However, on the other hand, at least one noted academic in the area[26] is of the view that the Prescription Act 1832 does not apply during the transitional period and thus, if the 20-year user period ends during the transitional period, the user would not be able to acquire a prescriptive right, and would, essentially, have to restart the clock. This is a highly unsatisfactory situation, and the matter can only be resolved by a decision of the courts.

In relation to the new mode of acquisition of an easement under the 2009 Act, again, it is unfortunate that the law in this area offers very little clarity. One view is that the new 12-year statutory mode of prescription cannot be claimed until 2021.[27] While this is one interpretative view of the legislation, there are indications in the legislation, and consequential Land Registration Rules, that would suggest the contrary. In a conference paper delivered by Professor John Mee, the view adopted was that the new mode of acquisition under the 2009 Act can be claimed during the transitional period from 1 December 2009 to 30 November 2021.

There has been significant confusion and concern, particularly in the farming community, about the effect of s 35(1) of the 2009 Act, which provides that "An easement or profit à prendre shall be acquired at law by prescription only on registration of a court order under this section".

---

[25] JCW Wylie, *Irish Land Law* (4th edn, Bloomsbury Professional 2010) 423.

[26] J Mee (2014) Reforming the Law of Prescription: A Cautionary Tale from Ireland, *Modern Studies in Property Law*, Volume 8; pp 31–38 (Hart Publishing 2015).

[27] P Bland, 'A Hopeless Jumble: The Cursed Reform of Prescription' (2011) 16 Conveyancing and Property Law Journal 54.

There are two important points to be made about s 35(1). First, it refers to an easement claimed under the new law, the 12-year relevant user period - the first such claim cannot be made until 1 December 2021.[28] Secondly, it refers to an easement acquired "at law". In the past, if there was a claim in court to an easement (usually a right of way), and the claim succeeded, the court would declare the existence of an easement, which would then be registered as a burden on the servient lands if those lands were registered lands. However, if there was no dispute, and the dominant lands benefitted from the use of an easement for upwards of 20 years, this use would often simply be evidenced by an affidavit of the current owner stating the length and nature of use, the name and address of the owner of the servient lands and, perhaps, a description of how the use started. This was because there was no dispute and the conveyancing or legal practice was that a statement of use in a sworn document was sufficient to prove the existence of the easement, in fact or in equity. The claimant had a right in equity to the easement, even though there was no court order. The right was not established "at law" but was recognised in conveyancing practice.

### Practical Implications

The experience of lawyers, farmers and the Property Registration Authority is that the 2009 Act has radically changed conveyancing practice. Because of the reference in s 35 to an easement being acquired in law by prescription only on registration of a court order under the section, in practice, if a property is now being sold or mortgaged with the stated benefit of a right of way by long user, the purchaser's or bank's solicitors now look for more than a statutory declaration of use, something which was previously considered sufficient where the affidavit was clear and unambiguous.

Since the passing of the 2009 Act, solicitors started to insist on production of a grant of right of way in the form of a document or a declaration by a court order, and, if the servient lands were registered lands, as evidence of registration of the easement as a burden on the relevant folio. Unless the law was amended, this could have led to a large number of court applications.

---

[28] As noted previously, there are opposing views on whether the 12-year statutory mode of prescription can be claimed, and, until a court addresses this issue, it is not free from doubt.

## New Procedure

Due to the confusion created by the 2009 Act, the 2011 Act was enacted, and this provided for a new procedure to claim a prescriptive right of way, particularly in cases where there is no dispute.

This is done by way of direct application to the Property Registration Authority, without the necessity of first obtaining a court order. The current method is by application under s 49A of the 1964 Act, as amended by the 2011 Act, in Form 68 of Land Registration Rules 2012-2013. The Land Registry has also published a detailed Practice Direction about prescriptive rights of way.[29] The right to apply to court still exists, and a claimant does not have to lodge a Form 68 application in the first instance, but may often prefer to do so in the hope of avoiding the expense of the court action, in situations where there is no dispute. The Form 68 application is served on the owner of the servient lands. The Land Registry adjudicates on these applications. If the landowner disputes the facts, and registration does not proceed, the claimant can still apply to court for a declaration that the right of way exists.

If the person makes an application to court and succeeds, the court will declare that the right of way exists, will identify the route and nature of the way, and may order registration of the right as a burden on the folio, (if the title is registered in the Land Registry, as distinct from the Registry of Deeds).

While the new procedure is helpful, it is also complex, particularly if ownership of the roadway, path or other route of the right of way is divided between a number of different owners. Put simply, if a farmer travels from part of his lands to the public road through a private roadway which runs through four other farms, he or she may have to claim a right of way over four different folios. Alternatively, two adjoining farmers may own a roadway which appears to run between their lands. Inspection of the new digitalised mapping of the Land Registry may show that one half of the road is within the first farmer's folio and the other half is within the second farmer's folio. Each owns one half of the roadway and each has used the other half for upwards of 20 years. If the first farmer travels from part of his lands to the

---

[29] Property Registration Authority, 'Easements and Profits à Prendre Acquired by Prescription under Section 49A' (2013).

<www.prai.ie/registration-of-easements-and-profits-a-prendre-acquired-by-prescription-under-section-49a/> accessed 30 July 2016.

public road over a private roadway which is not registered on a folio in the Land Registry, the case presents particular challenges, which are seemingly not anticipated in the legislation, when seeking to register a right of way.

## Specific Type of Easement

### Rights of Way

Many people enjoy rights of way without ever really thinking about them. For example, a person may access his or her house or land through a neighbour's private lane or roadway.

That person does not own the private lane or roadway, it is not a public route maintained by the local authority, but he or she is entitled to use it, because he/she has a legal property right.

A right of way, in its simplest form, is a right of one person, known as the owner of the dominant tenement, to pass back and forth over the land of an adjoining landowner, known as the owner of the servient tenement.

It should be noted that, if a right of way is established for a particular purpose, it cannot normally be expanded into different or broader purposes.[30] A good example is that of a right of way acquired for travel only by foot. In the normal way, a right so acquired would not automatically carry with it the right to use vehicles. However, the purpose could be expanded over time.[31] For example, it is well established that a right of way for use by horse and cart can be extended to use by a tractor and trailer. The nature of the right of way will depend on the historic usage of the right of way.[32] In the remainder of this chapter, unless otherwise stated, the only easements that will be dealt with are rights of way.

### Right of Way by Necessity

It has long been accepted in law that, if a landowner disposes of part of his holding, and the effect of such disposal is to make the remainder of that holding landlocked, with no other means of access apart from over the lands disposed of, there is an implied right of way, by necessity, over the

---

[30] *Maguire v Browne* [1921] 1 IR 148.

[31] *Brynes & Anor v Meakstown Construction Ltd.* [2009] IEHC 123.

[32] *Maguire v Browne* [1921] 1 IR 148 at 170.

part disposed of.[33] The person who has made the disposal must choose the most convenient means of access and must then stick to that route thereafter. This is referred to as a right of way by necessity.[34] It is very important to understand that this right only assists a person who is making a disposal of part of his or her holding. The principle does not, in any way, help somebody who is foolish enough to buy a landlocked, or poorly accessed, holding.

Another important point to consider is that the nature of a prescriptive right of way is determined by the use made of the dominant lands.[35] For example, if a farmer uses an access way into his farm and farmhouse for a long period, the prescriptive right of way arising is for mixed residential and agricultural purposes. But if the user was, and is, only to access farmlands and not a residence also, the prescriptive right of way arising is confined to user for agricultural purposes, and the use of the way may not support development of a site or sites for houses on the agricultural lands. There is some authority for the proposition that a right of way for agricultural purposes may be enlarged to a right of access in respect of one's private dwelling house.[36] However, the law is unclear, and great caution should always be exercised before buying a property where the extent and nature of the right of way is not absolutely clear. What is absolutely clear is that the owner of the dominant holding is not entitled to unreasonably increase the burden of the right of way.[37] For example, a right of way in respect of access for one private dwelling could not be enlarged to allow access for a commercial development or an estate of houses. Legal advice should always be sought.

Essentially, the effect of the 2009 Act is that a right of way arising by user or implication (e.g. necessity) can be lost by 12 years' non-user,[38] and this is a further incentive to have a right of way declared in court, registered on foot of Form 68, or granted in a document. This position represents a significant change to the old common law position, which was that a right of way could only be lost by a minimum of 20 years' non-user, coupled with

---

[33] Land and Conveyancing Law Reform Act 2009, s 40(2).

[34] Land and Conveyancing Law Reform Act 2009, s 40(2).

[35] *Maguire v Browne* [1921] 1 IR 148.

[36] *Carroll v Sheridan and Sheehan* [1984] ILRM 451.

[37] *Barrett v Linnane*, unreported, High Court, 20 March 2002.

[38] Land and Conveyancing Law Reform Act 2009, s 39(1).

a clear intention of abandonment, such as failure to object to the erection of an obstruction across the right of way in question.

The law in relation to prescriptive easements has been, and continues to be, difficult for lawyers and lay people alike, and it has been a source of much litigation in Ireland. There are still many properties accessed by old country roads or lanes which have not been taken in charge. The best advice that can be given to any property owner who is gaining access to all or part of his or her property by means of such a roadway or track, where the use is not declared by court order and is not registered as a burden or set out in a document of grant, is to take legal advice about the particular case. The issues arising can vary depending on the nature and history of the route, the number of other landowners involved, their title, how the use of the way commenced and the transactions which the property owner may enter into in the future.

It is strongly advised that any person who enjoys the benefit of a right of way should register that right well in advance of the deadline set out in the 2009 Act. Apart from the time required to prepare the necessary map and the application, additional time may be required if a court order must be obtained. One cannot necessarily assume that the landowner over whose property the right is enjoyed will consent to the application. Even if there is no dispute, the existence of an unregistered right of way, claimed on foot of long user, could delay a mortgage, sale or gift of all or part of property for the benefit of which the prescriptive right of way is claimed.

The best advice that can be given to any farmer who is accessing all or part of his or her property by a roadway or track, where the right of way is not registered on title, is to consult a solicitor.

### Preventing a Right of Way Coming into Being

(i) Approach the person utilising the piece of ground as a way in an amicable manner and request that he/she stop doing so;

(ii) If the request is not acted upon, fence off the access route;

(iii) Erect an appropriate sign if necessary;

(iv) Instruct a solicitor. It may be necessary to write to the user informing him or her that the use amounts to a trespass, and that, if he or she does not stop immediately, court proceedings will issue;

(v) If damage has been caused to the land by the trespasser, inform An Garda Síochána immediately.

## Summary

In a situation where a farmer or other property owner enjoys a right of way over another landowner's land, there are three options available to him or her in order to protect such right:

1.    Approach the landowner and ascertain whether he or she would be willing to sign a deed of easement to formally recognise the right, and then, once signed, register it in the Property Registration Authority (Land Registry or Registry of Deeds);
2.    Apply to the Land Registry pursuant to s 49A of the 1964 Act; or
3.    Where agreement cannot be reached with the landowner, apply to court, and, following a successful court application, register the court order in the Property Registration Authority (Land Registry or Registry of Deeds).

## Purchasing Agricultural Land

Buying agricultural land is probably the most expensive purchase a farmer will ever make. When purchasing property, one enters into a contract for sale. The concept of a contract lies at the heart of everyday business, and is the method by which all business, from the simplest to the most complex, is done.

In the context of acquiring property, a contract for sale is a legal agreement for the exchange of two items. The first is the property in sale and the second is the consideration, usually in the form of money that is paid as the purchase price. To be legally binding, a contract must have two essential components:

1.    Agreement; and
2.    Consideration.[39]

Normally, once a contract for sale has been signed by the vendor and the purchaser and a full deposit is paid, a legally binding contract comes into being. In some cases, there may be conditions inserted into the contract for sale so that it is only when the conditions are fulfilled, that a legally

---

[39] Consideration is the ingredient that makes a contract enforceable. In *Currie v Misa* (1875) LR 10 Ex 153, the court defined consideration as "... some right, interest, profit or benefit accruing to one party, or some forbearance, detriment, loss or responsibility, given, suffered or undertaken by the other".

binding contract comes into existence. An example of such a condition would be a purchase that is conditional upon the granting of a full grant of planning permission by the local authority.

Before signing a contract for sale, it is very important that a purchaser instructs a competent engineer to:

- Prepare a building condition report of the buildings on the land holding, including utilities, such as water, sewer, electricity, gas etc.;
- Prepare a structural survey of the property to ensure the structural integrity of the buildings on the land;
- Carry out a boundary inspection to ensure that the acreage of the land on the ground corresponds with the map attached to the contract for sale;
- Ensure the septic tank is registered and that it was certified by a competent engineer during its installation;
- Ensure compliance with planning permission and building regulations, and that a full planning search is carried out; and
- Ensure the buildings have Building Energy Rating (BER) certificates to provide information in relation to the energy efficiency of the buildings.

If obtaining a loan and charging or mortgaging the lands in favour of a financial institution, it will be necessary to produce evidence that the buildings, if any, on the land being given as security, have the benefit of full planning permission and are in compliance with any planning permission granted. It will also be necessary to ensure that the maps of the lands are in order.

A common cause of delay in such transactions is where the life assurance or fire insurance has not been put in place in time. Failure to arrange such matters as life policies, direct debit mandates, engineer's reports, buildings insurance etc., as required by the financial institution, can often cause delays in completing a lending transaction.

To draw down the loan cheque, mortgage protection insurance must usually be put in place. Securing this may take longer than expected, particularly if the borrower has had previous health issues. On rare occasions, financial institutions may waive this requirement.

If a borrower is giving part only of a holding as security, a map may need to be prepared by a competent engineer, marking out the property to be charged or mortgaged.

If a farmer is considering making a gift of, or selling, a site at a later stage, it is important that he or she does not mortgage these lands, as it will not be possible to gift or sell the lands in question without the written consent of the bank.

It is always important to consider the future, including family members' future requirements and plans, such as a child with ambitions of building a house on the land.

If access to the lands is gained by means of a right of way over a neighbour's lands, a deed of right of way must be put in place, or, as noted already, a court order obtained to confirm the existence of the right of way. Alternatively, one may enjoy access to a well and water supply which is located on a neighbour's land. In this situation, a document known as a deed of wayleave must be put in place to formalise the arrangement as it exists on the ground.

## Case

The High Court decision in *Byrnes & Nealon v Meakstown Construction Ltd*[40] shows the potential complexities arising in the sale of a property if a deed of right of way is not in existence. In that case, the purchasers agreed to purchase an apartment for €330,000, subject to contract and good marketable title. The issue that arose pertained to a right of way over county council lands from a roadway to the land upon which the property was located, as the site did not have direct access to the public road. The vendor eventually produced a deed of grant of right of way from the county council in which the council consented to the registration of the deed as a burden on the land. The purchasers took the view that the granting of a right of way by the county council required a resolution of the council which had not been obtained. The High Court held that the deed of grant of right of way and the council's assent to the registration of the deed as a burden on the land gave the purchasers the assurance they needed that they had a sufficient right of way and that this would be registered as a burden. As a result, the High Court found that the purchasers were not entitled to rescind the contract for sale.

---

[40] *Byrnes & Nealon v Meakstown Construction Ltd* [2009] IEHC 123.

In addition to the borrower entering into a deed of charge, it is common that a lender may also insist upon a guarantee by a third party to be answerable for the default of another. In this instance, it is vitally important that the proposed guarantor obtains independent legal advice in relation to the nature and effect of giving the guarantee.

Solicitors are prohibited from acting on behalf of both a borrower and a lender in a commercial property transaction, because of the inherent conflict of interest.[41] Accordingly, the bank will appoint its own solicitor to represent its interest in the transaction. The borrower will also need to appoint his or her own solicitor. The borrower may also be responsible for the bank's solicitor's fees. It is important to check this in advance with the financial institution.

It is important to factor into the budget any stamp duty, legal and Land Registry fees payable in order to complete the purchase.

Following signing by the purchaser of the purchase deed, his or her solicitor will proceed to stamp it with the Revenue Commissioners, and then register it in the Land Registry or Registry of Deeds. The current rates of stamp duty are 2% of the purchase price of non-residential land and 1% of the purchase price on residential property (on property with a value of up to €1 million) and 2% on consideration above that amount.[42] A purchaser who is eligible for relief as a young trained farmer (dealt with in the chapter entitled "Transferring the Family Farm") will not have to pay stamp duty on the non-residential property.

### Auctions

In recent years, property auctions have become a more popular method of disposing of properties, especially so-called distressed properties, quickly. This method of disposal of properties increases the risks for proposed purchasers and their legal teams, as the available time for carrying out full

---

[41] Solicitors (Professional Practice, Conduct and Discipline – Commercial Property Transactions) Regulations 2010, SI 2010/366, reg 3. See also, Law Society of Ireland, *A Guide to Good Professional Conduct for Solicitors* (3rd edn, Law Society of Ireland 2013).

[42] Revenue, 'Stamp Duty Rates' (2016) <www.revenue.ie/en/tax/stamp-duty/rates.html> accessed 30 July 2016.

due diligence enquiries on the property is usually limited. To mitigate the risk of buying a 'pig in a poke', it is advisable that:

- An inspection of the property be undertaken. The purchaser should view the actual property and not just the photographs. It has long been the law that a purchaser is bound by anything that is reasonably visible on physical inspection, such as a right of way;
- A copy of the property brochure be obtained from the auctioneer, or that the purchaser visits the website, reads the legal pack, and obtains a copy of the contract for sale and title documents;
- Legal advice be sought as soon as possible. Each property at auction should have a legal pack which contains all information relevant to the property. A solicitor will also have the opportunity of reviewing the title and agreeing to the insertion of any conditions into the contract for sale for his or her client's benefit with the vendor's solicitor; and
- A competent engineer be instructed to inspect the property, and carry out a full due diligence before bidding, as it is 'buyer beware' once the hammer drops in an auction.

## Case

A Circuit Court case in 2015 demonstrated the importance of ensuring that the map outlining the property being purchased is checked by a competent surveyor in advance of purchase.[43] In that case, the plaintiffs purchased a house at auction for €750,000 in the Leeson Street area of Dublin. A builder friend had used "a compass and a ruler" to measure the back garden! The plaintiffs sued the defendants, the next door neighbours, for trespass, alleging that they had wrongly built a dividing wall four feet into their garden. Groarke J found that the map used in the sale had not properly outlined the back garden of the property and no warranty had been given by the vendor, who had specifically refused to identify boundaries. Groarke J impressed upon house buyers the importance of having experts check out what they are actually purchasing.

It goes without saying that an intended purchaser should always have funds arranged in advance of buying at auction. A person who is the highest bidder at an auction and is successful, is obliged to sign the contract immediately and to pay a deposit there and then. The deposit is

---

[43] Ray Managh, 'Next door neighbours row over four-foot wall measured by compass and ruler' *Irish Independent* (Dublin, 6 February 2015).

normally 10% of the purchase price. The intended purchaser will normally be required to complete the purchase within four to six weeks of the auction. After contracts have been signed and the deposit paid, the purchaser is then legally bound to complete the purchase of the property. A purchaser who fails to do so may lose his/her deposit and is also liable to be sued for failure to complete. Thus, it is critical that finances are arranged prior to the auction.

## Compulsory Purchase Orders (CPOs)

The compulsory purchase of land is widely utilised by local authorities and semi-state bodies throughout Ireland for the construction of new roads, gas pipelines and ESB cables.

The statutory process involved in compulsory purchases is very complex, and has evolved over a period of 200 years. This section is designed to provide the reader with a basic knowledge and understanding of CPOs, something which may be helpful in advance of a meeting with his or her legal advisor.

The various pieces of legislation governing CPOs are interrelated and complex. There is also a large body of case law on CPOs, where the courts have attempted to clarify some of the issues that have come before them.

The entitlement to compensation and the procedures involved in CPOs vary according to the acquiring public authority and the legislation under which that body operates.

The legislation that primarily governs CPOs in Ireland is contained in the Land Clauses Consolidation Act 1845 (hereafter 'the 1845 Act'), the Housing Act 1966 (hereafter 'the 1966 Act'), the Acquisition of Land (Assessment of Compensation) Act 1919 (hereafter 'the 1919 Act') and the Planning and Development Acts 1963 and 2000 (hereafter 'the Planning Acts').

The compulsory purchase of land has certainly affected the farming community in recent years, due to the large amount of land that has been acquired for the widening of existing roads and the construction of new roads. It is important to understand that the procedure adopted under the

1966 Act is the bedrock for compulsory acquisition of land by local authorities under a number of different statutory codes. The 1960 Act confers a general statutory power of acquisition for the purpose of housing, but also for the acquisition of land for other purposes such as road building. Land acquisition for road building is being achieved under the 1966 Act.[44] Section 10 of the Local Government (No. 2) Act 1960 as amended by s 86(1) of the 1966 Act provides:

> Where –
>
> a) A local authority intend to acquire compulsorily any land, whether situate within or outside their functional area, for purposes for which they are capable of being authorised by law to acquire land compulsorily,
> b) those purposes are purposes other than the purposes of the Housing Act 1966, or are purposes some only of which are purposes of that Act, and
> c) the local authority consider that it would be convenient to effect the acquisition under that Act,
>
> The local authority may decide so to effect the acquisition.

The vehicle for compulsory acquisition for non-housing purposes is found in s 10(3)(a) of the Local Government (No.2) Act 1960. That section reads as follows:

> Where a local authority makes a decision under subsection (1) or (2) of this section, they may be authorised to acquire the land compulsorily by means of a compulsory purchase order as provided for by section 76 of the Housing Act 1966, and the third schedule thereto and for the purposes of this paragraph any reference to a housing authority in the said section 76 or the said third schedule shall be construed as a reference to a local authority.

Section 213 of the 2000 Act restates these powers and essentially provides that the local authority may, for the purposes of performing its functions, acquire land, wayleaves, easements, water rights or other rights over or in respect of any land, temporarily or permanently, by agreement or compulsorily.

It is noteworthy that the planning authority also has general powers to develop or secure the development of land under the 2000 Act. The specific

---

[44] Local Government (No 2) Act 1960, s 10(1), as amended, by substitution, by the Housing Act 1966, s 86(1).

powers are contained under s 212(1) of the 2000 Act, allowing the planning authority to:

(a) secure, facilitate and control the improvement of the frontage of any public road by widening, opening, enlarging or otherwise improving;

(b) develop any land in the vicinity of any road or public transport facility which it is proposed to improve or construct;

(c) provide areas with roads, infrastructure facilitating public transport and such services and works as may be needed for a development;

(d) provide, secure or facilitate the provision of areas of convenient shape and size for development;

(e) secure, facilitate or carry out the development and renewal of areas in need of physical, social or economic regeneration and provide open spaces and other public amenities;

(f) secure the preservation of any view or prospect, any protected structure or other structure, any architectural conservation area or natural physical feature, any trees or woodlands or any site of archaeological, geological, historical, scientific or ecological interest.

### Roads Act 1993

It is also important to note that Part IV of the Roads Act 1993, as amended, (hereafter 'the 1993 Act') provides for the making of a scheme for a motorway, service area, busway or protected road by a road authority or the National Roads Authority (NRA).

In order for a road authority to proceed with any of the aforementioned proposed developments under this part of the 1993 Act, two steps must be taken before land can be compulsorily acquired for a scheme under the 1993 Act.

First, the road authority must submit any scheme (i.e. scheme for a motorway or road etc.) made by it[45] to An Bord Pleanála for approval.[46] The second step is the preparation of an environmental impact statement (EIS).[47] This assessment relates to the proposed road and the Board must consider any submissions made in relation to the development. In essence, an approval

---

[45] Roads Act 1993, s 47(1).

[46] Roads Act 1993, s 49(1).

[47] Roads Act 1993, s 51(1).

from the Board, pursuant to s 49 of the 1993 Act, has the effect of authorising the road authority to acquire the land necessary for the development as if it were a confirmed compulsory purchase order.

## Compulsory Purchase

For any local authority, it may be necessary to acquire lands for the performance of its functions, and the most obvious approach is to acquire such lands by agreement. However, there are often circumstances where this is not possible and compulsory purchase is the only option.

There are three distinct parts to the compulsory acquisition process:

- Making of the CPO;
- Confirmation of the CPO; and
- Assessment of compensation (in the event that a CPO is confirmed).

The CPO procedure was brought into place for the common good. However, in serving the common good, the interests of landowners are often adversely affected. Achieving a balance between the two is not always easy.

### Making of the CPO

In the event that a local authority exercises its powers of compulsory acquisition, it must be in a position to show that the acquisition is clearly "justified by the common good".[48] In order for a CPO to be properly made, a notice in the prescribed form must be served on every owner, lessee and occupier of any land to which the order relates.[49] It is important that the notice describes the effect of the order and that it specifies the time within which, and the manner in which, objections can be made.

Once an order has been made, and publication of the notice has been completed, an oral hearing can be called by An Bord Pleanála if objections have been raised.[50] However, the decision to grant an oral hearing is at the discretion of the Board.

---

[48] *Clinton v An Bord Pleanála (No. 2)* [2007] 4 IR 701, SC at para [52].

[49] Housing Act 1966, Sch 3 art 4(b).

[50] Oral hearings have been put in place to replace the local public inquiry.

### Confirmation of the CPO

The local authority is permitted to confirm a CPO, provided there is no valid subsisting objection.[51] One of the following conditions must be satisfied before the power can be exercised:

(i) No objections are received by An Bord Pleanála or the local authority, as the case may be, within the period provided for making objections;

(ii) Any objection received is subsequently withdrawn at any time before An Bord Pleanála makes its decision; or

(iii) An Bord Pleanála is of opinion that any objection received relates exclusively to matters which can be dealt with by a property arbitrator.

Where none of the conditions are satisfied, the CPO must be confirmed by An Bord Pleanála before it has effect. There are certain time restraints in relation to submitting an order to the Board for confirmation. Once a local authority has complied with the notification provisions in relation to a CPO under paragraph 4 of schedule 3 to the Housing Act 1966, it is required to submit the order to the Board for confirmation within 6 weeks of complying with those provisions.[52] It is the duty of the local authority to satisfy An Bord Pleanála that "the acquisition of the property is clearly justified by the common good".[53] It should be noted that, if a CPO has been confirmed under the Housing Acts, there is a requirement under s 78(1) of the 1966 Act to publish and serve a notice of the confirmation within 12 weeks of the making of the order.[54]

Once a CPO becomes operative and a local authority intends to proceed with acquiring the land, the local authority must serve any notice which is required to be served in order to treat for the purchase of the interests in the land within 18 months. Furthermore, it is important to point out that a confirmation is not required under every scheme and, for that reason, legal advice should be sought in relation to this area.

---

[51] Planning and Development Act 2000, s 216(1).

[52] Planning and Development Act 2000, s 217(3).

[53] *Clinton v An Bord Pleanála (No 2)* [2007] 4 IR 701 at 724.

[54] Planning and Development Act 2000, s 217(4).

## Compensation

The primary legislation providing for the assessment of compensation is contained in the 1919 Act. The 1919 Act makes provision for the appointment of an arbitrator to assess the compensation payable.

The property is valued as at the date of the notice to treat.[55] A landowner who receives a notice to treat must submit a notice of claim within one month after receiving the notice to treat. Essentially, the notice of claim should state the claimant's interest in the land affected and also specify the compensation claimed. It is important to understand that failure to submit the notice of claim containing sufficient particulars, and within the prescribed time period, can result in the imposition of costs.[56]

The assessment of compensation will generally fall under a number of headings of claim. These include:

- The value of the land acquired. The landowner is entitled to the market value of his or her land at the date of the notice to treat. The market value can be based either on the existing value of the land or its development value, whichever is the greater. Development value can be claimed only where development potential can be proven to exist;
- Diminution in value of the retained lands, if any. It can also be the case that the completed development has a negative effect on the value of the retained land. If so, then compensation for what is known as injurious affection, may also form part of the claim. Another possibility to consider is that the acquiring authority would purchase the retained land;
- Where a land holding is fragmented by a new road, additional issues to consider will include whether the local authority should be forced to buy the remaining inefficient portion of land, or accept an underpass. Most farmers initially opt for the underpass. It is not always the best long-term solution. A farmer should think about the practicalities and daily farming requirements. Consideration should be given to, among other things, how difficult it may be to move livestock, the practicalities for silage cutting, and use of large machines;
- The costs resulting from acquisition. The acquiring authority is obliged to fence and secure any properties affected by its action, or pay for the cost of doing so. How and where this is to be done

---

[55] Housing Act 1966, s 84.

[56] Acquisition of Land (Assessment of Compensation) Act 1919, s 5(2).

can have considerable long-term consequences. This should be discussed and documented;

- Disturbance. Where existing use value is being claimed, the landowner may be entitled to compensation for disturbance and severance;
- Loss of profit or goodwill. This is self-explanatory. A landowner who suffers a loss of profit or goodwill in his or her farming business as a result of the CPO is entitled to be compensated accordingly;
- Loss or depreciation of stock or trade. Again, this is self-explanatory. A landowner who suffers a loss or depreciation of stock or trade in his or her farming business as a result of the CPO is entitled to be compensated accordingly; and
- Professional fees necessary for acquisition. The acquiring authority normally pays the landowner's reasonable chartered valuation surveyor's fees and also the farmer's reasonable legal fees.

In theory, the affected farmer should be in no better or no worse a position after the acquisition has been finalised.

If a claim is not yet settled but the acquiring authority serves notice that it intends to enter the land, they are obliged to give the landowner not less than 14 days' notice.[57] The entry will not affect the landowner's rights to compensation, and interest can be claimed on the compensation from the date of entry.[58]

### Agreement and Arbitration

Sometimes, it will simply not be possible to reach agreement on compensation.

The National Roads Authority has recently renewed a cooperation agreement with the IFA and local authorities, allowing for a resolution between parties who are in dispute[59] in respect of land compulsorily acquired, or to be acquired, for the development of the national road network. While the agreement does not have statutory footing, and there is a right to appeal, it does offer an option to farmers when attempting to resolve disputes

---

[57] Housing Act 1966, s 80(1).

[58] Housing Act 1966, s 80(2).

[59] Department of Transport, Tourism and Sport, 'Agreement reached with IFA on compulsory land purchase for national road development – Ring' (2016) <www.dttas.ie/press-releases/2016/agreement-reached-ifa-compulsory-land-purchase-national-road-development-ring> accessed 30 July 2016.

between themselves and the relevant body. According to then Minister of State at the Department of Transport, Tourism and Sport, Michael Ring TD, "The renewed agreement outlines a fixed payment of €3,000 per acre being paid to landowners on all lands and associated areas acquired for national road improvement works in accordance with the terms in the agreement".[60]

Section 3 of the 1919 Act provides for such difficulties to be resolved through arbitration. Both parties, the landowner and the acquiring authority, are bound by the arbitrator's decision. The arbitrator must follow the legislation when assessing compensation. The arbitrator is completely independent of the acquiring authority. He or she will listen to both sides of the dispute and make an award accordingly, based on the evidence presented.

## Costs of Arbitration – Who Pays?

In general, arbitration should be used as a last resort. Costs of dealing with the claim up to arbitration are for the acquiring authority to pay. Costs of the arbitration are at the discretion of the arbitrator, and may be awarded against either party.[61]

A landowner is usually entitled to recover most of his or her reasonable costs from the acquiring authority if, in the course of the arbitration, an award is secured for compensation higher than what has been offered. Each case will be dependent on its own circumstances, for example, if an arbitrator is of the opinion that a landowner did not put forward adequate reasons to support his or her claim for compensation in good time to enable the acquiring authority to make a fair decision on compensation, it could be argued that the landowner should be responsible for the costs in that instance.

It is important to take comprehensive legal advice on all available options, both in relation to any objections to be made and also in relation to the procedures to be followed in progressing those objections to the fullest degree permitted. Even if a landowner does not wish to object to the proposed CPO, it is important that he or she has a full understanding of the process, and the implications of the exercise of the powers of purchase by the relevant body or authority.

---

[60] ibid.

[61] Acquisition of Land (Assessment of Compensation) Act 1919, s 5(4).

## Boundary Disputes

### Avoid if Possible

Boundary disputes are among the most bitterly fought and passionate cases brought before the courts. Such disputes are often totally out of proportion to the issue at hand and may permanently destroy neighbourly relations. In many cases, the financial cost of litigation exceeds the value of the land concerned. Often, the area of the land in dispute will be very small but litigation may ensue because of its critical location or strategic importance to the owners concerned.

Boundary disputes can arise over many different issues, including shared access ways, rights to light, drainage rights, overhanging trees, air rights, squatter's rights etc. Irrespective of the reason for the dispute, they have the potential to last for years and can have a terrible impact on the lives of all those concerned.

The best advice to any farmer at the outset is to avoid litigation at all costs. Always ensure that a competent engineer or surveyor is engaged to check boundaries before purchasing property. Every landowner should clearly mark out the boundaries to his or her property on the ground. This will help to avoid unnecessary confusion. If a dispute arises, it is important to try to remain amicable with the neighbouring landowner, in an attempt to resolve the dispute out of court. Arbitration is an alternative to court for dispute resolution and can be beneficial in a boundary dispute situation due to the reduced costs compared to court, and should always be given serious consideration.

Resolving boundary disputes requires the skills and expertise of both surveyors and solicitors, working together as a team. The role of the solicitor is to examine the deeds and interpret the title, while the surveyor will provide the solicitor with independent advice in relation to maps and boundaries.

### Deciding on Legal Proceedings — Factors to Consider

In the event that it is not possible to settle the issue with the neighbouring landowner, a solicitor should be consulted to review the deeds and maps. The solicitor will offer advice as to the costs of the dispute, whether it is financially worth bringing the claim and the likely merits of a case.

If a boundary dispute goes before the court, there will generally only be one winner and, usually, the costs of the case follow the event i.e. in addition to their own legal costs, the person who loses will have to pay the winner's legal costs. It is important, therefore, to be advised from the outset of the strengths and weaknesses of the case.

## Court

If the matter proceeds to court, the case is either heard by the Circuit Court or the High Court.[62] Usually, a plaintiff will institute court proceedings in relation to a boundary dispute, seeking a declaratory court order establishing ownership of a particular property, or seeking injunctive relief prohibiting trespass or occupation of a particular property. The court will examine the title deeds to the property in dispute and look at the maps. It will hear evidence from the parties to the dispute, and any relevant witnesses, such as engineers, where they can give an expert opinion as to ownership. The judge will weigh up the evidence of both parties and make a decision. Unfortunately, it will often happen that these decisions are not acceptable to one or both parties to the dispute.

## Conclusion

Irish society has had a long affection with land. Bull McCabe, in John B. Keane's *The Field*, did all he could to save the land he loved from being sold at public auction.

> No. It's my field. It's my child. I nursed it. I nourished it. I saw to its every want. I dug the rocks out of it with my bare hands and I made a living thing of it! My only want is that green grass, that lovely green grass, and you want to take it away from me, and in the sight of God I can't let you do that!

The law surrounding real property is old and complicated, partly due to our attachment to, and placement of value on, the land. It is important to ensure that individual property rights are protected, and that if one is facing a CPO, or has not yet registered a right of way, specialist legal advice be taken so as to protect those rights. It is equally important that every farmer and property owner fully appreciates that "the day you buy is the day you sell", before purchasing land, so as to avoid being stuck with a property that he or she may not be able to sell on at a later date.

---

[62] Depending on the rateable valuation of the land.

# CHAPTER TWO

# Defending Your Dwelling

## Criminal Law (Defence and the Dwelling) Act 2011

The Constitution declares that the State will vindicate the property rights of every citizen[1]. Article 40.5 of the Constitution provides that "The dwelling of every citizen is inviolable and shall not be forcibly entered save in accordance with law".

The protection afforded to the dwelling house of every citizen is a fundamental right which dates back to time immemorial. It has now been put on a statutory footing by the enactment of the Criminal Law (Defence and the Dwelling) Act 2011 (hereafter 'the 2011 Act'). The introduction of the 2011 Act is an attempt to afford protection to home owners, by allowing them to act to defend their homes against those who enter illegally. The 2011 Act recognises that even force which causes death can, in certain circumstances, be justified[2].

To gain the protection afforded by the legislation, the defender must believe that the person against whom the force is used is a trespasser who intends to commit a crime.[3] Furthermore, as will be seen later in this chapter, the defender must behave reasonably.[4]

### Definition of Dwelling

The 2011 Act defines "dwelling" as a building or structure, or a vehicle or vessel, which has been constructed or adapted for use as a dwelling, or any part of a dwelling.[5] The Act also applies to the curtilage of a dwelling, which is defined as "an area immediately surrounding or adjacent to the

---

[1] Article 40.3.2 of the Constitution.

[2] Criminal Law (Defence and the Dwelling) Act 2011, s 2(7).

[3] Criminal Law (Defence and the Dwelling) Act 2011, s2(1)(a).

[4] Criminal Law (Defence and the Dwelling) Act 2011, s 2(1)(b).

[5] Criminal Law (Defence and the Dwelling) Act 2011, s 1.

dwelling which is used in conjunction with the dwelling, other than any part of that area that is a public place".[6]

## Main Provisions of the 2011 Act

Section 2(1) of the 2011 Act states that:

> ... it shall not be an offence for a person who is in his or her dwelling, or for a person who is a lawful occupant in a dwelling, to use force against another person or the property of another person where–
>
> (a) He or she believes the other person has entered or is entering the dwelling as a trespasser for the purpose of committing a criminal act, and
> (b) The force used is only such as is reasonable in the circumstances as he or she believes them to be–
>    (i) to protect himself or herself or another person present in the dwelling from injury, assault, detention or death caused by a criminal act,
>    (ii) to protect his or her property or the property of another person from appropriation, destruction or damage caused by a criminal act, or
>    (iii) to prevent the commission of a crime or to effect, or assist in effecting, a lawful arrest.

In essence, it shall not be an offence for any person in his or her dwelling or the curtilage of his or her dwelling, to use force against a person, or his or her property, in the circumstances as outlined above.

Interestingly, a person can rely on the 2011 Act even in the event that the person had a "safe and practicable opportunity to retreat".[7] Section 3 of the 2011 Act provides that a person is not obliged to retreat from his or her dwelling[8] or require a lawful occupant in a dwelling to retreat from the dwelling.[9]

## What is Reasonable Force?

The all-important question of what amounts to reasonable force is, of necessity, something of a grey area, and not something that one can be clear

---

[6] Criminal Law (Defence and the Dwelling) Act 2011, s 1.

[7] Criminal Law (Defence and the Dwelling) Act 2011, s 2(5).

[8] Criminal Law (Defence and the Dwelling) Act 2011, s 3(a).

[9] Criminal Law (Defence and the Dwelling) Act 2011, s 3(b).

and precise about. In seeking to clarify the position, the Court of Appeal has held that there must be both a subjective and an objective component to the test used to assess the appropriate degree of force.[10] The 2011 Act sets out the test for justifiable force in defence of the dwelling.

## The Subjective Element

It seems that the subjective element to be applied in determining whether someone acted reasonably in protecting himself or herself or another person from injury, in protecting their property, or in preventing the commission of a crime, is to focus on the mind-set of the owner or occupier, their intentions, and their foresight. The 2011 Act specifically states that:

> ... it is immaterial whether a belief is justified or not, if it is honestly held, but in considering whether the person using the force honestly held the belief, the court or the jury, as the case may be, shall have regard to the presence or absence of reasonable grounds for the person so believing and all other relevant circumstances.[11]

## The Objective Element

In addition to a subjective element, an objective element is also applied, requiring consideration of whether an ordinary, reasonable man in the same circumstances would have acted in the same way.

## Further Analysis of 'Reasonable Force'

The determination of what amounts to reasonable force will depend on the circumstances of the intrusion, and, as a consequence, it is difficult to define a hard and fast rule that will cover every circumstance. Caution must be exercised, as any person wishing to avail of this defence must still satisfy the court that he or she believed that the person entering the dwelling was a trespasser with the intention of committing a criminal act, and that the force used against that person was reasonable.

In dealing with the interpretation of reasonable force under the 2011 Act, it is useful to refer to the Dáil debates to glean the intention of the

---

[10] *The People (DPP) v Barnes* [2007] 3 IR 130 at 151.

[11] Criminal Law (Defence and the Dwelling) Act 2011, s 2(4).

legislature. In the course of the debates the former Minister for Justice and Law Reform, Dermot Ahern, stated that:

> The occupier will obviously have a judgment call to make when using force against an intruder as to the level of force required. Such an event, in most cases, is likely to occur in a situation of great tension and anxiety. The force that may be used is such as is reasonable in the circumstances as the occupier believes them to be at the time of the attack. This will be the case whether the force results in the death of the intruder or not.[12]

The present state of law would suggest that, given the circumstances of the particular situation, if a person uses force that is not objectively justified, and an intruder is killed, then it would follow that this person would be guilty of manslaughter. The rationale for this logic is found in a decision of *DPP v Dwyer*,[13] where Butler J neatly summed up the law of self-defence in the following passage:

> A person is entitled to protect himself from unlawful attack. If, in doing so, he uses no more force than is reasonably necessary, he is acting lawfully and commits no crime even though he kills his assailant. If he uses more force than may objectively be considered necessary, his act is unlawful and, if he kills, the killing is unlawful. His intention, however, falls to be tested subjectively and it would appear logical to conclude that, if his intention in doing the unlawful act was primarily to defend himself, he should not be held to have the necessary intention to kill or cause serious injury. The result of this view would be that the killing, though unlawful, would be manslaughter only.[14]

This passage provides useful guidance in determining what is reasonable force, in light of the 2011 Act.

## Civil Liability

In the years prior to the introduction of the 2011 Act, there were many instances where intruders made civil claims for personal injuries arising out of assaults by home owners. In addressing this issue, s 4(3) of the 2011 Act has stipulated that a person who uses such force in accordance with

---

[12] Dáil Deb 20 October 2010, vol 719, col 403.

[13] *DPP v Dwyer* [1972] IR 416.

[14] [1972] IR 416, 429.

the provisions of the Act will not be liable in tort in respect of injury, loss or damage sustained as a result of the use of such force. Where a person enters a premises for the purpose of committing an offence, the occupier is not liable for injuring that person, or damaging property intentionally, unless a court determines otherwise. Section 5 of the 2011 Act provides that no liability will arise for the occupier who uses force against an intruder with criminal intent.

## Conclusion

Rural crime has been very much in the media spotlight in recent times, amid genuine fears that members of the rural and farming communities are being targeted by criminal gangs. While the 2011 Act is both welcome and helpful, the rights given to those defending their homes must be exercised with extreme caution, as any person who wishes to rely on the defence provided by the Act will ultimately still be relying on a court, after it has examined the facts of the case, to determine whether or not he or she used force in a manner that was reasonable against another person, or the property of another person, where that other person had entered, or was entering, the dwelling as a trespasser for the purpose of committing a criminal act.

# CHAPTER THREE

# Occupiers' Liability

Occupiers' liability is a field of tort law, codified in statute, which concerns the duty of care owed by those who occupy real property, whether as owners or tenants, to people who visit or trespass. It deals with the potential liability that may arise from accidents caused by the defective or dangerous condition of the property. A "tort" is a wrongful act or an infringement of a right (other than under contract), which gives rise to legal liability. This chapter deals with the obligations on landowners or occupiers, including farmers, to people entering on their land, whether with or without consent. It concludes by making reference to the statutory notices or agreements that can be put in place, and which may serve to limit liability.

## Occupiers Liability Act 1995

In recent decades, Irish people have become much more legalistic in their attitude towards their rights and duties. As a result, there has been an increase in litigation arising from breach of duties or the enforcement of rights, and Irish farmers have become increasingly conscious of their exposure to potential personal injury claims arising from accidents on their lands. Agricultural lands, like other open spaces, are attractive to recreational visitors. As healthy living has moved from a drab obligation to a popular pastime, more and more people are taking to rambling across farmers' land. Accidents are an inevitable and unfortunate consequence of this trend. With an increased number of claims, farmers have become accustomed to paying increased premiums for their public liability insurance.

The law governing the duty of care owed by owners and occupiers of land, including farms, towards visitors, recreational users, and trespassers on that land, is contained in the Occupiers' Liability Act 1995 (hereafter 'the 1995 Act').

## Definitions under the 1995 Act

### Occupier

Section 1(1) defines an *"occupier"* as

> ... a person exercising such control over the state of the premises that it is reasonable to impose upon that person a duty towards an entrant[1] in respect of a particular danger[2] thereon and, where there is more than one occupier of the same premises, the extent of the duty of each occupier towards an entrant depends on the degree of control each of them has over the state of the premises[3] and the particular danger thereon and whether, as respects each of them, the entrant concerned is a visitor, recreational user or trespasser.

An occupier can be the landowner or a tenant of the land, and this includes a farmer.

### Visitor

Section 1(1) defines a *"visitor"* as

> an entrant who is present on premises by reason of the permission or invitation of the occupier or his or her family or a person ordinarily resident on the premises or an entrant present for social reasons. It also includes an entrant, other than a recreational user, who is present on premises by virtue of an express or implied term in a contract, and an entrant as of right.

### Recreational User

Section 1(1) defines a *"recreational user"* as

> ... an entrant who, with or without the occupier's permission or at the occupier's implied invitation, is present on premises without a charge (other than a reasonable charge in respect of the cost of providing vehicle parking facilities) being imposed for the purpose of engaging in a recreational activity.

---

[1] Occupiers' Liability Act 1995, s 1(1). *"Entrant"* is defined as "a person who enters on the premises and is not the sole occupier".

[2] Occupiers' Liability Act 1995, s 1(1). *"Danger"* is defined as "a danger due to the state of the premises".

[3] Occupiers' Liability Act 1995, s 1(1). *"Premises"* is defined as including "land, water and any fixed or moveable structures thereon and also includes vessels, vehicles, trains, aircraft and other means of transport".

### Recreational Activity

"*Recreational activity*" is defined in s 1(1) as

> … any recreational activity conducted, whether alone or with others, in the open air (including any sporting activity), scientific research and nature study so conducted, exploring caves, and visiting sites, buildings of historical, architectural, traditional, artistic, archaeological or scientific importance.

This includes activities carried on by hillwalkers, tourists, ramblers, and huntsmen.

### Trespasser

"*Trespasser*" is defined in s 1(1) of the 1995 Act as "an entrant other than a recreational user or visitor".

## Duty of Care

### Duty Owed to Visitors

Section 3(1) states that "[a]n occupier of premises owes a duty of care ("the common duty of care") towards a visitor".

Section 3(2) defines "*The common duty of care*" as

> … a duty to take such care as is reasonable in all the circumstances (having regard to the care which a visitor may reasonably be expected to take for his or her own safety and, if the visitor is on the premises in the company of another person, the extent of the supervision and control the latter person may reasonably be expected to exercise over the visitor's activities) to ensure that a visitor to the premises does not suffer injury or damage by reason of any danger existing thereon.

### Duty Owed to Recreational Users and Trespassers

Section 4(1) states,

> In respect of a danger existing on premises, an occupier owes towards a recreational user of the premises or a trespasser thereon ("the person") a duty,

> (a) not to injure the person or damage the property of the person intentionally and

(b)   not to act with reckless disregard[4] for the person or the property of the person,

except in so far as the occupier extends the duty in accordance with section 5.[5]

The duty is to take care and measures for the safety of all persons entering upon the land, and not to allow obvious or hidden dangers to remain on the land which would cause injury to a person who has entered.

The duty owed by the occupant to the entrant is based on the test of foreseeability, in that the law states that, where it is foreseeable that a person would enter the land and would be injured, the landowner or the occupier of the land would be liable in negligence for such injury caused to a person entering his or her land. It is foreseeable, for example, that traps laid inside a boundary wall for the purpose of catching a wild animal, would present a risk of injury to entrants. The position is similar where the landowner has hidden caves or unsafe ground on his or her land near a boundary leading on to a public right of way, laneway, or roadway. The further the land is from the public roadway or places where the public congregate, the less foreseeable the danger is considered to be. Local beauty spots and places of cultural interest attract the public, and accordingly, the law requires that an occupier ensure that his or her land has no hidden dangers that might cause injury to the public.

The 1995 Act provides that an occupier of a premises owes a duty of care to the following classes of persons who enter on his or her land.

### Visitor

As mentioned earlier, a visitor is defined as an entrant who is present on a premises by reason of the permission or invitation of the occupier or his or her family or a person ordinarily resident on the premises or an entrant present for social reasons.

It includes an entrant who is so present and is:

(a)   A member of the occupier's family who is ordinarily resident on the premises;

---

[4] "Reckless disregard" is not defined in the 1995 Act, but s 4(2) provides some guidance.
[5] Occupiers' Liability Act 1995, s 5(1) states that "An occupier may by express agreement or notice extend his or her duty towards entrants under sections 3 and 4".

(b) An entrant who is present at the express invitation of the occupier or such a member or;

(c) An entrant who is present with the permission of the occupier or such a member for social reasons connected with the occupier or such a member.[6]

The case of *Vega v Cullen*[7] provides an excellent example of the duty owed to visitors. The plaintiff was on a social visit to the defendant's property. At the time, the defendant was carrying out some repairs on the roof of his own property and had made his way onto the roof with a ladder that was leaning at a 45-degree angle against the wall of the house. The ladder was unevenly positioned, with one leg on a concrete surface and the other on a softer surface, which was at a slightly lower level. The plaintiff climbed the ladder in order to speak with the defendant, but as he began to descend, the ladder shifted to the right and the plaintiff fell to the ground.

In the High Court, Peart J held that it was the duty of the defendant to take reasonable care in ensuring that the plaintiff did not injure himself on the property. The defendant was held liable for the injuries sustained by the plaintiff, and Peart J found that the plaintiff's fall "resulted from the negligence of the defendant in leaving the ladder so positioned and in the particular circumstances of the case, by failing to warn the plaintiff not to ascend the ladder". The court also held that the plaintiff failed in his duty to take care for his own safety, finding that the plaintiff was 30 per cent liable for his own failure in duty.

### Recreational Users

As already stated, a recreational user is an entrant who is present on a premises with or without permission or implied invitation free of charge for the purposes of engaging in recreational activity.[8] Of particular relevance to the present day is the fact that hillwalkers fall into this category. Section 4 of the 1995 Act provides that an occupier owes a restricted duty of care to recreational users by ensuring not to injure

---

[6] Occupiers' Liability Act 1995, s 1(1).

[7] *Vega v Cullen* [2005] IEHC 362.

[8] Occupiers' Liability Act 1995, s 1(1).

them intentionally or act with reckless disregard for them. Section 4(4) of the 1995 Act provides that:

> ... where a structure on premises is or has been provided for use primarily by recreational users, the occupier shall owe a duty towards such users in respect of such a structure to take reasonable care to maintain the structure in a safe condition.

The legal principles applicable in this area can be seen in the case of *Weir-Rodgers v SF Trust Ltd.*[9]

The plaintiff in this case had eaten dinner in Donegal town and she decided to walk to a nearby beach in order to observe the sunset. She accessed an embankment overlooking the beach and rested on an area of flattened grass that appeared to be a viewing area over a stony gradient that led onto the beach. When she attempted to leave the viewing area, she slipped and fell down the cliff and into the water, sustaining multiple injuries.

The plaintiff brought personal injury proceedings in the High Court, claiming that the defendant, the occupier, was liable for her injuries, first, by acting in reckless disregard in failing to fence off the isolated area she had accessed overlooking the beach, and secondly, by failing to adequately warn users of the cliff.

On appeal to the Supreme Court by the defendant, the Court, by unanimous decision, dismissed the plaintiff's claim, taking the English approach to the question of occupiers' liability, namely that the occupier could not be under a duty to prevent people from taking risks inherent in the activities that they undertook. Geoghegan J described such inherent risks that would not attract a duty of care as follows:

> The person sitting down near a cliff must be prepared for oddities in the cliff's structure or in the structure of the ground adjacent to the cliff, and he or she assumes the risk associated therewith. There could, of course, be something quite exceptionally unusual and dangerous in the state of a particular piece of ground which would impose a duty on the occupier, the effect of which would be that if he did not put up a warning notice

---

[9] *Weir-Rodgers v SF Trust Ltd* [2005] 1 IR 47.

he would be treated as having reckless disregard. But this is certainly not such a case.[10]

The thrust of the decision imposes the concept of common sense on both hillwalkers and landowners alike. For example, if there is a danger-ous structure on the land, the farmer is obliged to make that structure safe, while also erecting sufficient warning notices for users of the land. Similar actions should be taken in ensuring the safety of a disused mine shaft. The farmer should flag this danger and have it fenced off. However, a farmer cannot be held liable for a walker who falls over a boulder or trips on an uneven surface, as the visitor or trespasser must make efforts to look out for his or her own safety.

## Trespassers

As already stated, a trespasser is defined as "an entrant other than a recrea-tional user or visitor".[11] Such entrants do not have permission or authority to be present on a property. A burglar falls within this definition. The duty owed to trespassers is set out in s 4 of the 1995 Act, and is similar to that owed to recreational users. However, an occupier may not be liable for injury or damage unintentionally caused to a person who enters on land or a premises for the purposes of committing an offence, unless the court determines otherwise.[12] The decision of the court will be based on the particular facts of the case.

In *Williams v TP Wallace Construction Ltd*,[13] the entrant plaintiff did not have permission or authority to be on the property in question. The defendant company had hired the plaintiff to install guttering at a shop-ping centre. On the day of the accident, the plaintiff attended the defend-ant's premises unannounced, in order to establish whether the job was being carried out properly. The plaintiff proceeded to inspect the site without express permission, as the site workers were on a break and the architect was not present. The plaintiff sued the defendant for injuries he sustained as a result of a fall from a ladder, which was not tied to the scaffolding. The plaintiff contended that the defendant was negligent in

---

[10] [2005] 1 IR 47, 58.

[11] Occupiers' Liability Act 1995, s 1(1).

[12] Occupiers' Liability Act 1995, s 4(3)(a) and (b).

[13] *Williams v TP Wallace Construction Ltd* [2001] IEHC 231.

failing to have the ladder secured. The court held that the plaintiff was not a visitor, but was, instead, a trespasser, because he was not on the site by invitation or arrangement. The court found in favour of the defendant and dismissed the plaintiff's case on the basis that the failure to tie the ladder to the scaffolding was not an act of reckless disregard, and the defendant did not breach his duty to the plaintiff, a trespasser, in this regard.[14]

### Children

The 1995 Act does not draw a distinction between an adult and a child and, as a result, a child is owed the same duty of care as that owed to an adult. However, in gauging the standard of reckless disregard, the court must have regard to all the circumstances of the case, such as the conduct of the person, and the care which he or she may reasonably be expected to take for his or her own safety while on the premises, having regard to the extent of his or her knowledge.[15] Naturally, a child is not as aware of dangers as an adult would be, and they may ignore or fail to understand warning signs. As a result, the courts have traditionally afforded more leniency to children who come onto a premises as a trespasser, if it could be shown that the child was at an age that he or she would "follow a bait as mechanically as a fish" and the occupier's premises contained "an allurement".[16] The question then arises as to what amounts to an "allurement". The case law states that, in order for something to be an allurement, it had to be both "fascinating and fatal".[17] In *O'Leary v John A Wood Ltd*,[18] Kingsmill Moore J held that "an object should not be considered an allurement unless the temptation which it presents is such that no normal child could be expected to restrain himself from intermeddling even if he knows that to intermeddle is wrong".[19]

---

[14] *Williams v TP Wallace Construction Ltd* [2002] [2001] IEHC 201, Judgment of Mr Justice Frederick Morris, p 10.

[15] See s 4 of the 1995 Act.

[16] McMahon BME and Binchy, W, *Law of Torts* (Bloomsbury, Professional 2013) p 416.

[17] *Latham v Johnson* [1913] 1 KB 398.

[18] *O'Leary v John A Wood Ltd* [1964] IR 269.

[19] [1964] IR 269, 277.

In the case of *Michael Ryan v Golden Vale Co-operative Mart Ltd*,[20] the court held that the item which caused injury must be a dangerous item. The minor plaintiff was injured when he was struck by a metal gate. It was contended on behalf of the minor plaintiff in alleging negligence on the part of the defendant, that the "defendants ought to have known that this gate was an allurement for boys such as these and should have ensured that the gate was locked so that this type of incident could not happen."[21] The court disagreed with this view and held that the gate was simply a gate and it could not be considered an allurement.[22]

Clearly, the allurement approach in these types of cases is of great benefit to children, but the courts appear to have taken a restrictive approach, so as to ensure that the net for liability is not cast so widely as to be unjust.

Academic commentary in this area suggests that this more onerous duty of care towards the child trespasser, borne out of judicial goodwill, is still an option for the judiciary now that trespassers and recreational users are distinguished from other visitors under the 1995 Act.[23]

## Contractors

Section 7 of the 1995 Act provides:

> An occupier of premises shall not be liable to an entrant for injury or damage caused to the entrant or property of the entrant by reason of a danger existing on the premises due to the negligence of an independent contractor employed by the occupier if the occupier has taken all reasonable care in the circumstances (including such steps as the occupier ought reasonably to have taken to satisfy himself or herself that the independent contractor was competent to do the work concerned) unless the occupier has or ought to have had knowledge of the fact that the work was not properly done.

---

[20] *Michael Ryan v Golden Vale Co-operative Mart Ltd* [2007] IEHC 159.

[21] ibid 2.

[22] ibid 5.

[23] McMahon BME and Binchy W, *Law of Torts* (Bloomsbury Professional 2013) paras 12.27–12.33.

## Notices or Agreements

One of the most interesting aspects of the provisions in the 1995 Act in respect of the duty to visitors, is the ability of the occupier to vary his or her duty by appropriate agreement or notice. This is consistent with the objective of achieving a balance between the rights of entrants, on the one hand, and the rights of occupiers on the other. The theory is that, if the occupier has gone to the trouble of warning entrants of the limits of his or her potential exposure for liability, then the entrant is put on notice that he or she ought to take particular care of himself or herself, and he or she ought to be bound by that.[24] The prudent occupier ought to take full advantage of this provision. In certain circumstances, a warning may be sufficient to absolve an occupier from all liability.

The 1995 Act illustrates the importance of notices in modifying the duty of occupiers to entrants on their lands. Notices should be simple, clear, reasonable, placed in prominent positions, and carefully drafted to enable occupiers to restrict or exclude their duties under the Act.

In this regard, s 5(2)(b) states the following:

> (b) Such a restriction, modification or exclusion shall not bind a visitor unless: -
>   (i) it is reasonable in all the circumstances, and
>   (ii) in case the occupier purports by notice to restrict, modify or exclude that duty, the occupier has taken reasonable steps to bring the notice to the attention of the visitor.
> (c) For the purposes of paragraph (b)(ii) an occupier shall be presumed, unless the contrary is shown, to have taken reasonable steps to bring a notice to the attention of a visitor if it is prominently displayed at the normal means of access to the premises.

An example of a notice used to limit liability to a visitor to one's property is provided hereunder:

---

[24] Interpreted from s 5(1) and s 5(3) of the 1995 Act.

NOTICE

OCCUPIERS' LIABILITY ACT 1995

IF YOU PASS BEYOND THIS POINT YOU ARE ON A PREMISES

TAKE NOTICE THAT THE OCCUPIER OF THIS PREMISES

GIVEN THE NATURE, CHARACTER AND ACTIVITIES OF THIS
PREMISES HEREBY IN ACCORDANCE WITH SECTION 5(2) OF
THE OCCUPIERS' LIABILITY ACT 1995

EXCLUDES THE DUTY OF CARE

TOWARDS VISITORS

UNDER SECTION 3 OF THE ACT

**WARNING**

UNAUTHORISED ENTRY IS PROHIBITED

## Practical Suggestions for Occupiers

Having set out the legal requirements, and the possible repercussions for occupiers arising therefrom, a number of practical suggestions may be of assistance for farmers:

- Ensure that slurry tanks have sufficient manholes and a grid that cannot be easily removed or dislodged by children;
- Cover or fence off all slurry tanks and lagoons;
- Make a safe play area for children and never allow young children to be unaccompanied on the farm;
- Keep children away from streams, rivers, barrels, wells, and tanks. Make sure these are 'no-go' areas. Where possible, provide fencing to close off dangerous areas;
- Assess and control risks to children and the elderly;
- Keep children away from areas where the work conditions may affect their health;
- Do not allow children unsupervised access to the farmyard;
- Use ladders safely. Ladders must always be solid and properly secured;

- Fence off silage pits, silos, bulk storage hoppers, grain pits, and areas where there are stacks of hay or straw bales, pallets, sacks, and stacked timber; and
- Place warning signs near dangerous areas, such as silage pits.

## Conclusion

It is strongly advised that all landholding farmers have public liability insurance, whether or not there is recreational activity on their land. Such an insurance policy should be of a type that covers all major risks to third parties coming on to the land, whether they be visitors, recreational users, or trespassers. A farmer who has no policy of insurance in place leaves himself or herself open to a claim by a third party, with potentially catastrophic results.

# CHAPTER FOUR

# Transferring the Family Farm

The transfer of ownership of property from one generation to the next can be one of the most problematic phases in any business operation, and this is especially so in the case of farms that are family-owned and run. A farm is more likely than any other family business to be transferred from one generation to the next.

This chapter offers practical advice on how to approach the planning of succession. It focuses on the importance of communication and research of all options before any paperwork is signed. It also discusses the Fair Deal Scheme and its implications for family farm transfers. It goes on to deal with the various taxes involved when transferring the farm, both for the transferor and the transferee and concludes by examining the practicalities to be attended to in order to finalise the transfer.

## Start Succession Planning Early

The most important advice for any farmer who wishes to transfer farm-land to a child is not to leave it until the last minute and, as a result, end up rushing into it. The transfer should not take place on the eve of a 35th birthday, which is the age limit for claiming Young Trained Farmer Relief in relation to stamp duty on lifetime transfers.[1] Neither should it be left to the final few days of the year, when holidays and other circumstances might intervene and result in a deadline being missed. Finally, it goes without saying that, in the absence of exceptional circumstances, the transfer should not be undertaken from the hospital bed of a dying parent.

If some uncertainty exists regarding whether to transfer the family farm during the lifetime of the farmer or, in the alternative, to allow it to pass

---

[1] Stamp Duties Consolidation Act 1999, s 81AA.

under a will upon death, it is vitally important, that, while a decision is being made, a valid will is in place to cover the event of an untimely death.

Transfer of the family farm is much more than merely a simple business transaction. It is a major decision with potentially far-reaching consequences, not just for the transferor and transferee, but also for other family members whose circumstances must be taken into account. In considering any proposed farm transfer, a number of complex issues must be addressed. These include the following:

(1) Family members, siblings, or children may need to be catered for. Educational needs of brothers and/or sisters of the transferee may need to be addressed, as well as entitlements to live and/or be supported in the family home on the farm. In general, transferors attempt to be fair to all their children and to ensure harmony amongst them;

(2) As the transferor is proposing to transfer significant assets during his or her lifetime, he or she must consider what income he or she will then have into the future. This must be considered in conjunction with the need of the transferee to have his or her own income from the property transferred. Much will depend on the particular circumstances. The person handing over ownership of the farm will need to ensure that he or she can live comfortably for the rest of his or her lifetime. The Contributory State Pension is modest and, on its own, unlikely to provide an adequate income to the retiring farmer;

(3) Tax – Is transfer to the next generation financially viable? What are the costs involved?

(4) The family home is normally located on the farm. Should it be transferred now or left in the ownership of the transferor, to be dealt with subsequently, under a valid will?

These issues can be difficult to deal with and the process may seem overwhelming at first. It is important to approach the area of property succession one step at a time. Succession planning should be viewed as a process rather than an event.

It is critical to explore the proposed transfer of farmland from every perspective. A farmer should initially attempt to establish whether or not the contemplated plan is tax efficient and can work in a practical way. He or she should also seek to ascertain and understand all of the benefits and drawbacks of what is planned. A farmer needs to make an informed decision before deciding on a course of action.

It is always a good idea to start by making appointments with professionals as early as possible. It is important to speak with an accountant or tax consultant in relation to the potential tax consequences arising from the transfer. Both the transferor and transferee will require tax advice. Consult a solicitor well in advance. Make an appointment with a Teagasc advisor, if necessary. The relevant financial institution must also be contacted in order to obtain consent for the transfer, if the lands are mortgaged. This may take time.

Farmers are self-employed and they should establish their position with the Department of Social Protection in relation to their PRSI contributions and eligibility for the Contributory State Pension.

The spouses of farmers, in particular, should also make enquiries with the Department of Social Protection. Under the rules of social insurance, a husband, wife, or civil partner who is employed by his or her spouse or civil partner is excluded from social insurance cover.[2] Prior to 2014, spouses or civil partners who received payments in respect of assisting in his or her spouse's or civil partner's trade were also excluded from social insurance cover.[3] Complicated social insurance scenarios can arise in the case of employment and involvement with farming partnerships and limited companies. Similarly, if a spouse or civil partner has been working in partnership with his or her spouse or civil partner for years, but no formal arrangement was in place, he or she will need to obtain advice in relation to his or her particular set of circumstances.

The social welfare office can provide farmers with a detailed PRSI history and information on any entitlement to benefits as a result of those PRSI contributions. An accountant or tax consultant can advise in relation to the farmer's PRSI status and any opportunities to maximise benefits through varying his or her status for PRSI purposes, in conjunction with changing

---

[2] For further information, see Department of Social Protection 'Family Employments & PRSI - SW102' (2015) <www.welfare.ie/en/Pages/Family-Employments-_-PRSI---SW-102.aspx> accessed 23 June 2016.

[3] Social Welfare Consolidation Act 2005, s 12(1)(a).

his or her business structure. In practice, many spouses may have been working in informal partnerships, with only one spouse declaring income and paying PRSI. Following representations by the Irish Creamery Milk Suppliers Association (ICMSA) in 2008, the Government agreed that farmers would be allowed to apply to the Department of Social Protection to have informal partnerships, and the years for which a wife was farming in an informal partnership with her husband, recognised.[4] These years would be counted towards establishing whether the spouse was entitled to the State pension in his or her own right.[5] It is important that a farmer and his or her spouse check that he or she qualifies for a medical card or GP Visit Card.

Good advice will make the task less daunting. Succession planning takes time, research, and clear communication. It should not be done in haste. Implementing an effective succession plan involves more than minimising the tax payable. Succession should be considered from every angle.

## Ask the Important Questions

To assist farmers in preparation for succession, there is a list of useful questions set out below. Every farmer who is considering transferring his or her farm should ask him or herself these questions. The answers may help to clarify what direction the farmer will take, and what he or she hopes to achieve in the succession process:

1. Will I leave the farm to pass under my will or will I transfer it in my lifetime?
2. Will I transfer the entire farm, or only part of it at this stage?
3. Will I transfer the family home or leave it to pass under my will?
4. To whom will I transfer the farm? Who is interested in farming?
5. Do I wish to provide for building sites for my other children?

---

[4] For more information, see Department of Social Protection, 'Working with your spouse or civil partner: how it affects your social welfare contributions and entitlements' (2014) <www.welfare.ie/en/downloads/sw124.pdf> accessed 23 June 2016.

[5] For more information, contact your local office of the Department of Social Protection, see <www.welfare.ie> or phone 1890 66 22 44.

6. Will I be emotionally secure once I transfer the farm? Am I comfortable with letting go of the reins?
7. Will I be financially secure once I transfer the farm?
8. How will the machinery be transferred – gift, sale, lease?
9. How will livestock be transferred – gift, shared income for a few years or livestock share lease?
10. Have adequate housing arrangements been made for the long term? Do I need to register a right of residence in the house?
11. Do I need to register a right of maintenance over the farm to cover the fact that I may need financial assistance in the future?
12. If I wish to work on the farm after the transfer, what is the method and rate of compensation? How much will I be expected, or want to work on the farm after retirement? Who will be responsible for what? Who will be responsible for and manage the livestock, crops and machinery, farm records, employees etc.?
13. How will work be divided? Are hours and vacation times agreed?
14. What are the arrangements for the transition of management? Who is responsible for overall decision making? In other words, who has the final say?
15. What about the other children? Have I looked after them? Are they financially independent?
16. How will the debt be handled? Do my children assume the existing debt, borrow elsewhere, or pay off the old debt?
17. How much tax will be payable? How much will it cost my child or children? How much will it cost me?
18. Have I discussed my succession plan with my entire family? Do I know what their hopes and expectations are?
19. What am I hoping to achieve at the end of this process?

## Talk to Family

For some farmers, deciding what to do with the farm business can be both stressful and troublesome. How can he or she pass the farm business to the next generation, while, at the same time, avoiding the creation of animosity or envy between the children? If he or she divides the farm equally between all the children, will it create such small fragments that the successor child cannot make a living from operating it? If one child is required to buy out his or her siblings, will the business create enough income to make this a feasible and viable option? Is dividing the farm equally between all of the children always a fair solution? Experience has shown that every situation and family is unique, but, whatever is ultimately decided upon, an honest and open approach from the outset, with clear communication with all of the children in the family, should assist the process.

The farmer who is considering transferring the farm should organise his or her thoughts and, at an early stage, have a discussion with the entire family. An open conversation, with all those involved, is required, so as to avoid any misunderstandings. The farmer who is planning to retire, and the proposed transferee of the farm, should be involved in the preparation process. This includes spouses and in-laws. Spouses and in-laws who are informed about the process, and are actively involved in the process, often offer support. They can also bring a unique perspective to succession planning, and help to achieve a fulfilling end result.

In the absence of special circumstances, the farmer should involve all of his or her children in the transfer process, and should communicate to them the proposed plan for transfer and distribution of assets. Ideally, this communication should be entered into while the farmer is in good health and of sound mind. Doing so may help to avoid catastrophic familial acrimony, will generally ensure a smooth transition, and, most importantly, may help to keep sibling relationships intact. Usually, those who are consulted will understand the reasons behind a farmer's decisions, and they will respect and accept them.

One of the most difficult dilemmas faced by many farm families is how to transfer the farm to a young son or daughter who is at home farming the land, while, at the same time, being fair to the non-farming children.

What is fair? In the dictionary, the word 'fair' is defined as treating people equally without favouritism or discrimination.[6] When it comes to succession planning and transfer of the family farm, being fair does not necessarily require that every child should receive assets or farmland of the same value. Instead, it involves every child receiving what they reasonably need in order to be independent. Fairness does not always mean equal treatment of all children. Sometimes, treating all children equally in succession planning can result in a very unfair outcome for the child who is at home farming on a full time basis. Dividing a farm is rarely an option, unless the holding is very large. In most cases, if a farm is to remain viable, it will have to remain intact, and not be divided up so as to achieve equality between a number of children.

---

[6] *Concise Oxford English Dictionary* (OUP, 2011).

There are many reasons which may justify what might, at first glance, appear to be unequal treatment of a farmer's children:

1. Non-farming children may have received college tuition, a down payment on a house, a site, or other compensation, so that, in effect, they have received their inheritance early. In other words, they have been assisted in setting up their lives;

2. The farming child will generally have helped to create part of the final estate of their parents, by actively contributing to their parent's business over the years. As a consequence, they may be entitled to more. The issue of 'contribution versus compensation' must be considered. 'Fair' does not always mean 'equal'. 'Equal' does not always mean 'fair'. Non-farming children often leave the farm in their teenage years to pursue careers elsewhere. They may have no interest in farming, or in receiving a transfer of part of the farm. In many instances, they will not have contributed in any meaningful way to the ongoing farming activity;

3. Parents often want the farm to be kept in the family. Consequently, they may wish to give more to the farming child whose goal it is to stay on the farm for this purpose, and in the hope that their child will eventually pass the farm on to a grandchild at some future time;

4. Effectively, the farming child is receiving delayed compensation for work performed in years when he or she was underpaid. The farming child may have foregone foreign travel and other luxuries to stay at home farming the land in question. The child may already have invested a great deal of 'sweat equity' into the business;

5. In many cases, a farming child has been, or will be, attending to most of the physical and other needs of their parents in their declining years.

Undoubtedly, the vast majority of farmers want to be fair to all of their children. They do not want non-farming children to feel that they have been unfairly treated or slighted, but, in reality, if a farmer were to divide the farm enterprise into equal pieces between more than one child, it is questionable whether each equal slice would be of adequate size to create a viable business. In most cases, it would not. For this reason alone, it is important to have a family meeting at which a farmer can communicate his or her wishes for the future of the farm to all children.

## Tax

The tax payable, if any, depends on the circumstances of each case, and a detailed discussion with a solicitor and a tax consultant or accountant is required in advance of any transfer taking place.

The three taxes to be considered when a farm is transferred during the lifetime of a farmer are:

1. Stamp Duty;
2. Capital Acquisitions Tax (also known as 'Gift Tax');
3. Capital Gains Tax.

Each of the aforementioned taxes are principally governed by the Capital Acquisitions Tax Consolidation Act (CATCA) 2003, Taxes Consolidation Act 1997, and Stamp Duties Consolidation Act 1999, as updated to the Finance Act 2015.

It should be noted that this section outlines the basic principles and some of the reliefs available, but it is very important to seek advice in relation to one's particular set of circumstances in advance of transferring a family farm, or any assets.

## Stamp Duty[7]

Stamp duty is a tax on a document ('instrument'),[8] such as a Deed of Transfer or a Deed of Conveyance, used to transfer or convey land or farm buildings. It should be noted that Basic Payment entitlements, livestock, or machinery are not liable to stamp duty, as they do not pass by virtue of a Deed of Transfer or Deed of Conveyance. The general rate of stamp duty on non-residential property, including land, is 2%.[9] The general rate of stamp duty is 1% on residential property with a market value of up to €1 million. Stamp duty on the excess over €1 million is 2%.[10] The provisions dealing with the stamp duty payable on gifts are found in s.30 of the Stamp Duty Consolidation Act 1999.

Current legislation provides for Consanguinity Relief.[11] This applies to transfers of non-residential property between certain blood relatives, for example, a parent, a child or a nephew or niece. With the benefit of this relief, duty is charged at half the normal rate i.e. it is reduced to 1%.

---

[7] Stamp Duties Consolidation Act 1999.

[8] Defined in the Stamp Duties Consolidation Act 1999, s 1, as including every written document.

[9] Stamp Duties Consolidation Act 1999, sch 1.

[10] Stamp Duties Consolidation Act 1999, sch 1.

[11] Stamp Duties Consolidation Act 1999, sch 1, para 5.

There were proposals to abolish this relief on 1 January 2015. However, it has been extended for another three years, provided the transferor is under the age of 67 years at the time of the transfer. It is to remain in place until 31 December 2018.[12]

In addition, in order to avail of Consanquinity Relief the individual to whom the land is transferred or conveyed must, from the date of execution of the transfer or conveyance:

- farm the land for a period of not less than six years[13];
  or
- lease it for a period of not less than six years to an individual who will farm the land.[14]

In addition the person who farms the land (be the recipient or the tenant) must either:

- be the holder of (or, within a period of four years from the date of the conveyance or transfer, become the holder of) a qualification set out in Schedule 2, 2A or 2B to the SCDA; or
- spend not less than 50% of the individual's normal working time farming land (including the land conveyed or transferred).

The relief is only applicable to farmland, and is not available in respect of other transfers, such as the transfer of a site to a child or the transfer of residential property.[15]

### Young Trained Farmer Relief[16]

There is another stamp duty relief, known as Young Trained Farmer Relief, which provides a full exemption from stamp duty for those who meet the necessary criteria.[17]

---

[12] Stamp Duties Consolidation Act 1999, s 81AA as amended by Finance Act 2015, s 563.

[13] Finance Act 2014, s 77(1).

[14] ibid.

[15] Revenue Guide to Farming Taxation Measures in Finance Act 2014 Part 5.2 and Stamp Duties Consolidation Act 1999, Paragraph 5, Schedule 1.

[16] For further information, see Revenue, 'Leaflet SD2B' (2016) <www.revenue.ie/en/tax/stamp-duty/leaflets/sd2b.pdf> accessed 22 June 2016.

[17] Stamp Duties Consolidation Act 1999, s 81AA.

A recipient of a gift of farmland, or the purchaser of farmland, qualifies for Young Trained Farmer Relief if he or she is under the age of 35 years at the date of the transfer and he or she satisfies the appropriate agricultural requirements.[18]

The transferee, including the partners, or the working director in the case of a company, must:

1. Be the holder of (or, within a period of 4 years from the date of the conveyance or transfer, become the holder of) an appropriate educational qualification (historically known as a 'green cert'); and
2. Spend not less than 50% of the individual's normal working time farming land (including the land conveyed or transferred).[19]

As is clear from the above requirements, Young Trained Farmer Relief is only available in the case of a transfer or sale of land, where the individual subsequently farms the land for the required period.[20] Young Trained Farmer Relief does not apply in the case where the land is subsequently let. Unlike the Capital Acquisitions Tax (Gift Tax) rules, discussed below, the Revenue Commissioners have not defined what is meant by 'normal working time', and, in light of this, persons hoping to benefit from Young Trained Farmer Relief should, in the interests of prudence, rely on the literal meaning and spend at least 50% of their working time farming.

There are a number of additional observations on the issue of Young Trained Farmer Relief.

The relief only applies where all purchasers or recipients have the appropriate qualifications. As such, a transfer of a share of a farm holding, such as putting the family farm into joint names with a successor son or daughter, would not benefit from the relief. The only exception to this rule is where the land is being transferred into the joint ownership of spouses or civil partners.[21]

---

[18] Stamp Duties Consolidation Act, 1999 s 81AA.

[19] Stamp Duties Consolidation Act 1999 Schedule 1 as amended by Finance Act 2014, s 77(1).

[20] Stamp Duties Consolidation Act 1999, s 81AA(8)(a).

[21] Stamp Duties Consolidation Act 1999, s 81AA(9).

Where a purchaser or recipient of farmland is under 35 years of age at the point of purchase or transfer, but has not obtained the relevant qualifications, stamp duty will apply on the purchase or transfer under normal rules. However, he or she can obtain a refund of the stamp duty paid where he or she acquires the necessary educational qualification within four years from the date of execution of the Deed of Transfer or Deed of Conveyance, and an application for the refund is made within the appropriate time frame.[22]

The exemption granted will be clawed back if the land is disposed of within five years from the date of execution of the Deed of Transfer or Deed of Conveyance and is not replaced by other land within one year of disposal.

Stamp duty does not apply in the case of transfers under a will or intestacy.

The current regime of Young Trained Farmer Relief is legislated for until 31 December 2018.

## Example 1

Patricia transfers her farmlands to her son, Kevin. Kevin is 38 years of age, so he is over the age which would have entitled him to qualify for Young Trained Farmer Relief. Patricia is 65 years of age. Consanguinity Relief applies, and stamp duty of 2% is reduced to 1%. The farmlands have a value of €1,000,000. The stamp duty payable is €10,000.

## Example 2

Daniel transfers his farmlands to his nephew, Joseph. Joseph is 33 years of age and has obtained an appropriate agricultural qualification. The farmlands have a market value of €2,000,000. He does not have to pay any stamp duty on the Deed of Transfer or Deed of Conveyance as he qualifies for Young Trained Farmer Relief.

---

[22] Stamp Duties Consolidation Act 1999, s 81AA(11).

## Capital Acquisitions Tax (Gift Tax)[23]

Capital Acquisitions Tax (Gift Tax) arises where a beneficiary receives a gift during the lifetime of the person making the gift. The beneficiary is responsible for paying the tax. The current Capital Acquisitions Tax (Gift Tax) rate is 33%.[24]

The gift is taxed if its value is over a certain limit or threshold. Different tax-free thresholds apply, depending on the relationship between the person giving the benefit and the person receiving the benefit. There are also a number of exemptions and reliefs that may be available, depending on the type of gift involved.

One very important exemption is one which is available to spouses and civil partners. Regardless of its value, a gift taken by one spouse or civil partner from the other is completely exempt and will not be liable to Capital Acquisitions Tax (Gift Tax).[25]

### Other Beneficiaries

For other beneficiaries, the potential liability to Capital Acquisitions Tax (Gift Tax) depends upon:

- the total value of all gifts and inheritances
- received by the beneficiary
- from the person making the gift, or from anybody else to whom the same group threshold applies
- in the period from 5 December 1991 up to (and including) the date of the gift which exceeds a tax-free element called the 'tax-free amount'.[26]

---

[23] Capital Acquisitions Tax Consolidation Act (CATCA) 2003.

[24] Capital Acquisitions Tax Consolidation Act (CATCA) 2003 Schedule 2, Irish Tax Institute Capital Acquisitions Tax and Stamp Duty Manual 2014/2015, pp 2 and 5.

[25] Capital Acquisitions Tax Consolidation Act (CATCA) 2003, s 70.

[26] Irish Tax Institute Capital Acquisitions Tax and Stamp Duty Manual 2014/2015, p 7.

## Capital Acquisitions Tax Thresholds
### (from 14 October 2015)

| | |
|---|---|
| Group A:<br>€280,000 | Applies where the beneficiary is a child (including an adopted child, a step-child, and certain foster children) or minor child of a deceased child of the disponer. Parents also fall within this threshold where they take an inheritance of an absolute interest from a child. This group threshold can also apply in the case of transfers to a 'favourite niece' or 'favourite nephew'.[27] Favourite nephew/niece relief entitles a beneficiary who is a child of the disponer's brother or sister or a child of the civil partner of the disponer's brother or sister to be treated as a "child" of the disponer, provided certain conditions are met. Where the relief applies, the niece or nephew is entitled to the Group A threshold instead of the Group B threshold.<br><br>The relief applies to a niece or nephew who has worked substantially on a full-time basis for the disponer for the period of five years ending on the date the disponer ceases to have a beneficial interest in possession in the business. The relief will only apply to assets used in connection with the business. Note that farming is a business for the purposes of the relief. |
| Group B:<br>€30,150 | Applies where the beneficiary is a brother, sister, niece, nephew, or lineal ancestor or lineal descendant of the disponer (e.g. grandchild, grandfather). This group threshold also applies in relation to gifts from a child to a parent.[28] |
| Group C:<br>€15,075 | Applies in all other cases i.e. strangers in blood.[29] |

---

[27] Revenue, 'Capital Acquisitions Tax Manual – Part 10' (November 2015) <www.revenue.ie/en/about/foi/s16/capital-acquisitions-tax/cat-part10> accessed 23 June 2016., CATCA 2003, Schedule 2, Part 1, Paragraph 1 and Finance Act 2013, s 85.

[28] CATCA 2003, Schedule 2, Part 1, Paragraph 1 and Finance Act 2013, s 85.

[29] Capital Acquisitions Tax Consolidation Act CATCA 2003, Schedule 2, Part 1, Paragraph 1 and Finance Act 2015, s 67.

## Are There Any Gift Tax Reliefs or Exemptions?

In addition to the exemption for a spouse or civil partner, there are a number of other important exemptions and reliefs which may be available. These include the following:

- Agricultural Relief[30];
- Business Relief[31];
- Dwelling House Relief.[32]

### Agricultural Relief[33]

Agricultural Relief, which is enormously important in farm transfers, operates by reducing the market value of agricultural property by 90%, so that Capital Acquisitions Tax (Gift Tax) is calculated on an amount known as the 'agricultural value', which is effectively one-tenth of the open market value.

### Conditions for the Relief

In general, the relief applies, provided the beneficiary qualifies as a 'farmer' as defined in the legislation.[34] The beneficiary qualifies as a 'farmer' if, on the valuation date,[35] the beneficiary's agricultural property[36] comprises 80% of his or her total property. The test is based on the valuation of the beneficiary's assets, and no account is taken of the beneficiary's liabilities in assessing his or her percentage of agricultural assets and non-agricultural assets, with one exception: debts or encumbrances in respect of a dwelling-house that is the only or main residence of the donee or successor can be deducted from the market value of that property.[37]

---

[30] Capital Acquisitions Tax Consolidation Act (CATCA) 2003, s 89, and Finance Act 2014.

[31] Capital Acquisitions Tax Consolidation Act (CATCA) 2003, s 90-102.

[32] Capital Acquisitions Tax Consolidation Act (CATCA) 2003, s 86.

[33] Capital Acquisitions Tax Consolidation Act (CATCA) 2003, s 89, and Finance Act 2014.

[34] Capital Acquisitions Tax Consolidation Act (CATCA) 2003, s 89(1).

[35] The valuation date is the date on which the market value of the property comprising the gift is established. In the case of a gift, the valuation date is the date of the gift. CATCA 2003, s 30(1).

[36] 'Agricultural property' is defined in the Capital Acquisitions Tax Consolidation Act (CATCA) 2003, s 89(1), and includes houses and other farm buildings appropriate to the property.

[37] Capital Acquisitions Tax Consolidation Act (CATCA) 2003, s 89(1).

In addition, anti-avoidance rules[38] circumvent any effort by an individual to temporarily deprive themselves of non-agricultural property with a view to satisfying the asset test and the valuations of non-agricultural property held by an individual must also include any 'interest in expectancy'.[39]

To qualify for the relief, the gift must consist of agricultural property, both at the date of the gift and at the valuation date. The valuation date is the date at which the property is valued for Capital Acquisitions Tax (Gift Tax) purposes.

## Example: The 'Farmer' Test

In 2016, John gave his farm to his son, James. The gift consisted of the following:

| | |
|---|---|
| Farmlands | €1,000,000 |
| Farmhouse | €150,000 |
| Stock | €50,000 |

James owns his own house, which is his principal residence. The house is valued at €300,000, and James has a mortgage on this property of €150,000. James also owns a jeep, valued at €15,000, and has savings of €10,000.

Is James a farmer?

To calculate:

$$\frac{\text{Agricultural property}}{\text{Agricultural property plus non-agricultural property}} \times 100$$

For James to qualify as a farmer, the answer must not be less than 80%.

$$\frac{1,200,000}{1,200,000 + (150,000 + 15,000 + 10,000)} \times 100 = 87.27\%$$

James is, therefore, considered to be a farmer.

---

[38] Capital Acquisitions Tax Consolidation Act (CATCA) 2003, s 89(1).
[39] Meaning a 'future interest'. Capital Acquisitions Tax Consolidation Act (CATCA) 2003, s 2.

James' mortgage can be deducted from the market value of his principal residence for the purposes of the farmer test.[40]

In addition, to pass the 'farmer' test, the beneficiary must:

1. Farm the agricultural property for a period of not less than six years commencing on the valuation date[41];
   or
2. Lease the agricultural property for a period of not less than six years commencing on the valuation date. The agricultural property may be leased to a number of tenants as long as each lease and tenant satisfies the conditions of the relief.[42]

In addition, the beneficiary (or the lessee, where relevant) must:

1. Have an appropriate agricultural qualification;
   or
2. Farm the agricultural property for not less than 50% of his or her normal working time.[43]

The agricultural property must also be farmed on a commercial basis and with a view to the realisation of profits.[44]

As a matter of practice, the Revenue Commissioners accept, for the purpose of the relief, that 'normal working time', including on-farm and off-farm working time, approximates to forty hours per week. This will enable farmers with off-farm employment to qualify for the relief, provided they spend a minimum average of twenty hours per week working on the farm. Where the individual can show that their 'normal working time' is somewhat less than 40 hours a week, then the 50% requirement will be applied to the actual hours worked, subject to the overriding requirement that the land is farmed on a commercial basis and with a view to the realisation of profits. In the majority of situations it should be clear from the level of farming activity being carried on whether the normal working time requirement is satisfied. If there is any doubt, the Revenue Commissioners

---

[40] Capital Acquisitions Tax Consolidation Act (CATCA) 2003, s 89(1).
[41] Revenue Commissioners Cat Manual Part 11, p 5.
[42] Revenue Commissioners Cat Manual Part 11, p 5.
[43] Revenue Commissioners Cat Manual Part 11, p 6.
[44] Revenue Commissioners Cat Manual Part 11, p 7.

will consider all information (including farming records) provided by a farmer in relation to his or her normal working time and farming activities. If, in exceptional situations it can be shown that, on an ongoing basis, certain farming activities, such as the occupation of woodlands, are carried out on a commercial basis and with a view to the realisation of profits, but do not require 50% of a person's normal working time/20 hours per week, the Revenue Commissioners will take this into consideration in deciding whether the relief is due.[45]

Again, be aware that this relief will be disallowed if the property is disposed of within six years, including the transfer into joint names with a spouse or civil partner within that six-year period.[46] Rules cater for a continuation of the relief where the proceeds are reinvested in alternative agricultural property within a period of 1 year of a disposal.[47] In the case of development land, the relief will be disallowed where a disposal is within a period of ten years.[48]

## Example I

Michael gifts his farmlands, farm machinery, and stock, with a market value of €500,000, to his daughter Angela. Angela qualifies as a 'farmer', having passed the farmer test and having committed to farming the property for 6 years from the date of the transfer. Angela has not received any other gifts or inheritances within her Group A threshold.

The agricultural value of the property is calculated as follows:

| | |
|---|---|
| Market value of agricultural property | €500,000 |
| Relief: 90% reduction of market value | €450,000 |
| Agricultural value of property | €50,000 |
| Annual small gift exemption[49] | (€3,000) |
| Taxable value | €47,000 |

---

[45] Revenue Commissioners Cat Manual Part 11, p 6.

[46] Capital Acquisitions Tax Consolidation Act (CATCA) 2003, s 89(4).

[47] Capital Acquisitions Tax Consolidation Act (CATCA) 2003, s 89(4)(ii).

[48] Capital Acquisitions Tax Consolidation Act (CATCA) 2003, s 102A.

[49] Capital Acquisitions Tax Consolidation Act (CATCA) 2003, s 69(2).

Angela is treated as having received a gift of €47,000. As her group threshold is €280,000, she is treated as having used up €47,000 of her tax-free threshold, and no Capital Acquisitions Tax (Gift Tax) is payable.

### Example 2

Assume that, in the previous example, Angela paid €20,000 in consideration for the agricultural property, and €10,000 in expenses and costs associated with the transfer. The amount of the consideration, the expenses, and the costs deductible in arriving at the taxable value of the property, are calculated using the following simple formula:

## Costs and Expenses

(Agricultural value of property/Open market value of property) × Cost and Expenses

$$(€50,000/€500,000) × €10,000 = €1,000$$

## Consideration

(Agricultural value of property/Open market value of property) × Consideration

$$(€50,000/€500,000) × €20,000 = €2,000$$

Therefore, the taxable value of the property for Capital Acquisitions Tax (Gift Tax) purposes is:

| | |
|---|---|
| Market value | €500,000 |
| Relief: 90% | €450,000 |
| Agricultural Value | €50,000 |
| *Less:* Allowable proportion of: | |
| – Consideration | €2,000 |
| – Costs and expenses | €1,000 |
| – Annual tax free exemption | €3,000 |
| Taxable value | €44,000 |

Angela is treated as having received a gift of €44,000. As her group threshold is €280,000, she is treated as having used up €44,000 of her tax-free threshold, and no Capital Acquisitions Tax (Gift Tax) is payable.

## Example 3
Margaret transfers her farm, with a market value of €1 million, to her son, Paul. Paul does not qualify for Agricultural Relief, and is liable to Capital Acquisitions Tax (Gift Tax) for any gift above €280,000, at a rate of 33%[50] on the balance. Such a situation is uncommon but illustrates the significance of qualifying for agricultural relief.

An inheritance tax return (IT 38) must be filed in order to successfully claim agricultural relief and pay inheritance tax.[51] Where the valuation date arises between 1 January and 31 August in any year the filing date is the 31 October that same year; if the valuation date is on or after the 1 September the filing date is the 31 October the following year.[52] There are provisions for a later filing date if filing and discharging the tax via the Revenue on-line system (ROS) which may vary from year to year. A 5% surcharge applies, subject to a maximum of €12,695, where the tax return is delivered within two months of the filing date. A 10% surcharge, up to a maximum of €63,485, will be applied where the tax return is not delivered within two months of the filing date. Interest also arises for late payments.

## Business Relief[53]
Business Relief will amount to a reduction of 90% in respect of the value attributable to relevant business property taken by the beneficiary.[54]

Only relevant business property will qualify for the relief. Relevant business property is defined in s 93 of the CATCA 2003 and is complex and it can include property consisting of a business or interest in a business, any land or building, machinery or plant which, immediately before the gift, was used wholly or mainly for the purposes of a business carried on by a company of which the disponer then had control or by a partnership of which the disponer then was a partner.

---

[50] The Capital Acquisitions Tax (Gift Tax) rate in place at the time of writing.
[51] Capital Acquisitions Tax Consolidation (CATCA) Act 2003, s 46(2).
[52] Capital Acquisitions Tax Consolidation (CATCA) Act 2003, s 46(2A).
[53] Capital Acquisitions Tax Consolidation Act (CATCA) 2003, s 90-102.
[54] Capital Acquisitions Tax Consolidation Act (CATCA) 2003, s 92.

To qualify for the relief, the relevant business property must have been owned for a continuous period of five years prior to the date of the gift.[55]

The business must continue for a period of 6 years post transfer.[56]

The relief, as the name suggests, is only applicable in relation to businesses. As such, the transfer of land in isolation would not, by definition, benefit under Business Relief. By contrast, the transfer of a farm comprising of a collection of assets, such as land, machinery, stock, and payment entitlements as a going concern, could potentially benefit under Business Relief.

## Example

Finbarr receives the family business from his father, Thomas. The taxable value of the business is €1,000,000. Business Relief is calculated as follows:

| | |
|---|---|
| Taxable value prior to relief | €1,000,000 |
| Relief: 90% | €900,000 |
| Revised taxable value after relief | €100,000 |
| Annual exemption | (€3,000) |
| Taxable gift | €97,000 |

Finbarr is treated as having received a gift of €97,000. As his group threshold is €280,000, he is treated as having used up €97,000 of his tax-free threshold, and no Capital Acquisitions Tax (Gift Tax) is payable.

There is a clawback of Business Relief[57] in the event that, within six years, commencing on the date of the gift, the assets cease to qualify as relevant business property, or the business or any business that replaced it is sold, redeemed, or compulsorily acquired, unless the business assets are replaced within one year by other relevant business assets.[58]

---

[55] Capital Acquisitions Tax Consolidation Act (CATCA) 2003, s 94.
[56] Capital Acquisitions Tax Consolidation Act (CATCA) 2003, s 101(1).
[57] Capital Acquisitions Tax Consolidation Act (CATCA) 2003, s 101.
[58] There are exceptions, such as bankruptcy or if the company is wound up bone fide due to insolvency.

Where there is a clawback of Business Relief, the tax is recalculated on the benefit as though the asset on which the relief is to be clawed back was not a business asset.[59]

## Dwelling-House Relief[60]

Dwelling-House Relief provides that a gift of a dwelling-house, taken on or after 1 December 1999, will be exempt from Capital Acquisitions Tax (Gift Tax), provided that the following conditions are complied with:

- The beneficiary must have occupied the dwelling-house continuously as his or her only or main residence for a period of three years immediately prior to the date of the gift[61];
- The beneficiary must not be entitled to an interest in any other dwelling-house at the date of the gift[62];
- The house must be owned by the owner during the three-year period prior to the gift[63];
- The beneficiary must continue, except where such recipient was aged fifty-five years or more at the date of the gift or has subsequently died, to occupy that dwelling-house as his or her only or main residence for a period of six years commencing on the date of the gift.[64]

Rules cater for a sale and replacement of alternative property within the six-year period.[65]

# Capital Gains Tax (CGT)[66]

CGT is a tax payable by the transferor. It is a tax on the increase in value of assets, such as land and buildings, from the date on which the transferor

---

[59] Irish Tax Institute Capital Acquisitions Tax and Stamp Duty Manual 2014/2015, p 206.

[60] Capital Acquisitions Tax Consolidation Act (CATCA) 2003, s 86.

[61] Capital Acquisitions Tax Consolidation Act (CATCA) 2003, s 86(3)(1)(a).

[62] Capital Acquisitions Tax Consolidation Act (CATCA) 2003, s 86(3)(b).

[63] Capital Acquisitions Tax Consolidation Act (CATCA) 2003, s 86(3)(A).

[64] Capital Acquisitions Tax Consolidation Act (CATCA) 2003, s 86(3)(1)(b).

[65] Capital Acquisitions Tax Consolidation Act (CATCA) 2003, s 86(7) and 86(8).

[66] Taxes Consolidation Act 1997, ch 3. For more information, see Revenue, 'Guide to Capital Gains Tax' (July 2015) <www.revenue.ie/en/tax/cgt/leaflets/cgt1.pdf> accessed 20 June 2016, and Revenue, 'Guide to Farming Taxation Measures in Finance Act 2014' (December 2014) <www.revenue.ie/en/tax/cat/leaflets/guide-farming-taxation-measures-fa2014.pdf> accessed 20 June 2016.

acquired the assets to the date he or she transfers them.[67] The current tax rate is 33%.[68]

The main saviour in relation to CGT is Retirement Relief,[69] which can greatly reduce or completely eliminate the tax.

In the context of the sale or transfer of a family farm, the conditions which must be met in order to avail of Retirement Relief are as follows:

- The transferor is over the age of 55 years[70];
- The transferor has farmed the relevant land for a period of at least 10 years[71];
- The transferor has owned the relevant land for over 10 years[72];
- In relation to the sale or disposal to a child (including a favourite niece or nephew), a limit of €3 million applies where the transferor is over the age of 66 at the time of the transfer.[73] No such limit applies where the transfer occurs prior to the individual's 66th birthday.[74] Special rules must be adhered to in order that a niece or nephew can be considered a child for the purposes of this relief[75];
- In relation to a sale or transfer to a third party, a limit of €750,000 applies where the transfer occurs prior to the individuals 66th birthday, with a limit of €500,000 applying where the sale or transfer occurs after this period.[76]

For the purposes of establishing the taxation application, the value of all relevant disposals are aggregated.

It is important that specialist advice be sought before any transfer takes place. In general, most farmers will be in a position to transfer to a child free from Capital Gains Tax, but it is important to obtain advice in relation

---

[67] Irish Tax Institute Capital Gains Tax Manual 2014/2015 Page 2.
[68] Taxes Consolidation Act 1997, s 28(3).
[69] Taxes Consolidation Act 1997, s 598 and s 599.
[70] Taxes Consolidation Act 1997, s 598(2).
[71] Taxes Consolidation Act 1997, s 598(1).
[72] Taxes Consolidation Act 1997, s 598(1)(a).
[73] Taxes Consolidation Act 1997, s 599(1)(b)(iia).
[74] Taxes Consolidation Act 1997, s 599.
[75] Taxes Consolidation Act 1997, s 599(1)(a).
[76] Taxes Consolidation Act 1997, s 598.

to one's particular set of circumstances. The following points are also relevant;

- To claim the relief, retirement is not necessary;
- In the case of land which has been let, but previously owned and farmed by that individual, such a person disposing of such land can also potentially benefit from Retirement Relief, where such land has been first let within a twenty-five-year period up to the date of its disposal, and where other relevant criteria are satisfied.[77] Land which is let by conacre, which is destined to be sold or transferred to any person other than a child, will not qualify for Retirement Relief post 31 December 2016. A temporary concession allows landowners who currently let their land by way of conacre to potentially benefit from Retirement Relief past this deadline, where they convert from conacre arrangements to leasing for a minimum lease period of 5 years (with successive leases on each lease expiration), or instead, such owners may potentially be in a position to avail of Retirement Relief where they dispose of their land prior to 31 December 2016[78];
- For the purposes of the relief, a child is deemed to include certain other persons, such as a grandchild, where the intermediate child of the owner or parent of the grandchild is deceased[79];
- Of course, it is important to establish, in the first instance, what quantum of tax liability could arise on a future sale or transfer under the benefit of Retirement Relief, in deciding whether to take action to secure such a benefit, either by conversion to leasing or transfer prior to 31 December 2016.

## Example

Frank is 62 years of age and transfers the farm to his son, David. The farm assets have a market value of €2 million. Frank has owned the land for the past 30 years, and has farmed it for the past 30 years prior to the transfer to David. Frank qualifies for Retirement Relief and the full value is exempt from Capital Gains Tax.

---

[77] Taxes Consolidation Act 1997, s 598(1)(a).

[78] Revenue Commissioners Notes for Guidance – Taxes Consolidation Act 1997 – Finance Act 2015 Edition – Part 19, p 112.

[79] Taxes Consolidation Act 1997, s 599(1)(a) and s 599(6).

## Ensuring Emotional and Financial Security after the Transfer

One major concern for the older generation, and something that should be borne in mind by their legal advisors, is that of their welfare and security after they have retired and have transferred all, or some, of their assets. The great majority of farmers will feel that, having worked on the farm all their lives, they have a right to expect some form of income from it after they retire. Good advance planning will ensure that timely and appropriate steps are taken to provide a nest egg for the future, such as a pension or a retirement plan. In the absence of such a pension or plan, it may be necessary to secure an income from the farm.

Every family and set of circumstances is unique, and each farmer will obviously want to do what is best for his or her children. It is particularly important to ensure, insofar as is possible, that the farmer who is considering the transfer of his or her farm will be emotionally and financially secure following such transfer.

Each farmer must ask him or herself if he or she is emotionally ready to transfer the farm and let go of ownership and control. This can be difficult for many farmers, especially if they have been the sole decision maker for many years and will be leaving it to someone else to take control of the reins. The farmer must acknowledge the reality of retirement and all that it entails. Among the questions that he or she must ask him or herself is whether or not he or she has a retirement plan to provide an income during his or her retirement. Retiring farmers must consider their plans, hopes, dreams and any goals that they would like to achieve.

Probably the most important issue to be faced is that of the financial security of the farmer after the farm has been transferred. Another key issue is whether or not the family home should be transferred at the same time as the farm, or, alternatively, be retained and then dealt with under a valid will, which would take effect only upon death. In many cases, the farmer may wish to transfer the family home at the same time as the farm, and retain a right of residence in the property for his or her lifetime. A right of residence is a right to reside in a property. A right of residence normally extends to the entirety of a dwelling-house, although historically, in older transfers or wills, provisions were made for a right to reside in a room or portion of a dwelling-house only.

A right of residence can be exclusive or non-exclusive, and whether it is one or the other will depend on the wording used. Normally, for an exclusive right of residence to be created, the word 'exclusive' or similar words should be used. In circumstances where the family home is transferred with the lands and outbuildings, a right of residence should be reserved for the retiring farmer and his or her spouse. In appropriate cases, consideration should also be given to retaining actual ownership of the family home and some of the farm assets, in order to provide some security.

From a taxation perspective, the transfer of the farmhouse at the time of the transfer of the land (albeit with the retention of a right of residency), can result in a more tax efficient outcome than an initial transfer of the farmland with a subsequent transfer of the farmhouse upon, say, the passing of the last surviving parent. Should the latter occur, the benefit of the farmhouse would not, as a result of the separation of the assets, qualify for Agricultural Relief, meaning that a significant liability to Capital Acquisitions Tax (Gift Tax) can arise. The retention of a right of residence is regarded as equivalent to the partial retention of property by the transferor, meaning that, upon the termination of the right of residence (e.g. on the passing of the transferor), a beneficiary will be treated as receiving a subsequent partial benefit. Special care should be taken in respect of rights of residence and exclusive rights of residence, as a result of the complicated taxation implications of each.

Sometimes the farmer may wish to gift the family home to another member of the family. However, it is advisable to be practical here. The recipient of the farmland will usually need to live nearby. This is particularly relevant, for example, at times when cows are calving in the middle of the night. It is important to strike the right balance while, at the same time, being practical.

Some farmers wish to retain building sites or valuable pieces of land, which can be sold in the short term, or later, or might possibly be used as a means of providing gifts to other children. Such sites may need to be marked out by a competent engineer in advance of the transfer, in order to clearly identify them and to avoid disputes or difficulty at a later date.

Some farmers may wish to include, in the Deed of Transfer or Deed of Conveyance, a proviso that the recipient will pay a certain amount of monies over an agreed number of years in consideration of the gift, in order to provide an income. Other farmers may wish to include a covenant, in the Deed of Transfer or Deed of Conveyance, that a certain amount of monies will be paid by the recipient to other members of the family within a stated time. Some retiring farmers may wish to retain ownership of some of the farm for life as security, and then lease it to the successor to generate income. Many Deeds of Transfer or Deeds of Conveyance will include a reservation of right of maintenance and support in favour of the farmer and his or her spouse for their respective lives. However, whilst this provides some security for the older generation, it may complicate matters for the transferee, if he or she needs to use the assets as collateral for a loan in the future.

While it is important for any transferor to ensure that he or she is financially secure after the farm has been transferred, it is equally important not to excessively burden the successor. He or she needs to earn a livelihood to support his or her own family, and must be given scope to grow the business.

## Fair Deal Scheme

The Fair Deal Scheme is governed by the Nursing Homes Support Scheme Act 2009 (hereafter 'the 2009 Act').

An important consideration which should be borne in mind by farmers is the fact that a person's income and assets are subject to a detailed examination by the Health Service Executive (HSE) in determining the level of contribution which must be made towards nursing home care costs as set out in the 2009 Act.

Section 5(2) of the 2009 Act states that:

> The Scheme is established for the purpose of giving financial support under this Act in respect of care services in accordance with this Act out of the resources allocated to the Scheme in each year .... and shall consist of the provision of financial support in respect of care services.

The Scheme was established primarily to help the elderly to meet maintenance costs in a nursing home. The amount of state support which a person receives is based on an assessment of his or her means.

The means assessment takes into account all the assets which the person holds, as well as his or her income. Basically, the Scheme looks at both the income and assets of an individual.

There is a duty on an applicant to provide all the information requested by the Health Service Executive (HSE) and there is a duty to be honest and truthful with all information provided.[80]

Section 9(5) of the 2009 Act states that:

> Any person who knowingly, or recklessly, gives the Executive information which is false or misleading in a material particular in, with, or in connection with, an application for State support is guilty of an offence and is liable on summary conviction to a fine not exceeding €5,000 or imprisonment for a term not exceeding 3 months or both.

## The 'Five-Year Look-Back' Rule

Part 3, Schedule 1 of the 2009 Act defines 'relevant assets' which are subject to assessment as

> … all forms of property whether situated in the State or not other than cash assets, including, options and incorporeal property generally in which the relevant person has a beneficial interest including transferred assets which would have been relevant assets if not transferred.

A 'transferred asset' is defined in the 2009 Act as

> … an interest of the person in an asset (whether a cash asset or a relevant asset) which has been transferred at any time in the period of 5 years prior to the date on which an application for State Support is first made by or on behalf of that person which transfer is made
> (a) for no consideration;
> (b) for nominal consideration; or
> (c) for consideration which is less than 75 per cent of the estimated market value of the interest of the person in the asset at the time of the transfer, but does not include the transfer of an asset made in respect of the settlement of any claim made in respect of the maintenance of a child or other matrimonial proceedings, and that the Executive is satisfied that such transfer was made for that purpose.[81]

---

[80] Nursing Homes Support Scheme Act 2009, s 9(2).
[81] Nursing Homes Support Scheme Act 2009, part 3, Schedule 1.

Essentially, for farmers, this means that there is a 'five-year look-back' rule, and assets, including the farm which they have transferred in the five-year period before applying for the nursing home Scheme, are included in the calculations to assess eligibility. A provision in the Scheme states that certain assets of a person who is to be in receipt of State support or ancillary State support, which were disposed of by the person within the five years before the application is made for the support, will nonetheless be included as assets in computation of the person's assessed means, whether those assets are cash assets or otherwise, disposed as a gift or at less than 75% of the estimated market value.[82]

The same rules apply to transferred income, which is income which the person would be entitled to receive, but, on account of some action taken by him or her, is now being received by a person other than the person whose means are being assessed.

The only 'safe' transfers are those where a clear five-year period has elapsed between the time of the transfer and the first application for State support. This is a relatively novel consideration, which farmers should take into account when deciding whether or not to transfer land in their lifetime.

From a financial and tax planning point of view, a farmer who wishes to maximise State support towards his or her nursing home care, should carefully consider transferring his or her farming assets well in advance of the time when the need for nursing home care is likely to arise, because, as outlined above, the financial assessment carried out by the HSE to determine an individual's ability to pay, takes into account any assets which have been owned in the past five years.

There are, of course, many other important considerations to take into account before transferring farming assets, and one must never rush into a decision, but the rules governing this Scheme certainly introduce a new aspect which must be borne in mind when preparing to enter into a voluntary transfer of farming assets.

---

[82] Nursing Home Support Scheme Act 2009, part 3, sch 1.

## After the Decision to Transfer is Made – What Next?

Once tax and financial advice has been obtained, family members have been consulted, all options have been researched and considered, and a decision is made to proceed, what is the next step?

The transferor (the person transferring the farmland) must instruct his or her own solicitor in relation to the proposed transfer. The transferor's solicitor will prepare the Deed of Transfer or Deed of Conveyance and all ancillary paperwork. A Deed of Transfer or Deed of Conveyance is the document used to transfer or convey some or all of the farmer's property. Usually, the transfer will be in favour of a close family member, during the landowner's lifetime. If the property is in the joint names of the farmer and his or her spouse, it will be necessary for both to sign the Deed of Transfer or Deed of Conveyance.

Both parties to the transfer, namely, the transferor and the transferee (the recipient of the farmland), must be independently advised, and, hence, two solicitors will be involved in the transaction. This has not always been the case, but it is now necessary under regulations introduced by the Incorporated Law Society.[83] The need for separate representation arises so as to avoid any possible conflict of interest on the part of a solicitor acting for either party.

Every situation and family farm transfer is unique. However, the transferor should bring the following paperwork and information with him or her when instructing his or her solicitor:

1. Title Deeds and an Auctioneer's Valuation of the property;
2. The name of the transferee's solicitor;
3. Civil Marriage Certificate, if the transferor is married;
4. Tax reference (PPS) number for the transferor;
5. Details of any conditions that are to be inserted into the Deed of Transfer, for example, a right of residence;
6. A Land Registry Compliant Map, prepared by a competent engineer, if, for example, only part of the lands is being transferred, sites are being retained, or if the title is a Registry of Deeds title (i.e. unregistered land);

---

[83] Solicitors (Professional Practice, Conduct and Discipline - Conveyancing Conflict of Interest) Regulation 2012, SI No 375 of 2012, reg 3.

7. A note of his or her herd number, if applicable;
8. The Property Tax Identifier Number (if the family home is being transferred);
9. Evidence that the property tax has been paid (if the family home is being transferred);
10. Evidence that the household charge has been paid (if the family home is being transferred);
11. Receipts for payments of the Non-Principal Private Residence Charge (NPPR) for 2009-2013 inclusive, if applicable;
12. A copy of any lease, if the lands are let;
13. Written confirmation from the transferor's appointed tax consultant or accountant that the transferor has been advised in relation to any Capital Gains Tax implications arising on the proposed transfer.

Once the paperwork has been prepared and the transferor is satisfied with it, he or she signs same and it is then sent to the transferee's solicitor for signing.

The transferee should bring the following with him or her when attending and instructing his or her solicitor:

1. Tax Reference (PPS) Number;
2. Written confirmation from the transferee's appointed tax consultant or accountant that the transferee has been advised in relation to any Capital Acquisitions Tax (Gift Tax) implications arising on the proposed transfer;
3. Original Birth Certificate;
4. Original Teagasc Qualification Certificates;
5. Original Letter of Equivalence from Teagasc;
6. Cheque or bank draft in respect of stamp duty (if payable) and Land Registry fees payable in respect of the Deed of Transfer or Deed of Conveyance.

Once the transferee is satisfied with the paperwork, he or she signs same. A copy is sent to the transferor's solicitor. The transferee's solicitor attends to the stamping of the Deed of Transfer or Deed of Conveyance and, thereafter, registration in the Property Registration Authority.

## Conclusion

Historically, farms passed to the successor, usually the eldest son, upon the death of the farmer, and with little or no advance planning. Nowadays, it is widely acknowledged that greater emphasis on planning for the handover of the family farm to the next generation is vital to ensure future viability and sustainability.

The absence of long-term succession planning can have negative consequences for the future of the farm, as the older generation struggle to maintain work levels and enthusiasm, and the younger generation become disillusioned with the lack of clarity and certainty as to their future. In addition, ineffective tax planning could lead to a tax bill or potentially lead to increased tax bills.

The famous quote, "Give me six hours to chop down a tree and I will spend the first four sharpening the axe"[84] highlights the importance of preparation. Timely advice from professional advisors will assist in finding the most suitable succession plan for every farmer and his or her farm.

---

[84] Abraham Lincoln.

# CHAPTER FIVE

# Wills, Administering an Estate and Enduring Powers of Attorney

Contemplating illness or death is never pleasant. Likewise, making a will is something that the vast majority of us prefer not to have to think about. A report entitled 'Will Making and Charitable Legacies', published by Amárach Research in September 2015,[1] dealt with the behaviour and attitudes of Irish people towards the making of wills. The research showed that only three in every ten people living in Ireland have made a will. Making a will is most popular with those aged over 55, with 57% of people in that age group having already made a will. Two thirds of those aged 25–34 have not yet made a will, while one fifth of 35–44 year olds have done so. The results from the 25–34 year olds are particularly surprising, when one considers that it is during this time period that most people buy a house, have children, or experience other significant life changes.

According to the *World Alzheimer Report 2015*,[2] over 46 million people suffer from some form of dementia, and it is estimated that, by 2050, this number will have risen to 131.5 million. In order to deal with the complicated legal and practical problems that can arise when somebody becomes of unsound mind, whether by reason of dementia or otherwise, a person can complete an enduring power of attorney. This document provides the framework under which that person's legal, financial and other affairs can be dealt, by their nominated attorney, in the event that he or she becomes mentally incapable. The nominated attorney has full power to attend to the affairs of the person who has completed a valid enduring power of attorney, whilst that person is mentally incapable of doing so. Thus, there is one less worry for his or her family members to deal with, particularly in a farming situation. Making a will and completion of an enduring power

---

[1] Amárach Research, 'Will Making and Charitable Legacies' (2015) Amárach Omnibus.

[2] Alzheimer's Disease International, *World Alzheimer Report 2015* (Alzheimer's Disease International 2015).

of attorney is dealt with in detail in this chapter. It goes on to deal with inheritance tax and, thereafter, the administration of an estate, which is the process undertaken after a person dies.

The law in relation to wills is contained in the Succession Act 1965 (hereafter 'the 1965 Act'). The law in relation to enduring powers of attorney is contained in the Powers of Attorney Act 1996 (hereafter 'the 1996 Act') and the Enduring Powers of Attorney Regulations 1996,[3] as amended by the Enduring Powers of Attorney (Personal Care Decisions) Regulations 1996.[4] As there are a number of technical words and phrases that regularly arise in this area, some useful definitions are set out below.

## Definitions

"Estate" – the extent of the assets, both real and personal, in the ownership of the deceased at the time of his or her death and which fall to be administered in accordance with his or her will or on intestacy.

"Intestate" – a person who dies without having made a valid will, or, despite making such a will, leaves some assets or beneficial interest in his or her estate undisposed of (partial intestate).

"Testate" – a person who dies leaving a valid will is deemed to have died testate.

"Bequest" – a legacy or gift of personal property (moveable) in a will.

"Devise" – a disposition in a will of real property (immovable), such as land or a house.

"Testator" – a person (male) who makes or executes a valid will. A female who does so is known as a testatrix. For the remainder of this chapter, the male version will be used.

"Executor" – a person (male) or institution appointed by a testator in his will and who is charged with the task of administering the estate of the

---

[3] Enduring Powers of Attorney Regulations 1996, SI No 196 of 1996.
[4] Enduring Powers of Attorney (Personal Care Decisions) Regulations 1996, SI No 287 of 1996.

testator and carrying out the terms of that will, in accordance with law. If such appointed person is a female she is known as an Executrix.

"Trustee" – a person who is given control, or powers of administration, over property which has been placed in trust by the owner of that property, with a strict legal obligation to deal with it solely for the purposes specified by the owner who has set up the trust. Very often, the trust is set up by a will.

"Guardian" – a person named in a will to act as guardian to a minor child.

"Probate" – the legal term for the process of proving a will. Taking out a grant of probate is the process of establishing the validity of a will to the satisfaction of the Probate Office, which is the office charged with the task of issuing all grants of probate and administration.

"Grant of Probate" – when a grant of probate has issued from the Probate Office, it means that the will has been proved as being formally correct, and the executor can proceed immediately to administer the assets of the deceased person. The grant is the legal document that gives the executor the title and authority to administer the estate of the deceased person.

"Grant of Letters of Administration" – a grant extracted by somebody other than an executor of a will. For present purposes, the most relevant one is a grant of letters of administration intestate.

"Grant of Letters of Administration Intestate" – a grant which issues in relation to the estate of an intestate person, after application to the Probate Office by the person or persons entitled to apply under the intestacy rules set out in the 1965 Act. Usually, those persons are the nearest next-of-kin of the deceased. The person to whom the grant issues is known as an administrator (male) or administratrix (female).

"Discretionary trust" – a trust under which the precise entitlement of each beneficiary is not fixed by the person setting up the trust, often a testator in his will, but is at the discretion of the trustees. It is particularly useful where the beneficiaries, usually a testator's children, are very young at the time of setting up the trust and it is considered prudent to wait for a number of years before distributing the assets and bringing the trust to an end.

In the case of farmers, this is especially important, as the trustees can wait and see which child is likely to be most suitable to take over the testator's farm, where the testator has died while his children are very young.

"Residue of the estate" – the part of a person's estate which is left over after payment of debts, funeral expenses, taxes, legal and other expenses incurred in the administration of the estate, as well as the transfer and payment of any gifts of specific assets or specific sums of cash to those entitled.

"Attorney" – the donee, or recipient, of a power of attorney under an enduring power of attorney.

"Donor" – the donor of an enduring power of attorney is the person who gives the power of attorney to the donee (attorney).

"Enduring power of attorney" (EPA) – an instrument (written document) creating the power, in favour of the attorney, to manage and administer the donor's property and affairs during any period of mental incapacity of that donor. It contains a statement by the donor to the effect that the donor intends the power to be effective during any subsequent mental incapacity of the donor.

"Mental incapacity" – incapacity on the part of an individual, by reason of a mental condition, to manage and administer his own property and affairs.

"Legal personal representative" – a general term to describe a person who is either an executor of a person's will, or is the administrator of a deceased person's estate by virtue of a grant of letters of administration. Thus, the term covers both executors and administrators.

## The Importance of Making a Will

There are many good reasons for making a will. For example:

- A person who makes a will can, subject to some statutory restrictions, notably a spouse's legal right share (which will be discussed later in the chapter), choose who will inherit his estate; he has, in legal parlance, freedom of testation. A will allows the person making it to nominate those who will inherit his assets and ensures that those assets pass to the beneficiaries chosen by the testator. On the other hand, where somebody does not make a will, and dies intestate, the distribution of his assets will be determined entirely by the rules of intestacy, as set out in Part VI of the 1965 Act;

- A person who makes a will chooses not only who will benefit under that will, but in addition, who will administer his estate. This is because the testator can name the person or persons, known as executors, who the testator believes are the most appropriate persons to administer the estate and who are the most likely to carry out the testator's wishes. If a person does not make a will, and dies intestate, the entitlement to act as administrator is determined by the rules of intestacy. This may have the unfortunate consequence of the estate ending up being administered by someone that the testator would never have chosen to fulfil that role;

- By making a will, a person can also choose, not only who will be entitled to his most valuable assets, but also who will inherit specific items, such as cars, jewellery, objects of sentimental value etc. and ensure that they pass to those likely to appreciate them most;

- In the case of those who have young children, wills are particularly important, as the parents can choose not only what assets are to be inherited by such children, but, equally importantly, who will act as their guardians with responsibility for the care of those children. In the case of parents with young children, the will is normally drafted so as to establish a trust fund for the childrens' benefit, and the appointment of guardians of the testator's choice to look after them;

- A carefully drafted will can have a significant impact on the level of inheritance tax that may be payable by the beneficiaries. It provides an opportunity to assess the position and consider what steps can be taken to minimise potential inheritance tax liability. The relatively small cost of making a will can represent excellent value when compared to the tax burden that may arise;

- A will provides an opportunity for flexibility in the manner in which assets can pass to a beneficiary. For example, a testator can create a life interest in favour of someone, in particular, a spouse or a child with special needs. A life interest entitles the holder to a right to enjoy the use of a property exclusively, or the income which that capital generates, during his lifetime. On the death of the holder of the life interest, the asset will automatically pass to the beneficiary nominated by the deceased in the will; and

- A person who is single, or separated, but living with a partner in a situation where that arrangement is not recognised in law as a civil partnership, will not benefit under the death of the other partner unless there is a will which specifically provides for the partner in question. A person who qualifies as a cohabitant of the deceased can make an application to court for a share in the deceased's estate in certain circumstances which are discussed later in the chapter and also Chapter 11 (Family Law).

## The Importance of Including Basic Payment Entitlements in a Will

The Minister for Agriculture, Food and the Marine (hereafter 'Minister for Agriculture') was called upon to clarify the situation of entitlements under the Basic Payment Scheme, with regard to the administration of estates and the position in the event that a will is silent on the issue of entitlements.[5]

The Single Payment Scheme was introduced to Ireland in 2005 and operated until 31 December 2014. Single farm payments were not attached to land, but to the farmer. As such, where payment entitlements were not specifically mentioned in a will, they formed part of the residue of the estate, and passed to those entitled to the residue i.e. the part of the estate left over after deduction of specific bequests, devises, tax, debts etc. This usually resulted in a person who was not farming receiving the payments, and, most of the time, this would not have been the intention of the deceased.

In 2015, the Basic Payment Scheme was introduced to Ireland.[6] Requests have been made to the Department of Agriculture, Food and the Marine (hereafter 'Department of Agriculture') to clarify what should happen when a will is silent in relation to basic payment entitlements.[7] At the time of writing, the position has not yet been confirmed.

The former Minister for Agriculture, Simon Coveney, stated, "The relevant Division within my Department is currently in consultation with my Department's Legal Services Division in relation to situations where a will is silent on payment entitlements".[8]

If the entitlements are to pass to the person who is to receive the farm, this should be expressly stated in the will, in order to avoid disappointment, uncertainty and difficulty for the intended beneficiary.

---

[5] Dáil Deb 28 April 2016, vol 907, col 8778.

[6] https://www.agriculture.gov.ie/media/migration/publications/2014/CAP2015 AnIntroductiontoDirectPayments260314.pdf, p 5.

[7] Dáil Deb 28 April 2016 vol 907, col 8778.

[8] ibid.

# When Does a Person Die Intestate?

There are four ways in which a person may die intestate. These are where:

1. He has made no will. This is self-explanatory. If the person has never made a will during his lifetime, then he will die intestate;
2. He has made an invalid will and no previous will exists;

## A Valid Will: Formal Requirments

There are various requirements that must be complied with in order for a will to be valid. A will, at the very least, must satisfy the following formal requirements:

- The testator must be over eighteen years of age[9] or be, or have been, married[10]; a person must be over the age of eighteen to marry[11];
- It must be signed at the foot or end of the will by the testator.[12] This can be done by making a mark in cases where the testator is illiterate. A testator may acknowledge a signature which has already been made, in the presence of the two witnesses, who must be present at the same time[13];
- The signature or mark of the testator must be at the end of the will[14];
- The two witnesses (neither of whom, nor their spouses, can benefit under the will),[15] must sign their names in the presence of the testator; however, they need not sign their names in the presence of each other[16];
- The will must be in writing[17];
- The case of *Hodson v Barnes*[18] is a bizarre and famous case. The deceased chose to write his will on an egg shell. After his death, amongst her late husband's belongings, his wife found an egg shell, which bore the message "*17-1925. Mag. Everything I possess*".[19] The court ruled that the will was invalid, but not for

---

[9] Succession Act 1965, s 77(1)(a).
[10] Succession Act 1965, s 77(1)(a).
[11] Family Law Act 1995, s 31(1)(a)(i).
[12] Succession Act 1965, s 78(1).
[13] Succession Act 1965, s 78(2).
[14] Succession Act 1965, s 78(1).
[15] Succession Act 1965, s 82(1).
[16] Succession Act 1965, s 78(2).
[17] Succession Act 1965, s 78.
[18] *Hodson v Barnes* [1926] 43 TLR 71.
[19] According to legend, it was actually written on an ostrich egg. Perhaps there was a shortage of paper in 1925!

the reason one might suspect. It was held invalid on numerous grounds, one being that the will was not properly witnessed. Interestingly, the court ruled that there was no reason whatsoever that a will could not be written on an egg shell. Though a will must be in writing, it need not necessarily be written on paper to be deemed valid. However, it goes without saying that, in practice, wills should always be written or typed on paper;

- The testator must be of sound disposing mind[20];
- In the case of *O'Donnell v O'Donnell*,[21] the deceased was a paranoid schizophrenic. Kelly J concluded that, at the time of the making of his will, the deceased's condition was under control and his personality disorder did not render him incapable of making a will. When considering whether or not someone was of unsound mind, the relevant time is that of the making of the will.

3.  The testator had revoked a previous will, leaving no will in existence.

    A person can revoke a will by destroying it with the intention of revoking it.[22] If this is done, and the person does not make a new will, he will be deemed to have died intestate.

    In the case of *Cheese v Lovejoy*,[23] the deceased wrote "revoked" and drew lines through the will and threw it in the waste basket. His housekeeper found the will and it was subsequently admitted to probate. The will was held to be valid. The reason for this is that there must not alone be an intention to revoke the will, but this must be coupled with the actual destruction of such will for it to amount to a valid revocation in law.

    Marriage also revokes a will, unless the will is clearly made in contemplation of that particular marriage.[24] It cannot be in contemplation of marriage generally;

4.  A testator has a will made, which does not dispose of all of his property. An intestacy follows in relation to the property not disposed of in the will.

Every will should contain a 'residuary clause', which is a section that sets out how property not specifically disposed of in the will should be distributed; for

---

[20] Succession Act 1965, s 77(1)(b).

[21] *O'Donnell v O'Donnell* (HC, 24 March 1999).

[22] Succession Act 1965, s 85(2).

[23] *Cheese v Lovejoy* (1877) 2 PD 251.

[24] Succession Act 1965, s 85(1).

example, "I leave the remainder of my estate to my daughter Ann". If a residuary clause is omitted from the will, and there are assets which have not been specifically disposed of, the person is deemed to have died 'partially intestate'. The residue will then be distributed in accordance with the rules of intestacy.

## Intestacy and the Division of the Estate

When a person dies without making a will, the rules of intestacy, as set out in Part VI of the 1965 Act, are applicable.[25] Those rules govern the entitlement to inherit the property of any person who dies intestate. Very often, the application of the rules of intestacy results in the deceased person's property being distributed in a manner that he would never have wanted. This is because the rules set out the order of priority of people who are entitled to receive shares in the deceased's property, as well as the amount of these shares. No account whatsoever is taken of factors such as preferences verbally indicated by the deceased during his lifetime, personal feelings held towards such persons, any existing disputes with them or, indeed, any other such factors.

The intestacy rules are as follows:

1.  Where the deceased leaves a spouse or civil partner only, with no issue (children), the entire estate passes to the surviving spouse or civil partner[26];
2.  Where the deceased leaves a spouse or civil partner and children, the spouse or civil partner inherits two thirds of the estate and the children inherit the remaining one third in equal shares[27];
3.  Where the deceased leaves children but no spouse or civil partner surviving, the estate is divided equally between the children.[28] If one of the children has pre-deceased the deceased, that child's share passes to his or her own children[29];
4.  Where the deceased leaves neither spouse nor civil partner nor children surviving, the estate is divided between the parents, if any, in equal shares. If only one parent survives, the surviving parent takes

---

[25] Succession Act 1965, Part VI (Distribution on Intestacy).

[26] Succession Act 1965, s 67(1), as amended by Civil Partnership and Certain Rights and Obligations of Cohabitants Act 2010, s 73.

[27] Succession Act 1965, s 67(2), as amended by Civil Partnership and Certain Rights and Obligations of Cohabitants Act 2010, s 73.

[28] Succession Act 1965, s 67(3), as amended by Civil Partnership and Certain Rights and Obligations of Cohabitants Act 2010, s 73.

[29] Succession Act 1965, s 67(4).

the entire estate.[30] It should be noted that, in this situation, even if there are surviving brothers and/or sisters, the surviving parent(s) inherit everything;

5. Where the deceased dies without a spouse or civil partner, children or parent surviving, the estate is divided equally between his brothers and sisters.[31] If a brother or sister has predeceased the deceased leaving children of his own, then that brother or sister's share will be divided equally between such children in equal shares[32];

6. Where the deceased dies without a spouse or civil partner, children, parent, brothers or sisters surviving, the estate is divided between all nephews and nieces equally[33]; There are further rules which apply to deal with the position where only cousins and more distant relatives survive[34];

7. Where there are no surviving relatives, the State takes the entire of the estate as ultimate intestate successor.[35] In practice, this is extremely rare.

## Examples

Mary dies and does not leave a will. She is survived by a husband and four children. As a consequence of Mary not making a will, her husband becomes entitled to eight twelfths of Mary's estate and her children become entitled to a one twelfth share each.

John dies and does not leave a will. He was a bachelor with no children and both of his parents have pre-deceased him. His estate is divided between his brothers and sisters in equal shares.

Paul dies and does not leave a will. He was married, but separated from his spouse and living with his partner for 5 years prior to his death. Paul had not entered in a deed of separation with his spouse, nor obtained a decree of judicial separation. He did not have any children. His wife takes his entire estate. However, there are provisions whereby his cohabitant (partner) may be able to make an application to court for a share in

---

[30] Succession Act 1965, s 68.
[31] Succession Act 1965, s 69(1).
[32] Succession Act 1965, s 69(2).
[33] Succession Act 1965, s 69(2).
[34] Succession Act 1965, s 70.
[35] Succession Act 1965, s 73.

Paul's estate,[36] depending on the circumstances, which will be discussed later. The partner has no automatic entitlement.

## Executors, Trustees and Guardians

### Executors

In making a will, executors should always be appointed. While one executor can act alone, it is always advisable to appoint at least two persons to fill this important role. In most cases, the same persons are appointed to act as both executors and trustees, though different persons can be appointed to the two roles.

The primary role or function of the executor is to take all the necessary steps to apply for a grant of probate and, thereafter, to administer the estate in accordance with the terms of the will and in accordance with law. Probate is the legal term for a procedure that gives the person named in a testator's will as the executor authority to carry out the testator's wishes as set out in the will. In order to administer the estate, the executor must first apply to the Probate Office for the grant of probate. This involves providing full details of the assets in the estate of the deceased person. The form on which this is done is known as an Inland Revenue Affidavit. It is also sometimes referred to as a Schedule of Assets, a name which very accurately describes it. The original will is also filed with the Probate Office. The Probate Office must be satisfied that the will is formally valid. If so satisfied, the Probate Office will issue the grant of probate. This, in effect, means that the will has been proved. The executor can then administer the estate. The grant of probate, the executor's document of title and authority, is then submitted to all banks, insurance companies, and other institutions where assets were held by the deceased. It also has to accompany documents lodged with the Property Registration Authority when the title to land or other property is being registered in the name of a new owner. The Department of Agriculture will always insist on obtaining either the original or a sealed and certified copy of the grant of probate before dealing with change of ownership of basic payment entitlements, herd numbers etc.

---

[36] Civil Partnership and Certain Rights and Obligations of Cohabitants Act 2010, s 194.

### Trustees

Trustees are the persons charged with the responsibility of dealing with and protecting the assets of another person, often someone who has died, for the benefit of named beneficiaries, usually the children of the deceased. Accordingly, trustees have an important role to play. For that reason, it is vital that the most appropriate person be selected to fulfil the role of trustee. In deciding whom to appoint as trustees, a testator should:

- Choose someone whom he knows, likes and can trust;
- Choose someone with the ability to make the right financial decisions for the benefit of the beneficiaries; and
- Where there is a farm involved, choose someone who is experienced in, and has a background in, farming.

Where there are infant children involved, the role of the trustee is to manage and look after the assets until those children reach the age specified in the testator's will, when they become entitled to the assets in their own right.

### Guardians

Where a testator has children under the age of 18 years, he should always appoint guardians in respect of those children. This can be a difficult decision. Guardians must take responsibility for the welfare of the infant children. The same persons do not have to be appointed as both trustees and guardians. It is advisable that a person chooses guardians whom his children already know and with whom they have some form of relationship. This might be difficult where children are very young and have not yet formed strong relationships. Any person who has made a will should bear in mind that he can change the will at any time. Thus, where a testator observes that it might be appropriate to choose different guardians because of changed family circumstances, then the will should be changed to reflect the new situation.

It is prudent and basic courtesy that any person who is thinking of making a will should always discuss the matter with potential guardians in advance, ensuring that the person being chosen is happy to take on this role. There is no point in nominating someone who is reluctant, or actually refuses, to fulfil such an important role. In practice, brothers or sisters (and their spouses or partners) are most often chosen to fulfil the role of guardians and/or trustees.

## Discretionary Trusts

In a farming situation, and where there are young children involved, it is generally advisable that a person making his will would consider setting up a discretionary trust under the terms of that will. A discretionary trust, as already noted, is a trust in which the shares and entitlements of each beneficiary are not fixed by the testator in the will, but are placed at the discretion of the trustees. This, of course, is subject to the overall guidelines and terms set out in the will.

In a typical and straightforward case, the trust is created when a parent directs in his will that the assets are to be given to named trustees and that those trustees must hold those assets for the benefit of the children. Once the children reach a certain age, usually, but not necessarily, twenty-one years, the trustees must hand over the trust property to those children.

A discretionary trust is especially useful in a farming situation, where the beneficiaries are young and time is needed to see which, if any, of the children might be interested in taking up farming. A person may also have a child with special needs who will require care for the rest of his lifetime. Specific provisions should be put in place for that particular child.

The trustees can pay out a portion of the capital of the estate or some of the income deriving from the assets, if it is required for the children. A typical example is the payment of monies to cover educational costs and needs, such as college fees, books and school uniforms.

The creation of a discretionary trust can be useful from a tax planning perspective. It can facilitate a phased transfer of assets to successors, ensuring that maximum tax reliefs and exemptions are claimed. In contrast, where assets are transferred to a successor in one fell swoop as a result of the death of a parent, the child is exposed to whatever taxation regime is in place at that time, and may not be in a position to avail of certain reliefs (such as agricultural relief) where they or the relevant assets do not satisfy relevant criteria at that particular time.

Where there are infant children involved, the role of the trustee is to manage and look after the assets until those children reach the age, as nominated in the testator's will, when they become entitled to the assets in their own right.

### Discretionary Trust Tax

Discretionary trust tax[37] is a tax payable on discretionary trusts. Where a discretionary trust remains in place after the youngest child attains the age of twenty one, discretionary trust tax is payable at a rate of 6% on the value of the trust on that date. In addition, there is an annual charge of 1% of the value of the trust assets thereafter until the trust comes to an end. If the discretionary trust is wound up within five years of the initial 6% charge arising, the charge is reduced from 6% to 3%, and an appropriate refund is payable by the Revenue Commissioners.

## Statutory Entitlements of Spouse/Civil Partner and Children

### The Spouse's/Civil Partner's Legal Right Share

Where one spouse or civil partner dies, leaving a will, and the surviving spouse or civil partner has not renounced his/her rights, then that surviving spouse or civil partner has a right, known as a "legal right share" to a share or portion of the deceased's estate. By virtue of s 111 of the Succession Act 1965, where there are no children, the surviving spouse or civil partner is entitled to one-half of the estate of the deceased spouse[38] or civil partner.[39] If there are children, the surviving spouse[40] or civil partner[41] is entitled to one-third of the estate.

If the deceased has made a will that gives the surviving spouse or civil partner a benefit, then such surviving spouse or civil partner is entitled to claim the legal right share provided for in s 111 of the 1965 Act instead of the gift in the will. To make this claim in the first instance, the surviving spouse or civil partner does not have to go to court. The executor, or administrator, is obliged to grant the share on application being made to him by the spouse/civil partner.[42] Section 115 of the 1965 Act provides for this, stating,

---

[37] The main legislative provisions in relation to discretionary trusts are set out in the Capital Acquisitions Tax Consolidation Act (CATCA) 2003, Parts 3 and 4.

[38] Succession Act 1965, s 111(1).

[39] Succession Act 1965, s 111(A)(1).

[40] Succession Act 1965, s 111(2).

[41] Succession Act 1965, s 111(A)(2).

[42] Succession Act 1965, s 112, as amended by Civil Partnership and Certain Rights and Obligations of Cohabitants Act 2010, s 82.

Where, under the will of a deceased person who dies wholly testate, there is a devise or bequest to a spouse or civil partner, the spouse or civil partner may elect to take either that devise or bequest or the share to which he is entitled as a legal right.

This is the so called "right of election".

There are strict time limits within which the right of election by a spouse or civil partner must be exercised. Section 115(4) of the 1965 Act states that:

It shall be the duty of the personal representatives to notify the spouse or civil partner in writing of the right of election conferred by this section. The right shall not be exercisable after the expiration of six months from the receipt by the spouse or civil partner of such notification or one year from the first taking out of representation of the deceased's estate, whichever is the later.[43]

It is also important to note that time does not begin to run against the surviving spouse/civil partner until the notice referred to has been served by the personal representative. From the point of view of the personal representative, it is vital that the notice is served as soon as possible.

It should be noted that there is no obligation on the executor, under the Act, to notify a surviving spouse or civil partner of the right to a legal right share. The Act only obligates the personal representitive to notify the spouse or civil partner of the right of election.[44]

## The Family Home

If the family home is held by both spouses or civil partners as joint tenants, the surviving spouse or civil partner automatically inherits the deceased spouse's or civil partner's interest. Property which is held in their joint names as joint tenants passes independently of a will. It is important to note that not all property held in joint names automatically passes to

---

[43] Succession Act 1965, s 115(4), as amended by Civil Partnership and Certain Rights and Obligations of Cohabitants Act 2010, s 85.

[44] Succession Act 1965, s 56(4), as amended by Civil Partnership and Certain Rights and Obligations of Cohabitants Act 2010, s 70.

the survivor. If joint property is held in a tenancy in common, then, upon the death of one of the tenants in common, that person's share in the property passes to his estate.

Section 56(1) of the 1965 Act confirms that the surviving spouse or civil partner may require that the family home be given to him instead of the legal right share, or of the share inherited on intestacy (right of appropriation). If the family home is valued at more than the legal right share, then, as a general rule, the spouse or civil partner would have to pay such difference into the deceased's estate. However, the surviving spouse or civil partner may apply to the court to have the dwelling house given to him either without paying the difference, or by paying such sum as the court thinks reasonable. The court may make such an order if it is satisfied that hardship would otherwise be caused, either to the surviving spouse or civil partner, or to a dependent child.[45]

This right of appropriation must be exercised by the spouse or civil partner no later than 6 months from the receipt by the surviving spouse/civil partner of the notification of his rights by the executor, or one year from the first taking out of the grant of probate to the deceased's estate.[46]

### Example

Patrick dies and leaves a will, dividing his farmlands and farmhouse, in which his wife Marie resides, between his three children. The net estate has a value of €600,000. In his will, he leaves the sum of €50,000 to Marie.

Marie has two options.

1. Marie can elect to take the €50,000 under the will; or
2. Marie can elect to take one third of the net estate, which is €200,000, and can also choose to take the family home as part of her legal right share, as she ordinarily resides there. If the family home is worth more than €200,000, Marie would have to pay the difference to the estate, as a general rule i.e. the difference in value between €200,000 (one third of the estate) and the value of the family home.

---

[45] Succession Act 1965, s 56(10)(b).
[46] Succession Act 1965, s 56(5), as amended by Civil Partnership and Certain Rights and Obligations of Cohabitants Act 2010, s 70.

# Rights of Children Under a Will

Unlike a spouse or civil partner, children have no absolute right to inherit any part of their parent's estate if the parent makes a will. However, if a child considers that he or she has not been adequately provided for, he or she may make an application to court to seek a declaration that the parent has "failed in his moral duty to make proper provision for the child in accordance with his means".[47]

Section 117(2) of the 1965 Act, as amended by s 86 of Civil Partnership and Certain Rights and Obligations of Cohabitants Act 2010, states that:

> The court shall consider the application from the point of view of a prudent and just parent, taking into account the position of each of the children of the testator and any other circumstances which the court may consider of assistance in arriving at a decision that will be as fair as possible to the child to whom the application relates and to the other children.

Each case is decided on its own merits and the court examines the situation from the point of view of a "prudent and just"[48] parent.

*McDonald v Norris*[49] concerned an acrimonious relationship between a father and son. The applicant, who was a son of the deceased, had been taken out of school at the age of fourteen and put to work on the family farm, due to his father being unable to work as a result of injuries sustained in an accident. The applicant received no remuneration for his work and was eventually ordered to move off the farm after he married. The father had made a will in which he gave his other son some of the farm and had, during his lifetime, sold another section of the land. When his father died, the applicant, being the son who had worked on the farm for many years, brought an application to the court, seeking a declaration that the deceased had failed to fulfil his moral duty to make adequate provision for him under the will. The court held that the son was entitled to the remainder of the farm on the basis that his father had deprived his son of an education and a chance of an independent career.

---

[47] Succession Act 1965, s 117, as amended by Civil Partnership and Certain Rights and Obligations of Cohabitants Act 2010, s 86.

[48] Succession Act 1965, s 117(2), as amended by Civil Partnership and Certain Rights and Obligations of Cohabitants Act 2010, s 86.

[49] *McDonald v Norris* [2000] 1 ILRM 382.

In *Re LB*,[50] the applicant was 40 years of age. He claimed that his mother had failed in her moral obligation to provide for him. Under her will, she gave most of her vast estate to charity. The son had a history of drug addiction. He was separated from his wife, was unemployed, and was an alcoholic at the time of his mother's death. The court held that she did not fail in her moral duty to him.

In *Re IAC*,[51] Finlay J declared that there is a relatively high onus of proof on the child applicant. The child must show a positive failure in moral duty on the part of the parent.

Prospective applicants in a s 117 claim should always be aware that the cost of such an application is at the discretion of the court. An unsuccessful applicant is not necessarily entitled to have the costs of the application paid out of the estate of the deceased. In some cases, a court can refuse the applicant the costs of the claim.[52]

Section 117(6) of the 1965 Act, as amended by s 46 of the Family Law (Divorce) Act 1996, states that the time limit within which a child must make such an application is limited to six months from the date of the first taking out of representation, which is acknowledged as being the date the grant of probate issues in the estate of the deceased.

## Cohabiting Couples

Cohabiting couples have no legal rights to each other's estate, but may be able to apply to the court for redress when one of them dies. Cohabiting couples may, of course, make wills in favour of each other, but, like the spousal situation, such wills do not affect the legal right share of a spouse[53] or civil partner[54] of the deceased cohabitant. In the case of a cohabiting couple, where the home in which they reside is held as joint tenants, the

---

[50] *Re LB* [1988]

[51] *Re IAC* [1989] ILRM 815.

[52] Succession Act 1965, s 117(5).

[53] Succession Act 1965, s 112.

[54] Succession Act 1965, s 112, as amended by Civil Partnership and Certain Rights and Obligations of Cohabitants Act 2010, s 82.

surviving partner automatically inherits the deceased partner's interest, but may be liable to pay inheritance tax.

The relevant legislation is the Civil Partnership and Certain Rights and Obligations of Cohabitants Act 2010. This Act provides that a "qualified cohabitant" as defined may apply to court for redress in the event of a cohabitant relationship ending.

## Definitions

"Cohabitant" – one of 2 adults (whether of the same or the opposite sex) who live together as a couple in an intimate and committed relationship and who are not related to each other within the prohibited degrees of relationship or married to each other or civil partners of each other.[55]

"Qualified cohabitant" – an adult who was in a relationship of cohabitation with another adult and who, immediately before the time that that relationship ended, whether through death or otherwise, was living with the other adult as a couple for a period—

(a) of two years or more, in the case where they are the parents of one or more dependent children, and
(b) of five years or more, in any other case.

In determining whether two adults are cohabitants, the court shall take into account all the circumstances of the relationship and in particular shall have regard to the following[56]:

(a) The duration of the relationship[57];
(b) The basis on which the couple live together[58];
(c) The degree of financial dependence of either adult on the other and any agreements in respect of their finances[59];
(d) The degree and nature of any financial arrangements between the adults, including any joint purchase of an estate or interest in land or joint acquisition of personal property[60];

---

[55] Civil Partnership and Certain Rights and Obligations of Cohabitants Act 2010, s 172(1).
[56] Civil Partnership and Certain Rights and Obligations of Cohabitants Act 2010, s 172(2).
[57] Civil Partnership and Certain Rights and Obligations of Cohabitants Act 2010, s 172(2)(a).
[58] Civil Partnership and Certain Rights and Obligations of Cohabitants Act 2010, s 172(2)(b).
[59] Civil Partnership and Certain Rights and Obligations of Cohabitants Act 2010, s 172(2)(c).
[60] Civil Partnership and Certain Rights and Obligations of Cohabitants Act 2010, s 172(2)(d).

(e)   Whether there are one or more dependent children[61];
(f)   Whether one of the adults cares for and supports the children of the other[62]; and
(g)   The degree to which the adults present themselves to others as a couple.[63]

In addition, the Act provides that a relationship does not cease to be an intimate relationship for the purpose of this section merely because it is no longer sexual in nature.[64]

It should also be noted that a person is not deemed to be a qualified cohabitant if one or both of the adults is or was, at any time during the relationship concerned, an adult who was married to someone else, and at the time the relationship concerned ends (cohabitant relationship), each adult who is or was married has not lived apart from his or her spouse for a period or periods of at least 4 years during the previous 5 years.[65]

A qualified cohabitant may, after the death of the other cohabitant, but not more than 6 months after representation is first granted in respect of that cohabitant's estate, apply for an order for provision out of the net estate.[66]

The court may, by order, make provision for the applicant that it considers appropriate, having regard to the rights of any other person having an interest in the matter, if the court is satisfied that proper provision in the circumstances was not made for the applicant during the lifetime of the deceased for any reason other than conduct by the applicant that, in the opinion of the court, it would in all the circumstances be unjust to disregard.[67]

---

[61] Civil Partnership and Certain Rights and Obligations of Cohabitants Act 2010, s 172(2)(e).
[62] Civil Partnership and Certain Rights and Obligations of Cohabitants Act 2010, s 172(2)(f).
[63] Civil Partnership and Certain Rights and Obligations of Cohabitants Act 2010, s 172(2)(g).
[64] Civil Partnership and Certain Rights and Obligations of Cohabitants Act 2010, s 172(3).
[65] Civil Partnership and Certain Rights and Obligations of Cohabitants Act 2010, s 172(6).
[66] Civil Partnership and Certain Rights and Obligations of Cohabitants Act 2010, s 194.
[67] Civil Partnership and Certain Rights and Obligations of Cohabitants Act 2010, s 194(3).

The court will only make an order if it is satisfied that the qualified cohabitant was financially dependent on the deceased.[68]

The applicant shall give notice of an application under this section to the personal representative of the deceased, any spouse or civil partner of the deceased, and to any other persons that the court may direct and, in deciding whether to make the order and in determining the provisions of the order, the court shall have regard to any representations made by any of those persons.[69]

Cohabitating couples' rights and the factors a court will take into account when deciding whether to make provision and how much provision to make, is dealt with further in Chapter 11 (Family Law).

## Challenging a Will

A will can be challenged on a number of grounds.

Some of the most common grounds of challenge are:

### Lack of Testamentary Capacity

The deceased must have been of sound disposing mind on the date on which the will was made.[70] If the deceased was not of sound disposing mind, the will may not be valid, and can be subject to challenge through the courts. However, there must be some evidence of lack of capacity, and the courts will not set aside a will lightly. In cases where a will is contested due to lack of capacity, the facts of the individual case will be crucial. Each case is dealt with on its own unique facts and circumstances. It is advisable that practitioners ensure, as far as is possible, that a prospective testator has the testamentary capacity to make a will. Appropiate evidence should be kept, in cases of doubt.

---

[68] Civil Partnership and Certain Rights and Obligations of Cohabitants Act 2010, s 194(5)(a).
[69] Civil Partnership and Certain Rights and Obligations of Cohabitants Act 2010, s 194(6).
[70] Succession Act 1965, s 77(1)(b).

### Case

In *Re Glynn*,[71] the deceased had given instructions for the making of a will. However, before executing the will, he suffered a massive stroke, which resulted in him being unable to communicate in written or oral form. Following this unfortunate occurrence, two independent witnesses returned to the hospital where he was being treated and read out the will to him. The deceased nodded his assent and placed an "X" by means of signature on the document, which was then attested by the two witnesses. The contention advanced by those contesting the will in these proceedings was that the will was invalid. However, the High Court held that the will was valid. This decision was appealed to the Supreme Court. On appeal, the Supreme Court also held the will to be valid, on the basis that the deceased had indicated his satisfaction that the document read out to him reflected his wishes. The court stipulated that, in order to prove that the will was invalid, it would require medical proof of incapacity.

### Case

In the case of *Banks v Goodfellow*,[72] the deceased testator thought that he was being pursued by a dead person and evil spirits. He was, however, capable of conducting his business affairs and was described as being careful with money. At the hearing of the case, the court was satisfied that he had the necessary testamentary capacity.

### Undue Influence

A will can also be challenged on the basis that the deceased was under the undue influence of another party and therefore did not make the will freely. An example of this is where an elderly person is wholly dependent on a relative for care and, as a result of this dependence, may feel under pressure to leave his estate to that person. Again, this ground of potential challenge depends on the individual facts of each case, and challenges under this category are dealt with on a case by case basis.

---

[71] *Re Glynn* [1990] 2 IR 326.
[72] *Banks v Goodfellow* (1870) LR 5 QB 549.

## Case

In the case of *Joy v Bannister*,[73] the concept of undue influence was usefully demonstrated. In that case, the deceased was befriended by a woman with the unfortunate name of Mrs. Death, who formed a close association with him until he made his will. After the will was made, Mrs. Death neglected her association with the deceased and treated him so cruelly that he was afraid to revoke his will. The court held that there was sufficient evidence of undue influence in this case and, as a consequence, the will was deemed to be invalid.

### The Validity of the Will

A will can be challenged on the grounds that it is invalid in law. For example:

- The will was not signed and witnessed properly (formal validity)[74]; or
- There is evidence of fraud or forgery in the will.

## Inheritance Tax

The tax, if any, depends on the circumstances of each case. The beneficiary is the person with primary responsibility for payment of the tax. Inheritance tax is governed by the Capital Acquisitions Tax Consolidation Act (CATCA) 2003, as updated by the Finance Act 2015.

It should be noted that this section outlines the basic principles and some of the reliefs available, and it is very important to seek advice in relation to the particular set of circumstances.

Inheritance tax may arise where a beneficiary receives an inheritance on the death of another person. The beneficiary who receives the inheritance is liable for the tax, if any. The inheritance is taxable if its value exceeds a certain limit, known as the threshold. If the value of the inheritance remains under the relevant threshold, no tax is payable. Different tax-free thresholds apply, depending on the relationship between the person giving the benefit and the person receiving the benefit. There are also a number of exemptions and reliefs from the tax that may apply, depending on

---

[73] *Joy v Bannister* (1617) BR 33.
[74] Succession Act 1965, s 78.

the nature of the inheritance. It should be noted, however, that divorced spouses or individuals who have dissolved their marriage or civil partnership are treated as strangers for inheritance tax purposes.[75] There is an exception to this rule, where transfers between spouses or civil partners take place on foot of certain court orders, and this is dealt with in further detail in Chapter 11 (Family Law).

### Spouse/Civil Partner as Beneficiaries

Inheritances taken by a surviving spouse or surviving civil partner from their deceased spouse or civil partner, are entirely exempt, regardless of the sum involved.[76]

For the avoidance of doubt, it should be noted that there is no stamp duty payable on inheritances. Generally, a death does not give rise to a liability for Capital Gains Tax. However, a Capital Gains Tax liability may arise on a subsequent disposal by a legal personal representative if there is an increase in the value of the property inherited between the date of death and such subsequent disposal by the legal personal representative.

### Other Beneficiaries

In the case of beneficiaries other than surviving spouses and civil partners, the potential liability to inheritance tax depends on whether or not the total value of all gifts and inheritances received by the beneficiary from the deceased, or from anybody else to whom the same group threshold applies, on or after 5 December 1991 (aggregation), exceeds the relevant tax-free threshold.[77]

The inheritance tax thresholds are set out in the following table;

---

[75] Irish Tax Institute, *Law of Capital Acquisitions Tax, Stamp Duty and Local Property Tax, Finance Act 2015* (Irish Tax Institute 2016) 59.

[76] Capital Acquisitions Tax Consolidation Act (CATCA) 2003, s 71.

[77] Irish Tax Institute Capital Acquisitions Tax & Stamp Duty Manual 2014/2015, p 7.

## Inheritance and Gift Tax Thresholds (from 14 October 2015)[78]

| | |
|---|---|
| **Group A: €280,000** | Where the beneficiary is a child (including an adopted child, step-child and certain foster children) or minor child of a deceased child of the disponer (e.g. as a result of a death). Parents also fall within this threshold, where they take an inheritance of an absolute interest from a child. This group threshold can also apply in the case of a favourite nephew or favourite niece.

Favourite nephew/niece relief entitles a beneficiary who is a child of the disponer's brother or sister or a child of the civil partner of the disponer's brother or sister to be treated as a "child" of the disponer, provided certain conditions are met. Where the relief applies, the niece or nephew is entitled to the Group A threshold instead of the Group B threshold.

The relief applies to a niece or nephew who has worked substantially on a full-time basis for the disponer for the period of five years ending on the date the disponer ceases to have a beneficial interest in possession in the business. The relief will only apply to assets used in connection with the business. Note that farming is a business for the purposes of the relief. |
| **Group B: €30,150** | Applies where the beneficiary is a brother, sister, niece, nephew or lineal ancestor or lineal descendant of the disponer. |
| **Group C: €15,075** | Applies in all other cases, (so called strangers in blood). |

---

[78] For further information on this relief, see Capital Acquisitions Tax Consolidation Act (CATCA) 2003, para 7, pt 1, sch 2.

### *Inheritance Tax Examples*

#### *Example*
Ann leaves an inheritance valued at €500,000 to her son, John. The inheritance comprises an investment property with a market value of €250,000 and cash of €250,000.

#### *Potential Tax Liability*
The inheritance received by John is valued at €500,000. The tax free threshold from a parent to a child is currently €280,000. The current tax rate is 33%.

| | |
|---|---|
| Inheritance Value | €500,000 |
| Less Group A Threshold | €280,000 |
| Taxable Inheritance | €220,000 |
| Inheritance Tax (€220,000@ 33%) | €72,600 |
| John pays €72,600 inheritance tax. | |

If Ann gave John the investment property without the gift of money, then the inheritance of the investment property would not be subject to inheritance tax, as it is valued at €250,000 and is therefore less than the tax-free threshold of €280,000. In that scenario, John will have no inheritance tax liability.

## Inheritance Tax Reliefs/Exemptions
In addition to the exemption for a spouse or civil partner, there are a number of other important exemptions and reliefs which may be available. These include:

- Agricultural relief;
- Business relief; and
- Dwelling house relief.

In preparing a will, it is worthwhile considering structuring one's affairs so that the tax exposure for beneficiaries is minimised. In some circumstances, this may involve redistribution of assets between beneficiaries or indeed the inclusion of a discretionary trust.

## Agricultural Relief[79]

The relief which is of greatest importance to farmers, and which is regularly availed of in the transfer of ownership of farms and other agricultural assets, is agricultural relief. This operates by reducing the market value of agricultural property by 90%, so that the taxable value, for inheritance purposes, of the agricultural assets, including land, stock, implements and machinery, is only 10% of the market value. This reduced value is known as "agricultural value" and it is on this figure that any inheritance tax is calculated. As the "agricultural value" is substantially less than the market value, most farm transfers and inheritances do not give rise to any liability for payment of inheritance tax. However, there are strict conditions that must be satisfied before the relief applies.

### Conditions for the Relief

In general, the relief applies provided the beneficiary qualifies as a "farmer".[80] The person will qualify as a "farmer" if, on the valuation date,[81] the beneficiary's agricultural property[82] comprises a minimum of 80% of the beneficiary's total property.

In addition, the inheritance must consist of agricultural property, both at the date of the inheritance and at the valuation date. The valuation date is the date at which the property is valued for inheritance tax purposes. In inheritance situations, this is normally the date the grant of probate or administration issues.

---

[79] Capital Acquisitions Tax Consolidation Act (CATCA) 2003, s 89, and Finance Act 2014.

[80] Capital Acquisitions Tax Consolidation Act (CATCA) 2003, s 89(1).

[81] The valuation date of an inheritance is complex and is set out in the Capital Acquisitions Tax Consolidation Act (CATCA) 2003, s 30(2), s 30(3), s 30(4), and s 30(5). In most cases, the valuation date of an inheritance is the date of delivery or payment to the beneficiary of the inheritance or else the date of its retainer on the beneficiary's behalf. In most cases, it is usually the date the grant of probate or the grant of administration issues. (Capital Acquisitions Tax Consolidation Act (CATCA) 2003, s 30(4)).

[82] "Agricultural property" is defined in Capital Acquisitions Tax Consolidation Act (CATCA) 2003, s 89(1), and includes houses and other farm buildings appropriate to the property.

The beneficiary must also satisfy what is known as the 'active farmer' test. He or she must:

1. Farm the agricultural property for a period of not less than six years commencing on the valuation date[83]; or
2. Lease the agricultural property for a period of not less than six years commencing on the valuation date.[84]

In addition, the beneficiary (or the lessee, where relevant) must:

1. Have an appropriate agricultural qualification[85]; or
2. Farm the agricultural property for not less than 50% of his or her normal working time.[86]

The agricultural property must also be farmed on a commercial basis and with a view to the realisation of profits.[87]

### Example 1

The 'Farmer Test'

Ann owns the following: a house valued at €180,000; a car worth €5,000; and she has €2,000 in a bank deposit account. She receives an inheritance of farmland valued at €1,000,000, plus livestock and farm machinery valued at €50,000.

Is Ann a Farmer?

The test is as follows:

$$\frac{\text{Agricultural property}}{\text{Agricultural property plus non-agricultural property}} \times 100$$

For Ann to qualify as a farmer, the answer must not be less than 80%.

---

[83] Revenue, 'Capital Acquisitions Tax Manual – Part 11 (February 2016) 6.
[84] Revenue, 'Capital Acquisitions Tax Manual – Part 11 (February 2016) 5.
[85] Revenue, 'Capital Acquisitions Tax Manual – Part 11 (February 2016) 5.
[86] Revenue, 'Capital Acquisitions Tax Manual – Part 11 (February 2016) 6.
[87] Revenue, 'Capital Acquisitions Tax Manual – Part 11 (February 2016) 7.

'Farmer Test' Calculation

| Asset | Agricultural Assets | Total Assets |
|-------|---------------------|--------------|
| Car | | €5,000 |
| House | | €180,000 |
| Bank Account | | €2,000 |
| Farmlands | €1,000,000 | €1,000,000 |
| Livestock and Farm Machinery | €50,000 | €50,000 |
| Total | €1,050,000 | €1,237,000 |

The gross market value of Ann's assets, after taking the inheritance, is €1,237,000. The gross market value of her agricultural assets is €1,050,000.

The farmer test calculation is as follows:

$$(€1,050,000 / €1,237,000) \times 100 = 84.88\%$$

Therefore, Ann is considered to be a farmer for the purposes of agricultural relief. She exceeds the 80% threshold. However, she must meet the criteria imposed as a result of the Finance Act 2014 to either farm the land or lease the land for the 6 years post transfer, as appropriate.

It should be noted that debts or encumbrances in respect of a dwelling house e.g. a mortgage, which is the beneficiary's only or main residence and which is not agricultural property, can be deducted for the purposes of the farmer test.[88]

It is also important to note that the test as to whether or not one is a farmer for the purposes of qualifying for the relief is based on both the nature of the assets held and the time spent farming. This can give rise to anomalies. A full-time farmer who happens to have significant non-agricultural assets, such as cash and/or investment property, might not qualify for the relief at all. On the other hand, someone who has never farmed at all, but who leases the land, such as a teacher, accountant or

---

[88] Capital Acquisitions Tax Consolidation Act (CATCA) 2003, s 89(1).

office worker, can qualify for the relief simply by meeting the asset test set out in the legislation. This anomaly makes it all the more important to ensure that immediate legal and taxation advice be sought by any person who has received an inheritance of agricultural property as, in many cases, it is possible to take steps to resolve matters, between the date of the inheritance on the one hand, and the valuation date for tax purposes on the other. It may also be possible for such a person to claim the alternative relief, known as business relief, in cases where agricultural relief is not available.

The Revenue Commissioners, who examine each claim, will usually accept, for the purpose of the relief, that "normal working time", including on-farm and off-farm working time, approximates to forty hours per week. This will enable farmers with off-farm employment to qualify for the relief, provided they spend a minimum average of twenty hours per week working on the land in question. Where the individual can show that his normal working time is somewhat less than forty hours a week, then the 50% requirement will be applied to the actual hours worked, subject, at all times, to the overriding requirement that the land is farmed on a commercial basis, and with a view to the realisation of profits. In the majority of situations, it should be clear from the level of farming activity being carried on whether the normal working time requirement is satisfied. If there is any doubt, the Revenue Commissioners will consider all information (including farming records) provided by a farmer in relation to his or her normal working time and farming activities.[89]

It is important to note that agricultural relief will be disallowed if the property is disposed of within six years of the date of inheritance.[90] Replacement provisions within the legislation do cater for the disposal or compulsory acquisition of the agricultural property and replacement with other property within one year from the disposal[91] or six years in the case of the property being compulsorily acquired.[92] In the case of agricultural property being sold as development land, the relief will

---

[89] Revenue, 'Capital Acquisitions Tax Manual – Part 11 (February 2016) 6.

[90] Capital Acquisitions Tax Consolidation Act (CATCA) 2003, s 89(4)(a)(i).

[91] Capital Acquisitions Tax Consolidation Act (CATCA) 2003, s 89(4)(ii).

[92] Capital Acquisitions Tax Consolidation Act (CATCA) 2003, s 89(4)(ii).

be withdrawn in the case of a disposal within a period of ten years.[93] Importantly, a transfer by a successor of his or her share or a partial share in the property to his or her spouse within the requisite period would amount to a partial withdrawal of relief, unless the successor availed of the replacement provisions.

In addition, agricultural relief is clawed back if any part of the agricultural property is not farmed by an active farmer, or by a lessee who is an active farmer, for at least 50% of the person's normal working time, or is not farmed on a commercial basis, throughout the 6-year qualifying period from the valuation date, or, if earlier, the date the activity started.[94]

## Example 2

Under his will, John leaves his farm to his son, Sean. The farm is valued at €3 million. If Sean does not qualify for agricultural relief as set out above, he is liable to payment of inheritance tax in respect of the value of the inheritance above €280,000, at a rate of 33% on the balance. In this case, it would be calculated as follows:

| | |
|---|---|
| Value of Inheritance | €3,000,000 |
| Less Group A Threshold | €280,000 |
| Taxable Inheritance | €2,720,000 |
| Inheritance Tax @ 33% | €897,600 |

However, provided Sean qualifies for agricultural relief, the inheritance tax payable is as follows:

| | |
|---|---|
| Value of Inheritance | €3,000,000 |
| Reduction of 90% of €3,000,000 | €2,700,000 |
| Revised taxable value after relief | €300,000 |
| Threshold (Category A) | €280,000 |
| Taxable Inheritance | €20,000 |
| Tax @33% | €6,600 |

---

[93] Capital Acquisitions Tax Consolidation Act (CATCA) 2003, s 102A.

[94] Revenue, 'Capital Acquisitions Tax Manual–Part 11 (February 2016) 7.

Sean must submit an inheritance tax return in order to successfully claim agricultural relief and pay inheritance tax.[95] Where the valuation date arises between 1 January and 31 August in any year, the filing date is 31 October that same year.[96] For example, Tim received an inheritance of farmland and the valuation date was 3 April 2016. Tim must file an inheritance tax return and discharge the inheritance tax, if any, no later than 31 October 2016. There are provisions for a later filing date, if filing and discharging the tax via the Revenue on-line system (ROS), which can vary from year to year. A 5% surcharge applies, subject to a maximum of €12,695, where the tax return is delivered within two months of the filing date. A 10% surcharge, up to a maximum of €63,485, will be applied where the tax return is not delivered within two months of the filing date. Interest also arises for late payments.[97]

## Business Relief[98]

Similar to agricultural relief, this relief, when it applies, operates by allowing a reduction of 90% of the market value of a gift or inheritance, so that the tax is calculated on the reduced value.[99] There are various conditions that must be met before the relief can be availed of. Only relevant business property will qualify for the relief.

'Relevant business property' is defined in s 93 of the Capital Acquisitions Tax Consolidation Act 2003. This is complex and can include property consisting of a business or interest in a business, any land or building, machinery or plant which, immediately before inheritance, was used wholly or mainly for the purposes of a business carried on by a company of which the disponer then had control or by a partnership of which the disponer then was a partner.

To qualify for the relief, the relevant business property must have been owned by the deceased for a continuous period of two years prior to the date of the inheritance.[100]

---

[95] Capital Acquisitions Tax Consolidation Act (CATCA) 2003, s 46(2).
[96] Capital Acquisitions Tax Consolidation Act (CATCA) 2003, s 46(2A).
[97] Capital Acquisitions Tax Consolidation Act (CATCA) 2003, s 53(A).
[98] Capital Acquisitions Tax Consolidation Act (CATCA) 2003, ss 90-102.
[99] Capital Acquisitions Tax Consolidation Act (CATCA) 2003, s 92.
[100] Capital Acquisitions Tax Consolidation Act (CATCA) 2003, s 94.

## Example

James inherits the family business upon the death of his father, Patrick. The taxable value of the business is €4,000,000. Business relief is calculated as follows:

| | |
|---|---|
| Taxable value prior to relief | €4,000,000 |
| Reduction of 90% | €3,600,000 |
| Revised taxable value after relief | €400,000 |
| Threshold (Category A) | €280,000 |
| Taxable Inheritance | €120,000 |
| Tax at 33% | €39,600 |

## Claw-Back of Business Relief

If the business, or any business which replaced it, ceases trading within a period of six years from the date of the inheritance, the relief will be withdrawn and clawed back,[101] unless the business is replaced within one year by other relevant business property. However, there will be no claw-back of the relief where the business ceases to trade by reason of bankruptcy or as a result of a bona fide winding-up on the grounds of insolvency.[102]

There is no claw-back on the death of the beneficiary.[103]

The relief will also be clawed back if, within that six-year period, the business, or the shares or securities in that business, are sold, redeemed or compulsorily acquired, and are not replaced within one year by other relevant business property.[104] There are exceptions to this, such as bankruptcy, or if the company is wound up bona fide due to insolvency.

In a case where land, which qualified for business relief, is disposed of, in whole or in part, by the successor, within the period commencing six years on the date of the inheritance and ending ten years after that date, then the

---

[101] Capital Acquisitions Tax Consolidation Act (CATCA) 2003, s 101.
[102] Capital Acquisitions Tax Consolidation Act (CATCA) 2003, s 101(2)(a).
[103] Capital Acquisitions Tax Consolidation Act (CATCA) 2003, s 101(2)(ii).
[104] Capital Acquisitions Tax Consolidation Act (CATCA) 2003, s 101.

relief granted will be clawed back in respect of the development value of that land at the valuation date of the inheritance.[105]

The relief, as the name suggests, is only applicable in relation to businesses. As such the inheritance of land in isolation would not by definition benefit under business relief. In contrast, the inheritance of a farm comprising of a collection of assets such as land, machinery, stock and payment entitlements as a going concern could potentially benefit under business relief.

From a farming perspective, the important issue here is that the entitlement to claim "Business Relief" is not dependent on an asset test, such as applies when claiming "Agricultural Relief". As a result, there may be cases where a person who cannot claim "Agricultural Relief", can, in the alternative, claim "Business Relief". This can have huge beneficial consequences for such a person. Finally, it should be noted that both reliefs cannot be claimed in respect of the one inheritance.

### Dwelling House Relief[106]

Dwelling house relief involves gifts or inheritances of a dwelling house taken on or after 1 December 1999, which will be exempt from inheritance tax, provided the following conditions are complied with:

- The beneficiary must have occupied the dwelling house continuously as his or her only or main residence for a period of three years immediately prior to the date of the inheritance[107];
- The beneficiary must not be entitled to an interest in any other dwelling house at the date of the inheritance[108]; and
- The beneficiary must continue, except where such beneficiary was aged fifty-five years or more at the date of inheritance or subsequently dies, to occupy that dwelling house as his or her only or main residence for a period of six years commencing on the date of the inheritance.[109] Otherwise, tax relief will be clawed back.

---

[105] Capital Acquisitions Tax Consolidation Act (CATCA) 2003, s 102(A).
[106] Capital Acquisitions Tax Consolidation Act (CATCA) 2003, s 86.
[107] Capital Acquisitions Tax Consolidation Act (CATCA) 2003, s 86(3)(a).
[108] Capital Acquisitions Tax Consolidation Act (CATCA) 2003, s 86(3)(b).
[109] Capital Acquisitions Tax Consolidation Act (CATCA) 2003, s 86(3)(b).

This relief is of particular importance to children of elderly parents, where those children have lived with, and taken care of, such parents, and then take a gift or inheritance of the house in question.

Rules cater for a sale and replacement of alternative property within the six-year period.[110]

## Administering an Estate

### It is Not Always Necessary to Take Out Probate

If the bank accounts of a deceased person contain less than a certain value, usually €25,000 and there is no real estate, such as land or houses, the bank will release the monies to the next-of-kin on condition that an indemnity is provided. In that case, no grant of probate or administration is required. Banks differ on the amount that they will release without production of a grant.

### Nominations

In many instances, the holder of an account or investment can nominate the person who will become entitled to the proceeds of that account or investment on his death. This procedure is most popular in the case of credit union and post office accounts, and often applies to some life assurance policies. Provided that a valid nomination form has been completed, the funds will generally be paid out to the person named as the beneficiary under that nomination, without the production of a Grant.

### Jointly-Owned Property

Where a person owns property jointly with another, the most important question is whether that ownership is on the basis of joint tenancy or tenancy-in-common. The difference is highly significant. A surviving joint tenant will, in the absence of exceptional circumstances, on the death of the other joint tenant, become automatically entitled to full ownership of the asset in question, regardless of the provisions of the deceased joint tenant's will. This automatic entitlement to ownership arises by right of survivorship (*jus accrescendi*). Joint tenancy normally applies in the case of property owned by married couples. The vast majority of such couples

---

[110] Capital Acquisitions Tax Consolidation Act (CATCA) 2003, s 86(7) and s 86(8).

now place their family home, along with many other assets, in their joint names as joint tenants, so as to ensure that, upon the death of one of them, the property will automatically pass to the survivor without the necessity of taking out a grant of probate to administer that joint property. This is both convenient and cost-effective.

On the other hand, where property is held in a tenancy in common, when one tenant-in-common dies, there is no automatic right of ownership in favour of the surviving tenant-in-common. Instead, the share of the deceased tenant-in-common will pass, either under the terms of his will, or to his next-of-kin in the event of intestacy. Ownership as tenants-in-common arises most often in the case of business property, where it would not be appropriate that the survivor would automatically secure sole ownership upon the death of one partner in the business.

It is also possible for one tenant-in-common to put in place a co-ownership agreement to regulate what happens to the property upon his death.

### The Probate/Adminstration Process

Section 2 of the 1965 Act states:

> The personal representatives of a deceased person shall distribute his estate as soon after his death as is reasonably practicable, having regard to the nature of the estate, the manner in which it is required to be distributed and all other relevant circumstances, but proceedings against the personal representatives in respect of their failure to distribute shall not, without leave of the court, be brought before the expiration of one year from the date of the death of the deceased.

There is a duty on the executor to administer the estate as soon as is reasonably practicable.

In reality, the time taken will depend on the size and nature of the assets in the estate. If the person who dies is the owner of a number of properties, including property abroad, and also has multiple bank accounts and life insurance policies, it may take considerable time to gather all the necessary information and valuations required to complete the papers to be filed with the Revenue Commissioners and Probate Office. In addition, where there are a large number of beneficiaries, it can also take time to secure the necessary information from them, such as their tax reference (PPS) numbers and details of any prior gifts and inheritances taken by them.

Once the personal representative, and the solicitor acting for him, are satisfied that they have located all of the assets, a Form CA24 (known as an Inland Revenue Affidavit, or a Schedule of Assets) is completed, and the application for the grant is then submitted to the Probate Office. The personal representative must also complete, and swear, on oath, a form known as the Oath for the Executor/Administrator. This is a promise by the personal representative that he will deal properly with the assets and will account for them, both to the Revenue Commissioners and to all beneficiaries. Depending on what queries, if any, may arise, the grant normally issues after a couple of months.

Once the grant issues, the personal representative is entitled to gather in all of the property of the deceased and distribute it in accordance with the directions in the will or on intestacy and in accordance with the law. Monies in the testator's bank account can be withdrawn, shares can be sold, title to houses and farmland can be vested in the beneficiaries' names or sold, and the estate can be finalised. One important matter for a personal representative to bear in mind is that, before the final distribution of the estate, he is obliged to give written notice of at least 3 months of his intention to distribute the estate, together with a copy of the Schedule of Assets to the Department of Social Protection. If requested in writing by the Minister for Social Protection within 3 months of the personal representative supplying the documents, the personal representative must ensure that sufficient assets are retained from the estate to repay any overpayment of assistance that might have been paid to the deceased. If the personal representative fails to comply with any of the above obligations, he may be prosecuted, and may also be liable to repay any overpayment due to the Department of Social Protection from his own assets.[111] A personal representative is also obliged to inform the Revenue Commissioners and to obtain tax clearance from any liability to the estate in advance of administering the estate of a deceased. Otherwise, the personal representative risks being personally responsible for any outstanding claim against the estate.

---

[111] Social Welfare Consolidation Act 2005, s 339.

### Inheritance Enquiry Unit (IEU)

The Inheritance Enquiry Unit (IEU) in the Department of Agriculture was put in place to help the legal personal representatives of a deceased farmer to administer the estate in relation to any scheme or programme in which the deceased was involved.

Following the death of a farmer, there are generally two issues to be dealt with:

1. A change to the registration details of the herd number/herdkeeper; and
2. Payment of any outstanding monies due to the estate of the deceased and the transfer of any entitlements held by the deceased.

When a Regional Veterinary Office is notified of the death of a farmer, it records the death of the farmer on the Department of Agriculture's systems and commences the process of herd transfer details, subsequently changing the registration details of the herdowner. Where appropriate, arrangements for the registration of a herdkeeper, with responsibility for the management and care of livestock in the herd, are made. Outstanding payments and/or the transfer of payment entitlements held by the deceased, are transmitted to the legal personal representative, who will deal with them in accordance with the deceased's will. There may be outstanding payments due to the estate of the deceased under various schemes.[112]

As soon as practicable, the executor/administrator of the estate of the deceased farmer and/or the solicitor dealing with the administration of the estate should contact the IEU.[113]

---

[112] Department of Agriculture, Food and the Marine, 'Arrangements for dealing with Department related issues following the death of a farmer' (2013) <www.agriculture.gov.ie/media/migration/customerservice/inheritanceenquiryunit/InheritanceEnquiryUnitInformationNote161213.doc> accessed 29 July 2016.

[113] Inheritance Enquiry Unit, Department of Agriculture, Food and the Marine, Eircom Building, Knockmay Road, Portlaoise, Co Laois. Email <inheritance@agriculture.gov.ie> or phone 1890 252 238.

## Statute of Limitations

Section 45 of the Statue of Limitations 1957 states that

> ...no action in respect of any claim to the estate of a deceased person or to any share or interest in such estate, whether under a will, on intestacy or under s 111 of the Succession Act 1965, shall be brought after the expiration of six years from the date when the right to receive the share or interest accrued.

Farmers should be aware of this time limit of 6 years within which to claim any interest to which they might be entitled; accordingly, delay should not be entertained when it concerns a right to an interest in an estate

# Enduring Power of Attorney

Regrettably, many families in Ireland have a family member who has suffered from some form of mental illness. Unfortunately, this may happen at any time or stage in life and, very often, there is little warning before it happens.

When a person does suffer a mental illness or incapacity, it makes what would normally be a simple daily routine of, for example, paying bills, running a farm and making basic financial decisions, very difficult, if not impossible. It goes without saying that, where a person becomes incapable of managing his or her affairs, enormous practical and legal problems arise. If someone becomes incapacitated through disability, illness or a progressive degenerative disease, their assets will often have to be frozen and, after that, only dealt with in accordance with strict legal rules. Bank accounts, farm entitlements, land, and other assets that are in a person's sole name, or joint names with a spouse, cannot easily be dealt with, if they can be dealt with at all.

From a financial and practical point of view, a person, while in good mental health, should create an enduring power of attorney (EPA). This is a legal document, which only takes effect in the event that the person becomes mentally incapacitated. This is an important point and one that is often misunderstood. The person creating the EPA is known as the donor, and in the event of his or her becoming incapacitated, power to deal with the donor's money and assets transfers to the attorney. The EPA becomes operative only if the donor becomes incapable of looking after his or her affairs and is registered in accordance with the provisions of s 7 of the 1996 Act. It continues in force until death, or until such time as the donor recovers his mental capacity. By planning ahead, and completing an EPA while he is of full sound mind, the donor places himself in a position to decide who will act as his attorney. Thus, he has a considerable degree of control over what happens in the unfortunate event of him becoming incapable of dealing with his own affairs at some stage in the future.

In order to complete a valid EPA, a person must be mentally capable of doing so. As will be readily appreciated, the choice of attorney is very important. In most cases, the persons chosen to act as attorneys are close family members, such as a spouse, partner, parent, sibling or friend. The choice of attorney is a personal matter, but a great deal of thought and careful consideration must be given to the nomination. In considering whom to appoint as attorney, a person should ask:

- Is this person suitable for the job?
- Do I trust them?
- Do they have the skills to manage my farming business and make decisions for me?
- Will this person act in my best interest at all times?

Once a person has become unable to manage his or her affairs, it is too late to make an EPA. For that reason, it should always be attended to while a farmer, like any other person completing an EPA, is in full health and in control of all his faculties. An EPA can be revoked at any time before it is registered.

Section 9 of the 1996 Act states that if, in the future, a person's attorney has reason to believe that the donor is becoming mentally incapable of managing his affairs, he must apply to have the EPA registered in the High Court. Before doing so, he must give notice to the donor of his intention to do so, as well as to the donor's two notice parties, named in the EPA.[114] The donor and the notice parties will be able to object if they disagree with the registration.[115]

---

[114] Powers of Attorney Act 1996, s 9(2).
[115] Powers of Attorney Act 1996, s 10(2).

To illustrate the importance of completing a valid EPA, it should again be noted that, in the event of a person becoming mentally incapable without having this document in place, his family will not be in a position to deal with his financial affairs or his property until he dies, or is made a ward of court beforehand. An application to be made a ward of court[116] is an extremely costly and time consuming process, which could significantly erode a person's assets. Furthermore, in wardship cases, it is the court which has the ultimate authority and power to deal with a person's assets and affairs. The procedure under which a person is made a ward of court generally involves the appointment of a person or persons, known as a committee. This committee must act, at all times, under the direction of the Office of Wards of Court. As will be appreciated, this can be cumbersome, time-consuming and expensive. In many ways, it is an outdated procedure, which is unsuited to the demands of the day-to-day operation of a farm. The committee may not necessarily comprise people whom the farmer would have appointed to look after his affairs in the first place, had he considered the matter whilst in full health.

It should be noted that the law surrounding enduring powers of attorney is set to change due to the Assisted Decision Making (Capacity) Act 2015, which introduces new provisions for individuals to make legally binding agreements, where they lack, or may lack, capacity to make decisions unaided.

In short, by taking legal advice and completing an EPA, extremely difficult circumstances can be made much less complex. Apart from anything else, the completion of an EPA may obviate the need for a wardship application to court, which can be cumbersome and expensive.

## Conclusion

The saying that, "nothing can be said to be certain, except death and taxes",[117] has stood the test of time. These certainties are a fundamental part of life, and a person must not shy away from addressing them. Nobody likes to think about the fact that they will die or may become of unsound mind, but it is incumbent upon each and every person to plan

---

[116] The procedure governing wardship is set out in RSC Ord 67.

[117] Letter from Benjamin Franklin to M Le Veillard (13 November 1789).

for these events. The first, and best, way to do this is by making a will and completing an enduring power of attorney. Where a person has made a will, it is important to review it regularly, as circumstances change. What may have been a perfectly appropriate and sensible will when it was made, can easily become out-dated and no longer appropriate, if the testator's circumstances change. This may happen where there are significant changes in family, financial or life circumstances. Similarly, it is worthwhile checking the tax efficiency of a will at regular intervals, as the tax code changes from year to year. Making a will and completing an enduring power of attorney may require considerable thought and consideration. However, taking these steps is not only advisable, but, once taken, provides peace of mind and contentment. Most farmers will experience a sense of relief once the documents are in place, happy in the knowledge that many potential legal and financial pitfalls are likely to be avoided in the future.

# CHAPTER SIX

# Land Leasing

The leasing of agricultural land was an unattractive prospect for most of the 19th and 20th centuries, due to the considerable rights to which tenants were entitled, such as compensation for disturbance and for improvements made by tenants on property leased from landlords.[1] As a consequence, conacre[2] and agistment[3] were the popular choices in Ireland as the means of allowing one person to occupy land owned by another. The advantage of the conacre or agistment arrangements was that the landowner secured the benefits of a normal letting arrangement in return for the use of the land, while, at the same time, enjoying absolute security, as the landowner remained in legal ownership and possession of the land.

However, many of the tenant's rights afforded under the legislation introduced in the 19th century were repealed by s 3 of the Land Act 1984. Long-term leasing of land is now commonplace. Many farmers who need to enlarge their holdings cannot afford the enormous cost of purchasing land and, for that reason, the leasing of land may be an attractive option. Landowners who have retired from farming, or those who have recently inherited farmland and do not intend to farm it themselves, are generally happy to lease their lands to active farmers who wish to expand their production. Measures introduced in recent budgets have provided a significant stimulus to encourage long-term leasing of agricultural land.

This chapter is mainly concerned with leasing, and, in particular, with the significant changes made in this area by the Property Services (Regulation) Act 2011 (hereafter 'the 2011 Act'). It also outlines, in some detail, long-term leases, the statutory rights of a tenant to renewal of a lease, the income tax exemptions available in relation to long term leasing of land, and how to

---

[1] Landlord and Tenant (Ireland) Act 1870.
[2] Conacre is the right to sow and harvest crops on another's land.
[3] Agistment is the right to graze livestock on another's land.

protect the Basic Payment Entitlements when entering into a long-term lease. In addition, the process of evicting a tenant is addressed.

At the outset, it is necessary to define a land lease, and then to contrast it with conacre and agistment agreements. A land lease is a written legal agreement between a lessor, the landowner, and a lessee, the active farmer, who takes the land from the landowner. The lessor is the person who owns the land and wishes to lease it out to another person. The lessee is the tenant, who leases the land with a view to farming it. Until recently, there was a statutory requirement to obtain the consent of the Irish Land Commission before agricultural land could be leased.[4] However, the enactment of s 12 of the Land Act 2005 repealed s 12 of the Land Act 1965, eliminating the necessity for the consent of the Irish Land Commission.

## Conacre and Agistment

Before dealing further with conacre and agistment agreements, each must be properly defined. Both are usually for a term of eleven months.[5] Conacre is the right to sow and harvest crops on another's lands. Some crops are particularly suited to conacre arrangements, such as potatoes, beet, and vegetables. Conacre, like agistment, has long been a feature of Irish agriculture. A useful overview of a conacre arrangement was provided by Pigot CB in *Booth v McManus*,[6] where he stated:

> I have been in the habit of considering the dealing of conacre to be one in which the owner of the land retains the occupation of the premises, the conacre holder having a licence to till the land, and a right, connected with that licence, of egress and regress, for the purpose of so tilling.[7]

Agistment is the right to graze livestock on another person's land.

Agistment or conacre agreements are usually on a seasonal basis, normally for 11 months but never for a full 12 months.[8] These arrangements are entered into in order to avoid a lease coming into being, and the person

---

[4] Land Act 1965, s 12.
[5] Per Doyle J in *Collins v O' Brien* [1981] ILRM 328 at 329.
[6] *Booth v McManus* [1861] ICLR 418.
[7] [1861] ICLR 418, 435.
[8] Per Doyle J in *Collins v O' Brien* [1981] ILRM 328 at 329.

taking the land acquiring the rights of a lessee.[9] It is well settled in Irish law that a person taking land under conacre and agistment does not acquire rights to which a lessee, under a lease, would be entitled, such as an automatic right to renewal of the lease.[10]

Under the old system, conacre agreements almost always involved an auctioneer. The landowner and the person taking the land generally signed a standard licence agreement.

The system has changed dramatically since the enactment of the 2011 Act, which led to the establishment of the Property Services Regulatory Authority (PSRA) in 2012.[11] The purpose of the new legislation is to protect the public, and the main function of the PSRA is to licence and regulate property services providers, for example auctioneers and letting agents. Section 11 of the Act gives the PSRA a number of functions, including controlling and supervising licensees so as to maintain and improve standards in property services, investigating complaints and implementing a redress system for consumers.

In relation to conacre or agistment, there is now a statutory requirement that a full 'letter of engagement', or contract, be signed by the landowner, or person appointing the auctioneer.[12] In the majority of cases under the new system, the landowner, and not the farmer, will now be obliged to pay the agent's fee. This is in contrast to what was traditionally the case. The agent is contracted to let the rights to sow or harvest crops (conacre) or the right to graze (agistment) on behalf of the landowner. The landowner is the client. Essentially, under the 2011 Act, conacre and agistment are now deemed property services.[13]

Section 43 of the 2011 Act confirms that a letter of engagement must be issued by an agent to a landowner within 7 days of agreeing, or beginning,

---

[9] See Crampton J in *Dease v O' Reilly* (1861) 12 ICLR 418 at 435–436 and *Carson v Jeffers* [1961] IR 44 at 47 (per Budd J).

[10] *Maurice E Taylor (Merchants) Ltd v Commissioner of Valuation* [1981] NI 236 at 245.

[11] Property Services Regulatory Authority. <www.psr.ie/website/npsra/npsraweb.nsf/page/index-en> accessed 8 July 2016.

[12] Property Services Regulation Act 2011, s 43(2)(b).

[13] Property Services Regulation Act 2011, s (2)(1).

to provide a property service, whichever is the earliest.[14] The landowner must return the letter of engagement, duly signed, within 7 working days.[15] If an agent does not receive a signed letter of engagement, returned from the landowner, they must cease to provide, or shall not start to provide, the property service.[16]

Sourcing of land for conacre and agistment is also a property service, whereby the agent is contracted to source the rights to sow or harvest crops (conacre), or to source the right to graze (agistment), on behalf of a farmer.

The farmer is the only party who can initially instruct an agent to source agricultural land in conacre and agistment, and, therefore, the farmer is the client. In this situation, the letter of engagement is between the farmer and the agent, and the farmer is liable to pay the agent's fee.

As a result of the 2011 Act, conacre and agistment transactions have now become similar to other property sales or letting transactions.

## The Importance of a Written Lease

As mentioned earlier, a lease document is a written legal agreement between a lessor (the landowner) and a lessee (the active farmer). A lessor is also known as a landlord and a lessee is also known as a tenant.

The lease sets out the obligations of both parties during the period of the lease, providing useful legal protection to all parties.

The lease must be signed by both parties. Signatures on the lease must be witnessed by an independent person or persons.

There are many benefits to be gained by putting in place a written lease. For example:

(a) In order to avail of the income tax reliefs and exemptions which are discussed later in this chapter, it is essential that the lease document is in writing, or evidenced in writing. A written lease is vital

---

[14] Property Services Regulation Act 2011, s 43(1).
[15] Property Services Regulation Act 2011, s 43(2)(b).
[16] Property Services Regulation Act 2011, s 43(2).

for lessors hoping to avail of the income tax exemptions on the rental income under s 664(1)(a) of the Taxes Consolidation Act 1997 (hereafter 'the 1997 Act');

(b) While legal advice is often sought in order to enforce the rights of a party after a dispute has arisen, it is generally better, in terms of finances, goodwill, and the well-being of the land, to seek such advice prior to entering into an agreement. Having a detailed lease agreement in place, especially for a long term letting, is the best way of avoiding future problems between a lessor and lessee;

(c) A written lease is practical, as it provides a record of what has been agreed between the parties, which may prove most useful after a period of time has elapsed and details might otherwise be forgotten. This is particularly important where one or other of the original parties dies, or becomes of unsound mind;

(d) A written lease provides a useful basis for both parties as they consider the proposed arrangement. It may assist the parties in anticipating and addressing any problems or stumbling blocks, when, or even before, they arise.

It should be noted that a lease agreement is a written document that specifies the terms and conditions of the lease arrangement for the period set out in the lease only.

## Squatters

Adverse possession or, as it is more commonly known, squatting, allows a person to claim a right over land which is owned by another person, on the basis that he or she has occupied the land continuously for over twelve years,[17] with the intention of excluding all others, including the true owner.

Adverse possession cannot be claimed if rent is being paid for the land on a regular basis. A properly drafted lease protects the security of the land and ensures that the occupier cannot claim adverse possession. Adverse possession is discussed in greater detail in Chapter 1.

## Statutory Rights of a Tenant to Renewal of a Lease

In certain circumstances, lessees may have a right to claim renewal of a lease when the term of the lease agreement expires.

---

[17] Statute of Limitations 1957, s 13(2).

The Landlord and Tenant (Amendment) Act 1980 (hereafter 'the 1980 Act') and the Landlord and Tenant (Amendment) Act 1994 (hereafter 'the 1994 Act') regulate the relationship between a lessor and a lessee by providing a number of statutory reliefs to the parties. Relief is provided to lessees by allowing them to claim renewal of the lease at market rent, where the property being leased consists predominantly of buildings, and where the land attached to those buildings is considered to be "subsidiary and ancillary" to the buildings, as per s 5 of the 1980 Act. A new tenancy is a further letting for a term of between 5 and 20 years, at the election of the lessee.[18]

For example, if a farm consists predominantly of buildings, such as cowsheds or slurry pits, the lessee has a right to renewal of the lease at open market rent after a term of five years has elapsed, as per s 13(1)(a) of the 1980 Act.

Many cases have come before the courts on the question of what is considered "subsidiary and ancillary".

The case of *Kenny Homes & Co Ltd v Leonard*[19] involved a filling station with a substantial car parking business, where payment for the car parking was being made in respect of part of the filling station. Lynch J found that the car parking area was not subsidiary and ancillary to the buildings and, in fact, the reverse was the case, in that the filling station was subsidiary to the substantial car parking area. Therefore, the premises did not constitute a "tenement", as defined in the legislation,[20] and, as a consequence, there was no right to a new tenancy.

Section 13(1)(b) of the 1980 Act provides that a lessee is entitled to seek renewal of a lease, where he or she has been in occupation for more than twenty years. Section 13(1)(c) of the 1980 Act provides that a lessee is entitled to seek a renewal of the lease where he or she makes substantial improvements to the property. However, under most lease agreements there is a prohibition on the tenant carrying out investments or improvements without the permission of the lessor.

---

[18] Landlord and Tenant (Amendment) Act 1980, s 13.

[19] *Kenny Homes & Co Ltd v Leonard* (SC, 18 June 1998).

[20] Landlord and Tenant (Amendment) Act 1980, s 5(1).

There are restrictions on the entitlement to a new tenancy set out in s 17 of the 1980 Act. That section is in two parts. The first part, s 17(1), deals with situations where the tenancy has been terminated by reason of some default on the part of the lessee, for example, for non-payment of rent or breach of covenant on the part of the lessee. Section 17(2) is applicable where a lessor wishes to obtain possession of the premises for his or her own purposes. Where the lessee loses the right to a new tenancy under s 17(2), he/she is entitled to compensation for disturbance. Compensation for disturbance is not payable where the right to a new tenancy is lost under s 17(1).

## Ways to Prevent an Automatic Right of Renewal

There are a number of ways in which lessees can be prevented from acquiring an automatic right to renewal of the lease. One such way is by granting a lease of the land only, and then granting a separate and distinct licence or letting for temporary convenience of the buildings on the land to the lessee.[21] In this situation, the lessee will not have a right of renewal after five years. A licence is a permission by the owner which allows another person to enter land. It does not create an interest in land. Without the licence, such entry on the land would amount to trespass.[22] A licensee is excluded from the statutory rights a lessee would acquire under the 1980 Act.[23] He or she has no entitlement to a new licence.

It would appear from some recent judgments of the High Court that the courts will not merely focus on the names or labels that the parties attach to their agreements, but will examine the actual documents and the real nature of the arrangements. Peart J, in *Noel Smith v CIE*,[24] followed the decision in the case of *Street v Mountford*,[25] holding that an agreement described as a licence was, in fact, a tenancy. The agreement in that case dealt comprehensively with the relationship between the parties, setting out in some detail the nature of the arrangement, and, indeed, stated clearly that it was not the intention of either party to create the relationship

---

[21] Landlord and Tenant (Amendment) Act 1980, s 5(1)(a)(iv).

[22] See *O' Keeffe v Irish Motor Inns* [1978] IR 85 at 94 (per O' Higgins CJ) and 100 (per Kenny J).

[23] Landlord and Tenant (Amendment) Act 1980, s 5(1).

[24] *Noel Smith v CIE* (HC, 9 October 2002).

[25] *Street v Mountford* [1985] AC 809.

of landlord and tenant. Notwithstanding the description in the heading of the agreement, Peart J focused on the true nature of the parties' relationship. In support of his conclusion, he quoted Lord Templeman in *Street v Mountford*, who stated that "there is no doubt that the traditional distinction between a tenancy and a licence lay in the grant of land for a term at a rent with exclusive possession".[26] Lord Templeman emphasised that the consequences in law of an agreement can only be determined by consideration of the effect of the agreement.[27] The decision of Peart J in *Smith v CIE* was recently referred to in the decision of McGovern J in *Esso Ireland Limited & anor v Nine One One Retail Limited*.[28]

A temporary convenience letting arises when a property is let for temporary convenience or necessity. Such lettings, if they are genuinely made for such purposes, fall outside the ambit of the 1980 Act and no right of renewal arises.

In the case of *Carton v Wilson*,[29] it was held that a mere statement of temporary convenience is not sufficient. The letting must actually be, bona fide, for temporary convenience. This type of letting is often employed to avoid statutory controls, in particular, the renewal rights which can accrue under the 1980 Act. Furthermore, a letting that is made for temporary convenience must be clearly expressed as such, according to the High Court in *Like It Love It Products Ltd v Dun Laoghaire-Rathdown County Council*.[30] Each case is, of course, determined on its own facts and circumstances.

Another possible method of ensuring that a lessee does not acquire statutory rights of renewal where there are buildings on the land, is by ensuring that the lessee signs a deed of renunciation.

A deed of renunciation is a document signed by the lessee renouncing his or her entitlement to a new tenancy. Section 4 of the 1994 Act provided for such a deed of renunciation. However, the 1994 Act was limited in its scope, in that it only applied to offices. Furthermore, a tenant

---

[26] *Street v Mountford* [1985] AC 809 at 6.

[27] ibid at 12.

[28] *Esso Ireland Limited & anor v Nine One One Retail Limited* [2013] IEHC 514.

[29] *Carton v Wilson* (1962) 96 ILT 92.

[30] *Like It Love It Products Ltd v Dun Laoghaire-Rathdown County Council* [2008] IEHC 26.

was required to enter into a renunciation of the right to a new tenancy prior to the commencement of that tenancy. Section 4 of the 1994 Act was eventually repealed by s 47 of the Civil Law (Miscellaneous Provisions) Act 2008. The entitlement to renounce the right to a new tenancy was extended to all types of property. Very importantly, the parties are now free to enter into such a deed of renunciation at any time. The requirement that the tenant obtains independent legal advice has been retained.

In practice, farmers and landowners enter into agreements by way of licence or temporary convenience lettings in relation to the buildings on a farm. This is another reason why farmers and landowners historically viewed short term leases more favourably. In reality, the majority of land leases do not involve any buildings, and, consequently, there is no automatic statutory right of renewal for the lessee. However, a landowner who is considering leasing buildings, along with his or her farmland, should consult a solicitor in relation to his/her particular set of circumstances, so as to ascertain the best possible approach.

From a taxation perspective, the income tax exemption extends to farm buildings that are leased as part of the overall lease of farmland.[31] As such, there may be a taxation incentive to taking the leasing approach.

## Important Clauses to be Inserted in the Lease

While lease agreement templates are widely available, and the Irish Farmers Association (IFA) has produced a precedent master agricultural lease,[32] it is advisable to seek the advice of a solicitor in order to adapt the lease agreement to the specific needs of both the lessor and the lessee in each individual case. There are a number of basic details which should form part of every lease, including:

(i)  *Lease Duration*
What is the term of the lease? Where investment by the lessee is required, in order to make the best use of leased land, it is important that the lease duration is sufficiently long to justify such investment.

---

[31] Taxes Consolidation Act 1997, s 664(1)(a).

[32] Irish Farmers' Association, 'IFA Master Lease of Agricultural Land' (2015). <www.ifa.ie/cross-sectors/farm-business-and-credit/land-lease-master-document/> accessed 8 July 2016.

### (ii) Annual Payment and Payment Procedures

How much rent is to be paid? How often? If applicable, how much of the basic payment entitlements are to be paid to the lessor? When should they be paid?

### (iii) Rent Review Clause

A farmer may be fearful of becoming locked into high or low land rents. This can be remedied by tailoring a lease agreement to include regular rent reviews, or by linking the rental charge to, for example, the annual price of milk or barley. Rent reviews are generally provided for every five years or so. Clauses should be inserted to provide that, in the event that agreement cannot be reached on the rent review, then the matter would be referred to an arbitrator, whose decision would be final and binding, thus avoiding legal proceedings and saving unnecessary costs.

### (iv) Details of the Land Use and the Upkeep of the Land

The upkeep of the land should be covered in the lease. The specific purpose for which the lessee intends to use the lands should be agreed. If cattle are to be placed on the lands, the lessee should covenant that no diseased animal will be present.

### (v) Insurance

The lease should specify that the lessee is obliged to put in place his or her own insurance, and that he must indemnify the lessor from all claims or liabilities arising from the lessee's user of the property. It is also important that the lessor has his or her own public liability insurance. This is necessary as the lessor and the lessee have an insurable interest in the property, however their interests are not the same.[33]

### (vi) Treatment of Basic Payment Entitlements

If a farmer is leasing the basic payment entitlements, appropriate clauses must be included in the lease. A private contract clause should also be signed to ensure that the basic payment entitlements revert to the lessor on the termination of the lease. It is also worth considering the inclusion of a clause to provide that, in the event of the lessee not receiving his or her basic payment entitlements, this

---

[33] *Andrews v Patriotic Assurance Co. of Ireland (No. 2)* (1886) 18 LR Ir 355.

should not affect the validity of the agreement, and that the monies will still be due and owing to the lessor. A further clause should also be inserted into the lease, obliging the lessee to process and lodge all paperwork with the Department of Agriculture by the required deadline for the purpose of claiming any entitlements payable, and further obliging the lessee to deal expeditiously with any queries that the Department of Agriculture may raise in connection with the application.

### (vii) Clause Preventing Subletting
A lessee should not have a right to sub-let the land without the lessor's prior written consent. This is to ensure that the lessor retains control over the identity of those who occupy his or her lands. Having entrusted possession of his or her lands to someone, a lessor will not want to see the lessee handing over the lands unilaterally to someone who may be considered undesirable.

### (viii) Farm Buildings
Farm buildings should be dealt with separately. This is important in order to ensure that the lessee does not have an automatic right of renewal of the tenancy, as noted earlier.

### (ix) Identity of lands
The land should be clearly identified by reference to maps and folio numbers, if applicable.

### (x) Termination provisions
Clauses covering the manner and time in which notice of termination by either party must be served are extremely important.

It is also important to consider matters which might arise in the future, such as a child who wishes to construct a dwelling house on part of the lands. It is important that any lease includes a clause which would entitle the lessor to release such site from the lease and transfer it to such child.

The above list is not exhaustive, and any farmer who is contemplating leasing his or her lands should consult a solicitor with experience in the area of agricultural leases, so as to ensure that he or she is fully protected against unexpected pitfalls.

## Income Tax Exemptions Available for Leasing Farmland[34]

Section 20 of the Finance Act 2014 sets out the income tax exemption thresholds, where a qualifying lease is entered into on or after 1 January 2015. These are as follows:

- €40,000 where all of the qualifying leases are for a minimum duration of 15 years or more[35];
- €30,000 where all of the qualifying leases are for a minimum duration of 10, but less than 15 years[36];
- €22,500 where all of the qualifying leases are for a minimum duration of 7, but less than 10 years[37];
- €18,000 where all the qualifying leases are for either 5 or 6 years.[38]

It should be noted that the limits apply in respect of the minimum period covered by the lease agreement.[39] As such, a 12-year lease with a break clause after 6 years will only benefit from the annual income tax exemption of €18,000, rather than the €30,000 annual exemption applicable to leases of between 10 and 15 years. The term of the lease must be in respect of a definite period in order to satisfy the statutory requirements.

### Conditions
- The farm land must be in the State[40];
- Leases between close relatives or connected parties do not qualify[41];
- The lease must be in writing[42];
- The lease must be for a definite term of at least five years[43];

---

[34] For more information, see Revenue, 'Leasing Farm Land' (2015) <www.revenue.ie/en/tax/it/reliefs/leasing-farm-land.html> accessed 6 July 2016, and Revenue, 'Revenue Operational Manual - Exemption of certain income from leasing farm land - Section 664 TCA 1997' (May 2016) <www.revenue.ie/en/about/foi/s16/income-tax-capital-gains-tax-corporation-tax/part-23/23-01-23.pdf> accessed 7 July 2016.

[35] Finance Act 2014, s 20(b)(iv)(A).

[36] Finance Act 2014, s 20(b)(iv)(B).

[37] Finance Act 2014, s 20(b)(iv)(C).

[38] Finance Act 2014, s 20(b)(iv)(D).

[39] Revenue Operational Manual 23.01.23 Exemption of certain income from leasing of farm land s 664 TCA 1997, updated May 2016

[40] Taxes Consolidation Act 1997, s 664(1)(a).

[41] Taxes Consolidation Act 1997, s 664(1)(a)(iii).

[42] Taxes Consolidation Act 1997, s 664(1)(a)(i).

[43] Taxes Consolidation Act 1997, s 664(1)(a)(ii).

- The lease must be made on an arm's length basis between one or more qualifying lessors and one or more qualifying lessees[44];
- The land must be let for the purposes of farming.[45]

The Revenue Commissioners, by concession, will accept a lease between an uncle and his nephew or niece, or an aunt and her nephew or niece, as qualifying in respect of the income tax exemption, where all other relevant criteria are satisfied. If the land is owned jointly with a spouse, each person is entitled to the annual exempt amount.[46] Income that may be exempt includes rent and the value of any Basic Payment Scheme entitlement paid back to the owner of the land under the lease.[47] It is not necessary to apportion the rent received between the land and the basic payment entitlements.

The amount payable under the lease remains subject to PRSI and USC taxes. The relief cannot operate to create a loss.[48] The relevant exemption limit applies irrespective of the number of qualifying leases held.[49]

However, a farmer who is considering leasing land should also consider other possible tax implications, such as the potential impact on Capital Gains Tax and Capital Acquisitions Tax in the event of a future disposal, especially the possible loss of retirement relief and/or agricultural relief.[50,51] This should be discussed with a tax advisor before entering into any lease.

## Stamp Duty

The Agri-taxation Review recommended that stamp duty relief be given in relation to certain leases of farmland to encourage more productive use of land.[52] This recommendation is now reflected in s 81D of the Stamp Duties Consolidation Act 1999. However, it is subject to a commencement order

---

[44] Taxes Consolidation Act 1997, s 664(1)(a)(iii).
[45] Taxes Consolidation Act 1997, s 664(1)(a).
[46] Taxes Consolidation Act 1997, s 664(3).
[47] Taxes Consolidation Act 1997, s 664(7).
[48] Revenue Operational Manual 23.01.23 Exemption of certain income from leasing of farm land Section 664 TCA 1997, Updated May 2016 Page.
[49] Taxes Consolidation Act 1997, s 664(1)(a).
[50] Capital Acquisitions Tax Consolidation Act 2003, s 89.
[51] Taxes Consolidation Act 1997, s 598 and s 599.
[52] Revenue Guide to Farming Taxation Measures in Finance Act 2014, 4.1.

by the Minister for Finance, and hence, stamp duty is still payable on agricultural leases.

A lease must be stamped by the Revenue Commissioners in order to permit a lessor claim the tax relief incentives on the lease income. Stamp duty[53] is charged at the rate of 1% of the annual rent. The lease must be stamped within 44 days of first execution of the lease.[54] The lease can now be stamped online through the Revenue Online System (ROS).

## Registration

Land leases must be registered by the lessee with the Property Services Regulatory Authority.[55] The relevant land leases are then entered into the Commercial Leases Register, which is freely accessible, online, to the public. The information available to the public in relation to any land lease includes:

- The address of the commercial property the subject of the lease;
- The date of the lease of the property;
- The term of years of the lease; and
- The rent payable in respect of the property.

This process can be completed by the lessee, or by a solicitor or auctioneer. There is no charge payable on registering the lease.

## Ensure Proper Procedure is Followed when Terminating a Tenancy

As with all arrangements, the selection of the right lessee is of utmost importance. The most common cause of disputes between lessors and lessees is non-payment of rent. This is more likely to arise if the rent is unrealistic, or the lessee is unreliable. Before agreeing a rent, it is important that a lessee knows all relevant costs of production and is satisfied that he or she can pay the agreed rent on time.

Terminating a lease can be a protracted, technical, and complicated process. Great care should be taken to check the terms of the lease to

---

[53] Stamp Duties Consolidation Act 1999, sch 1.

[54] Stamp Duties Consolidation Act, s 2, as amended

[55] Property Services (Regulation) Act 2011, s 88(1).

establish whether or not provision has been made for a specific method of termination. In some cases, the parties will agree that either or both of the parties have the option of terminating the lease in advance of the expiry of the term of the lease. This is commonly known as a break option. Such options will generally require the party exercising the option to give 6 to 12 months' notice of the exercise of the option. As options are, in law, regarded as a privilege, the conditions precedent to the exercise of the option must be adhered to, or the right to exercise the option may be lost.[56]

The parties to a lease or tenancy are generally free to terminate their relationship by agreement. This is known as surrender. Section 7 of the Landlord and Tenant Ireland Act 1860 provides that the estate or interest of any tenant under any lease or other contract of tenancy shall not be surrendered otherwise than by a deed executed, or note in writing signed by the tenant or his agent, or by act and operation of law. A lease or tenancy may be surrendered by operation of law where the tenant delivers up possession of the property and that delivery is accepted, for example, the handing over of the keys to the property.[57]

The most common methods of terminating or ending a commercial lease are as follows:

1. Notice to quit; and
2. Forfeiture.

### Notice to Quit

Notice to quit is used to recover the property where the lessee is overholding (remains in possession and continues to pay rent), after the term of the lease has ended. On the expiry of a fixed term lease or tenancy, a new tenancy may come into existence between the parties, which is known as a periodic tenancy. The tenancy may be a periodic tenancy from year to year, month to month or week to week. The precise nature of the relationship will depend on how rent is calculated under the agreement. The danger for lessors, where a lessee overholds on a fixed term lease or tenancy and where the rent is calculated on a yearly basis, is that a tenancy from year

---

[56] *Sunnybank Inn Ltd v East Coast Inns Ltd.* (11 May 1979) HC.
[57] *Grimmage v Legge* (1828) 8 B. & C. 324.

to year will arise by implication. Notices are very technical and should always be drafted by a solicitor.

A person who has received prior express authorisation may serve the notice to quit. Where the lessor is not serving the notice to quit, it is wise to arrange prior written authority to be given to the server. Such authority cannot be given retrospectively. It is important to bear in mind that such a matter could come before a court and it is prudent to obtain prior express authorisation.

There is no set form for the notice to quit, but it must contain a clear and unambiguous intention to terminate the tenancy.[58] A description of the premises must be given[59] and it must be clearly addressed to 'the lessee and all other persons in occupation'.[60] In the case of an agricultural holding the notice must be signed.[61]

### Length of Notice

The first step is always to check the written agreement to see whether or not there is an agreed procedure. Many leases and tenancy agreements specify that in the event that the lessee overholds, the tenancy can be terminated by the giving of one month's notice in writing.

The essential question is how the rent is reserved in the lease. A monthly tenancy requires one month's notice, expiring on a gale day.[62] A quarterly tenancy requires 3 months' notice, and this too, should expire on a gale day.[63] A tenancy from year to year requires 183 days' notice, expiring on the anniversary of the tenancy.[64]

Section 69 of the Landlord and Tenant (Ireland) Act 1870 states that any tenancy at will, or less than a tenancy from year to year, is created by a lessor after the passing of the Act, the lessee under such tenancy shall, on quitting his/her holding, be entitled to notice to quit and compensation

---

[58] Byrne, *Landlord and Tenant Law – The Commercial Sector* (Round Hall) Chapter 25, p 338.

[59] ibid.

[60] ibid, p 339.

[61] Landlord and Tenant (Ir) Act 1870, s 58.

[62] *Harvey v Copeland* (1892) 30 L.R. Ir. 412.

[63] *Kemp v Derrett* (1814) 3 Cam 510.

[64] *Doe v Matthews* (1851) 11 C.B. 675.

as if he or she had been a lessee from year to year. The provision only applies to pastoral or agricultural holdings. The provision does not apply where the letting or contract for the letting of land is made and entered into bona fide for the temporary convenience, or to meet a temporary necessity, either of the lessor or lessee.[65]

The lease should be checked to see if provision has been made for the mode of service of notice. Personal service is best, and, in the case of a limited company, notice should be served on the registered office of the company.

## Waiver of Notice

A notice to quit will be deemed to have been waived by any of the following:

- Service of a subsequent notice[66];
- A demand for rent[67];
- Acceptance of the rent which falls due after the end of the notice period.[68]

## Should a Lessor Accept Payment of Rent?

In practice, lessors are advised not to accept payment of rent, or else to mark the receipt of rent as mesne rates only. 'Mesne rates' is the term given to compensation for trespass when the trespasser is a former tenant who is overholding.[69] It is important not to demand rent beyond the commencement of the notice period, or at least not to incorporate any such written demand into the notice.

## Forfeiture

Forfeiture is only appropriate where the term of the lease is still running. It must be understood that a lessor has no right to terminate a lease prematurely, unless the lessee has been in breach of one or more of its terms.[70]

---

[65] Landlord and Tenant (Ireland) Act 1870, s 69.

[66] *May v Gorman* (1875) 10 ILT 20.

[67] *Pile v Kent* (1930) 64 ILTR 17.

[68] ibid.

[69] JCW Wylie, *Landlord and Tenant Law* (Third Edition, Bloomsbury Professional) Chapter 12, p 363.

[70] *Doe D David v Williams* (1936) 7 Car. & P. 322.

A lessor also loses the right to forfeiture if he or she fails to follow certain statutory procedures designed to give the lessee a reasonable opportunity to remedy any breach.[71] It is extremely difficult to forfeit a lease, especially if the parties are meeting in court for the first time. Forfeiture is an equitable remedy and the court has a wide discretion to grant relief to the tenant.

## Grounds for Forfeiture

Forfeiture can arise in the following ways:

1. Disclaimer by the lessee of the lessor's title[72];
2. Re-entry or ejectment where there has been a breach of a condition in the lease[73]; and
3. Re-entry or ejectment where there has been a breach of a covenant which provides for re-entry for such breach.

## Breach of Condition of Lease

A breach of a condition of a lease gives the lessor an inherent right to re-enter.[74] What is fundamental is that the lessor distinguishes between a condition and a covenant. A condition is a fundamental term in a lease.

## Breach of Covenant in a Lease

A breach of covenant in a lease will only give rise to a right to re-enter if the covenant broken also has a proviso for re-entry in the lease. Before forfeiture can take place, a specific notice must be served by the lessor on the lessee,[75] unless forfeiture is occurring for non-payment of rent.[76] In this case, there is strictly speaking no need for the said notice, but it is advisable to serve one. The notice calls upon the lessee to remedy the breach within a reasonable time. There is no prescribed form of notice.

---

[71] *Piggott v Middlesex County Council* [1909] 1 Ch. 134.

[72] *Congested Districts Board v Connor* [1916] 2 IR 611.

[73] *Doe D Henniker v Watt* (1828) 8 B. & C. 308.

[74] ibid.

[75] Conveyancing Act 1881, s 14(1) as amended by s 35, Landlord and Tenant (Ground Rents) Act 1967.

[76] Conveyancing Act 1881, s 14(8).

The lessor may elect to forfeit the lease either by way of court proceedings or by peaceable re-entry.

## Peaceable Re-Entry

If the notice is served and the time specified in the notice has elapsed without remedy of the breach, a demand again is made for possession, and the lessor may re-enter if it can be done peaceably.[77] If re-entry cannot be effected peaceably the lessor cannot use force.[78]

The lessee may apply to court for relief against forfeiture,[79] even after the lessor has taken possession of the property, and where possession has been obtained other than on foot of a court order for possession.[80] Although the granting of relief is at the discretion of the court, where a lease has been forfeited for non-payment of rent, relief against forfeiture will almost always be granted where the lessee discharges the outstanding rent together with interest and costs.[81] As forfeiture for non-payment of rent is regarded as security for payment of the rent, relief against forfeiture is granted on the basis that it would be unconscionable for a lessor who has received his full rent, with interest and costs, to insist on taking advantage of the right to forfeit.

## Court Proceedings

If the lessor is unsuccessful or cannot re-enter peaceably, then the lessor's remedy is to issue an ejectment civil bill and to seek an order for possession by the court.

## Conclusion

Long term leasing, which was once extremely rare, is now proving to be a very effective land use. With proper collaboration, it will almost always provide security for both parties. Most legal and professional advisors are very much in favour of the long term leasing of land, and are seeing, at first-hand, how well it can work for both the landowner/lessor and the active farmer/lessee. It is generally more progressive, results in better land use, and ensures that land and facilities are properly maintained

---

[77] *Bank of Ireland v Lady Lisa Ireland Ltd* [1992] 1 IR 404.
[78] Prohibition of Forcible Entry and Occupation Act 1971, s 2.
[79] Conveyancing Act 1881, s 14(2).
[80] ibid.
[81] *Rayan International Ltd v Murphy Flynn* [2009] IESC 28.

and enhanced. Landowners who wish, for whatever reasons, to step back from active farming, but who do not wish to retire fully, can opt to lease part of their farm, while continuing to farm the remainder of the lands themselves. Long-term leasing delivers access to land for a definite period of time, at a known cost. This provides certainty, allowing an operator to develop his or her farm enterprise. When considering long term leasing, it is important to choose a reliable party to lease to, and to have a well drafted, comprehensive agreement put in place, prepared by a solicitor who is experienced in these types of agreements, so as to ensure that the interest of the lessor is protected from the outset. It is equally important for the lessee that a written lease is in place and that he or she obtains legal advice in advance of signing any documentation.

# CHAPTER SEVEN

# Solar Farms and Wind Farms

The Renewable Energy Directive (RED) 2009[1] sets out binding targets for each Member State, with the stated aim being that, in the EU as a whole, renewable energy will account for a minimum of 20% of the overall energy consumption by 2020. Under EU 2020 renewable energy targets, the Irish government must achieve 40% of electricity generation from renewable energy sources, or face significant penalties.[2] At the end of 2015, wind turbines generated 22% of Ireland's average electricity demand[3]. In fact, most investment to date has been directed towards wind farms. However, proposals for new wind farms are increasingly encountering challenges at planning permission stage,[4] and solar photovoltaic (PV) is currently the only other proven renewable technology that can be rolled out in a timely manner, so as to allow Ireland reach the 2020 targets. Other forms of renewable technology include biomass and hydroelectric.

Ireland will be the last country in Europe to roll out utility-scale solar farms,[5] with construction of the first of those farms unlikely to commence until 2018. Whilst the cost of solar PV technology has fallen by 82% in the last 6 years,[6] subsidies will still be required in the short term to make the technology economically viable. In December 2015, the government published its *Energy White Paper*,[7] in which it indicated that it would

---

[1] Directive 2009/28/EC of the European Parliament and of the Council of 23 April 2009 on the promotion of the use of energy from renewable sources and amending and subsequently repealing Directives 2001/77/EC and 2003/30/EC OJ L140/16.

[2] Department of Communications, Energy and Natural Resources, *Energy White Paper: Ireland's Transition to a Low Carbon Energy Future 2015–2030* (2015).

[3] Eoin Burke-Kennedy (27 December 2015). "Over 23% of electricity demand now supplied through wind", *The Irish Times.*

[4] *Klaus Balz and Hanna Heubach v An Bord Pleanála*, High Court, 25 February 2016

[5] Independent 'Why do all other countries have solar and we don't?' Paul Melia, 23 July 2016.

[6] Lazard, *Lazard's Levelized Cost of Energy Analysis 9.0* (Lazard 2015) p 10.

[7] Department of Communications, Energy and Natural Resources, *Energy White Paper: Ireland's Transition to a Low Carbon Energy Future 2015–2030* (2015).

consider introducing subsidies for solar PV during 2016 to facilitate the roll out of solar farms. In addition to government subsidies, there are three other key pre-requisites to the successful development of a typical 5 megawatt (MW) solar farm:

1. Availability of a viable grid connection to an ESB Networks substation;
2. Access to 25 to 30 acres of land within a short distance (2km radius) of the substation, typically leased from the landowner for a 25 to 30-year term, and usually with an option to extend that term;
3. Planning permission for the development.

In the short term, the securing of a viable grid capacity with ESB Networks is likely to be the most challenging of these three requirements. At present, ESB Networks process solar grid applications below 5MW (known as Non-Gate Process Applications (GPA)), on a first come, first served basis[8] and, currently, only a handful of sites can be connected to a substation without the necessity for major upgrades to existing infrastructure. As of May 2016, ESB Networks had received over 400 2.4 gigawatt (GW) solar applications.[9] However, only 35% to 40% of these applications are likely to be viable without significant sub-station upgrades.[10] Going forward, new solar applications are likely to be much larger than the 5MW size, which is currently the norm. This will allow the developers to absorb the upgrade costs. However, the applications are likely to take 4 to 5 years to be processed, and are unlikely to have much impact on Ireland's ability to achieve its 2020 renewable energy targets.[11]

Over the past 15 years, many landowners have been actively canvassed by wind farm developers, seeking to secure locations for wind turbines on their lands. However, in the past two years in particular, the developers have shown a preference for land to facilitate the development of solar farm installations rather than wind turbines.

---

[8] ESB Networks 'Solar Connections on the Irish Distribution System' Ivan Codd Renewable Planning Manager, Asset Management, ESB Networks Engineers Ireland 6 April 2016, p 25.

[9] ESB Networks 'Solar Connections on the Irish Distribution System' Ivan Codd Renewable Planning Manager, Asset Management, ESB Networks Engineers Ireland 6 April 2016, p 43.

[10] Eirgrid, 'Offer Process Application Information' (2016). <www.eirgridgroup.com/site-files/library/EirGrid/Connection-Offer-Disclosure-of-Applications-as-published-31-March-2016.pdf> accessed 17 July 2016.

[11] Lazard, *Lazard's Levelized Cost of Energy Analysis 9.0* (Lazard 2015).

This chapter deals with exclusivity agreements, option agreements and leases. It explores some of the main clauses in the various agreements, and highlights particular areas of which landowners should be aware. The chapter concludes with a discussion on the tax implications of such agreements.

The prospect of additional income will always be welcomed by landowners, but great care should be exercised before signing contracts with developers. Such signing should never be done without taking legal advice and talking through the issues with an agricultural consultant, tax advisor and other professionals. Farmers who may be considering becoming involved in large-scale wind power or solar power schemes should think carefully, and consider the matter in full before committing to any agreement.

## Exclusivity Agreements, Option Agreements and Leases

Essentially, exclusivity agreements, option agreements and leases are contracts. A contract is a legally binding agreement between two or more parties in which they are obligated to do, or refrain from doing, certain things. A contract can be written, verbal, or implied, in a formal or informal manner. A breach of contract takes place when a contracting party fails to meet his or her terms and obligations under the agreement.

### Exclusivity Agreements

In the context of wind farms or solar energy projects, an exclusivity agreement is one made between a developer and a landowner, in which the landowner agrees to give the developer the right to apply for grid connection and carry out feasibility studies. The fundamental basis of an exclusivity agreement is the understanding that the landowner will not enter into any similar arrangement with another developer for the duration of the agreement.

An exclusivity agreement is usually a two page document, which identifies the site, by reference to a map. The term of the exclusivity agreement is usually for 12 months. The developer will want the landowner to sign an exclusivity agreement for a specific period of time, sufficient to enable the developer to deal with all preliminary matters and conduct feasibility tests on the land. During the term of the exclusivity agreement the landowner is prohibited from entering into any negotiations with another developer.

From the landowner's perspective, exclusivity agreements should be avoided wherever possible until full heads of terms have been agreed. The heads of terms document outlines the basis of the project. It usually contains, or makes reference to, the format of the option and lease agreements, and the rights of the developer. The heads of terms will also confirm the duration of the option and the lease. If heads of terms are not agreed before the signing of the exclusivity agreement, a landowner could easily find him/herself in a far weaker position when subsequently negotiating the terms of the option agreement and lease.

On occasion, there will be no exclusivity agreement at this stage, and it is sometimes incorporated into the later heads of terms. Exclusivity agreements and heads of terms agreements usually contain confidentiality clauses which prevent the landowner from discussing the terms with any other party. Usually, there is no payment made to the landowner on the signing of the exclusivity agreement or heads of terms. These agreements are essentially agreements to conduct business but can be legally binding, as is summarised in the aphorism "an agreement for a lease is as good as a lease",[12] as it can apply to all specifically enforceable agreements. Consequently, it is important to seek legal advice prior to signing an exclusivity agreement or heads of terms.

## Option Agreements

In the context of wind farms and solar farms, an option agreement is an agreement between a developer and a landowner which allows the developer the right, but not the obligation, to take a lease of all or part of the landowner's land, at an agreed price for an agreed term and, at some point within the specified term, to construct a wind farm or solar farm on the landowner's land.

An option agreement usually favours a developer rather than a landowner. It gives the developer greater flexibility in terms of what he or she proposes to do. This reflects the time and resources which the developer will be expending on the project. The developer must place him or herself in such a position as to ensure that the agreement can be terminated if the project is not progressing in a satisfactory manner, or becomes unviable. Effectively, by signing an option agreement, the landowner is restricting his or her land use to some extent.

---

[12] *Walsh v Lonsdale* [1882] 21 CH D9.

During the option agreement period, the developer will prepare and submit a planning application. The developer is usually required to consult with the landowner and to make available to him or her copies of all relevant planning documents and update the landowner of any objections to the planning permission application. The developer will require access to the site to carry out inspections and surveys etc. The developer may bring machinery and equipment onto the site during this time, and the landowner is obliged not to interfere with the developer in this work. The landowner will not be allowed to enter into any other agreements in relation to his or her land from the moment the option agreement has been signed.

Typically, on the signing of the option, an agreed non-refundable option fee is payable, usually €1,000 per year, the first payment being made upon the signing of the option agreement. Legal costs incurred by the landowner are normally discharged by the developer.

Developers generally seek an option term of between one and five years, depending upon the likely duration of the planning process. It is common practice to incorporate an option to extend the term of the agreement, usually by two years and conditional on payment of a further fee, to facilitate ongoing planning and other delays. If the developer requires the land, the developer is entitled to serve a written notice (option notice) on the landowner, which obliges the landowner to execute the lease, the terms of which will have already been agreed. Usually, two months' notice is provided for in the option agreement. At any time during the term of the option agreement, the developer can decide when, or if, he or she wishes to progress the option agreement into a lease. Typically, option agreements and leases are negotiated at the same time.

If the development cannot, or does not, go ahead, for example, where planning permission is refused or the application to the grid has been unsuccessful, the option will not then be exercised by the developer and the lease will not become operative. This brings the agreement to an end, with both parties free to go their separate ways. Consequently, the option payment will generally be all that is received by the landowner.

### Lease

A lease is a document which sets out the terms under which a landowner agrees to rent his or her property to a developer. A lease guarantees the lessee, (the tenant), the use of property, and guarantees the lessor, (the landowner), regular payments from the lessee over a specified number of years.

The lease also serves as an agreement between a developer and landowner, which obliges the developer to arrange for the design, planning, financing, and construction of the solar or wind energy plant and equipment on a landowner's property, at little or no financial cost to the landowner. The developer will remain responsible for the operation and maintenance of the plant and equipment for the duration of the agreement.

There is no standard exclusivity agreement, option agreement or lease and the documentation varies from developer to developer. Each agreement must be examined closely. Some of the more important terms are set out below.

## Planning

The cost of a planning application will normally be borne by the developer. If planning permission is refused, the developer will often be willing to pay a further fee to the landowner for the opportunity to re-submit an application, but landowners should be aware that some developers may withdraw from a project entirely if the planning problems are unlikely to be overcome. A landowner should be kept informed of all developments in relation to the planning application, should be notified promptly of any objections, and should be provided with regular progress reports. A landowner should also seek to establish a time frame within which the developer must have submitted the planning application to the local authority.

## Selling or Transferring Land

Landowners who are involved in these agreements will often wish to transfer the land involved to a son or daughter in future years and will not want to encounter any difficulty in doing so. Accordingly, when negotiating such an agreement, a landowner should also ensure that he or she makes any third party or successor in title fully aware of the implications of the agreement with the developer. The terms of such agreement will be binding on a successor in title, who will have no choice but to agree to be bound by same. The agreements do not usually restrict the landowner from assigning or transferring the lands, but any person to whom the lands are transferred will be bound by the terms of such agreements. Sometimes, the agreement will contain clauses which oblige the landowner to seek the written consent of the developer before transferring the lands. In that case, the landowner should insist that such a clause be removed, or, at least, that such consent shall not be unreasonably withheld or delayed.

## Practicalities

There is always a risk that the promise of potentially large income from the project will distract the attention of the landowner from other issues, which may, in fact, be very important. The landowner should look at the bigger picture, considering all potential personal and familial implications arising from the deal.

The following are just some of the important questions to be asked:

- How will the construction work and use of the new access routes affect the existing farming business and daily life?
- Is the proposed development near a landowner's family home? If so, will enjoyment of the home be adversely affected?
- How will it affect the layout of the farm?
- Will fences and gates have to be changed?
- What are a landowner's future plans for the land? What will be the impact on such plans?
- Is a landowner considering making a gift of a building site to a child at a later date? If so, will that site be adversely affected?
- Is the landowner thinking about transferring the farm to one of his or her children in the foreseeable future? If so, will those plans be affected by the current agreement?
- Are there any restrictions in the lease as to the uses to which a landowner can put the remainder of his lands? For example, is he or she considering afforestation on another part of the lands? If so, will the developer's consent to do so be required?
- Does the landowner have a legal entitlement to use all roadways constructed on his lands by the developer?
- Who is responsible for grazing the solar site and keeping weeds and vermin away?
- What about access to the site? Is this access shared with other parts of the farm?
- Who maintains the access?
- Will all gates be kept shut, and possibly locked, in order to stop unauthorised access?
- Will the landowner be entitled to graze stock on the land after the windmills or solar panels have been constructed?
- Will the proposed works and development interfere in any way with existing drains and/or watercourses?

- Does the landowner know the exact identity of the land which will form part of the agreement?
- In the case of wind farms, will there be a problem with noise levels? Will the developer be able to guarantee that the strict decibel levels laid down by the Department of the Environment will be adhered to?
- What happens if the developer becomes insolvent? Who will remove the equipment?

The lease should deal with access routes on the land to construct the panels, ancillary infrastructure, and deployment of on-site security fencing. It may also provide for access to, or wayleaves over, other land owned or leased by the developer, which could include access roads which may also be linking up with third party lands. The landowner has a right to retain usage of the lands, but this may be restricted to uses such as grazing sheep. A landowner should also ensure that he or she has an entitlement to use all access routes. A tricky part of these leases, from a farmer's perspective, is that they can include clauses restricting farmers from interfering with a solar or wind project by, for example, allowing livestock onto the project area, or creating a shadow by planting trees or erecting buildings in proximity to the solar panel footprint. It is important that any clause in the agreement which attempts to excessively, or unnecessarily, restrict the landowner's use of the land, be carefully considered.

### Maintenance

The developer is normally responsible for maintenance costs and should have his or her own insurance in the event of damage to equipment. The landowner may potentially earn further income by providing the company with services, such as grass-cutting and weed control. Where they arise, these services should be covered by a separate agreement, if not included in the main one.

It is important to ensure that, if at all possible, the landowner has the right to graze stock on the land, once the solar park has been built or the wind turbines have been erected. Some companies may allow only sheep, but not cattle, to graze around the panels or turbines. The position should be clarified in advance.

## Basic Payment Entitlements

Before a landowner enters into any agreement, he or she should consult with an agricultural advisor. Entitlements could be affected by the installation of wind turbines or solar panels on a farmer's land.

Generally, in relation to the wind farms, the developers agree to indemnify the landowner against any loss of payments.

It is important to note at the outset that there is no certainty at present as to how the basic payment entitlements will be affected by the presence of a solar farm on farmlands. The Department of Agriculture has stated that it "shall endeavour to facilitate such development while maintaining basic payment schemes, subject to EU Commission approval".[13] In addition, The Irish Farmers' Association (IFA) is continuing to lobby for confirmation by the Department of Agriculture in relation to the eligibility of lands for basic payment entitlements.[14] However, at the time of writing, the position in relation to basic payment entitlements and solar farms remains unclear.

Commentary in the area has suggested that the area taken up by the actual solar panels will not usually be eligible for basic payment entitlements.[15] Therefore, the landowner should deduct these areas from the basic payment entitlements application. In considering whether or not the rest of the land parcel is eligible, the landowner must consider whether or not he or she can demonstrate that the primary purpose of the land is agricultural. Very often, sheep can be grazed around the solar farm and under the solar installations. In that regard, it is worth bearing in mind that, if the primary function of the land parcel is for solar panels, then the entire land parcel will be ineligible for the payments. However, if the land around the panels and/or under the panels is grazed in line with normal grazing practices, then this land might be considered eligible, but the farmer must still deduct from his or her basic payment entitlements application any land which cannot be grazed.[16]

It should also be noted that a farmer's obligations under the option agreement or lease may affect his or her ability to comply with the conditions laid down by the Department of Agriculture for some schemes, and, consequently, his or her entitlement to receive the payments. The lease agreement should also contain a provision which indemnifies the landowner against

---

[13] Department of the Taoiseach, *A Programme for Partnership Government* (2016) 124.

[14] http://www.ifa.ie/ifa-seeks-basic-payment-eligibility-of-lands-used-for-solar/#.V5NfCoMrLcs.

[15] Independent Business Farming "Advice: Weigh up your options on solar energy contracts" Martin O' Sullivan, 9 March 2016.

[16] ibid.

any loss which might arise as a result of the Department of Agriculture refusing, or seeking to claw back, any payments, such as basic payment entitlements or forestry payments. It is important that legal and tax advice is sought in relation to these issues prior to entering into any such agreement, so that the landowner is in possession of up to date information regarding entitlements.

## Insurance

It is critical that a landowner insists on being entitled to production of a copy of the developer's insurance policy, and, thereafter, evidence of the renewal of such policy on an annual basis. Ideally, the policy should have the landowner's interest noted upon it, as this would guarantee that the policy could not be cancelled without notice to the landowner. The agreement should contain a clause under which the developer agrees to indemnify the landowner in relation to all claims arising out of the developer's use or occupation of the land. It is essential that the developer's policy would cover all risks, including accidents involving the developer's employees, on the landowner's property. The landowner must also have his or her own public liability insurance and must inform his or her insurance company of the existence of a wind farm or solar farm on the land. This is because the development of those facilities amounts to a material change in the land and, as such, is something that must be notified to the insurance company. The necessity for two separate insurance policies arises because, under insurance law, the landowner and the developer have separate insurable interests[17]. These insurance and indemnity clauses are an important consideration in the preparation of option agreements and leases, and can have serious consequences for landowners if not thoroughly examined.

## Removal of Equipment

One of the most important items to be agreed upon is that of the developer's obligation to re-instate the land so that it is not left in an unsatisfactory state at the end of the term of the lease. At that point, decommissioning of the project is essential. This includes the removal and disposal of the existing panels, wind turbines and access routes, together with the restoration of the land to make it suitable, once again, for agricultural use.

---

[17] *Andrews v Patriotic Assurance Co. of Ireland (No. 2)* (1886) 18 LR Ir 355.

It is only natural that landowners would be concerned about the prospect of wind turbines or solar installations remaining on their lands. For this reason, the lease should provide for the removal of the structures, as well as the access roads, and the reinstatement of the lands to their original condition at the end of the term of the lease. This is important because, as every farmer knows, the restoration of land can be expensive.

An important factor to be taken into account is that the company could become insolvent, be liquidated, or be dissolved, exposing the landowner to liability for the disposal of panels, plant, turbines, cables, and equipment of every nature, and to the costs of reinstatement of the lands. This could be very expensive. Ideally, there should be an insurance bond put in place by the developer to the effect that, in the event that the developer cannot, or will not, reinstate the land and remove all equipment, the bond will cover the cost. If not, the entire expense may unjustly fall to the landowner. The importance of securing an insurance bond to cover all of this loss cannot be over-emphasised, and it is one of the most critical clauses in any agreement of this type.

## Identity of the Lands

As obvious as it may seem, it is worth highlighting the importance of a landowner knowing the exact identity of the lands that he or she has agreed to make available to the developer. The area should be defined on a map, with reference to folio numbers, if applicable. It is also important that the definitions section of the agreement is accurate, and correctly reflects the property which it is intended to lease or grant an option over.

## Rent and Payment Clauses

The method of calculation of the payment can be complex, and should be examined carefully. It can vary from developer to developer.

Rent varies considerably, depending on the individual site, including light intensity, grid connection, number of turbines, development costs etc.

Most rental agreements are adjusted for inflation, but it is important to clarify exactly how the rent is structured, how often it is reviewed, and upon what basis it is agreed. Five yearly rent reviews are common in commercial leases, but reviews on an annual basis, in line with inflation, are common in the case of wind and solar farms.

When negotiating terms, it is important that the landowner, or his or her agent, ensures that he or she is fairly compensated for the risks and onerous terms involved.

### Payment for Wind Farms

As already mentioned, the normal duration of a lease for wind farms is from 25 to 30 years.

It is important that there be a minimum rental payment per megawatt of installed capacity, as distinct from exporting capacity. A landowner should also be entitled, on a pro rata basis, to a percentage proportion of the operating proceeds, either from the turbines on the land or from the overall development.

A landowner should seek to have a clause inserted into the agreement, entitling him or her to an independent auditor's certificate to vouch the operating expenses.

A clause should also be inserted to provide that, in the event of new, or more efficient, or more productive turbines being constructed, that a further payment be made.

The Irish Farmers' Association negotiated minimum terms with two major wind farm development companies (Element Power Limited and Mainstream Renewable Power Limited) in 2012.[18] The outcomes were as follows:

1. Annual payment during the option period of €1,000 per year[19];
2. Minimum annual lease payment of €6,000 (per megawatt (MW)) and €18,000 (per turbine)[20];

---

[18] Irish Farmers' Association, *Harnessing Ireland's Wind Resource for Renewable Energy Production* (2013) <www.ifa.ie/wp-content/uploads/2013/11/130919-IFA-Wind-Policy-1. pdf> accessed 17 July 2016.

[19] ibid, p 4.

[20] ibid, p 4.

3. Payment of 3% of energy price and green credits up to the year 2015, rising to 5% thereafter[21];
4. In respect of forestry lands;
   (a) Full compensation to be paid for grants clawed back, and those remaining to be paid;
   (b) The wind farm development company taking on full re-planting obligations; and
   (c) Landowners to receive full crop rotational value for any felled forestry[22];
5. In respect of agricultural schemes, full payment for any losses in Rural Environmental Protection Scheme (REPS), area aid and basic payment entitlements[23]; and
6. Consultation regarding location of access points and roads and fixed payment, on receipt of planning permission, of €10,000 to €18,000.[24]

These are basic terms which should provide a valuable starting point for a landowner and his or her advisor with which to commence negotiations.

## Payment for Solar Farms

Similar to wind farms, lease terms are usually for 25 to 30 years. Rent varies from between €800 to €1,500 per acre.

The lease rent will not normally be paid until electric current is flowing commercially from the solar farm and will be paid 3 to 6 months in arrears.

There is also scope to negotiate a lump sum payment when planning permission has been granted, or when the grid connection has been successfully concluded. Some developers are offering sums of in the region of €30,000 to €100,000.

In some cases, there may be scope to obtain a share of the revenues from the electricity generated on the site. It is important that the revenue figures are based on the gross turnover, independently certified by an auditor. In other cases, there may be an option to negotiate a supply of electricity

---

21 ibid, p 4.
22 ibid, p 4.
23 ibid, p 4.
24 ibid, p 4.

to a landowner's property at a reduced rate, or even free of charge as part of the rental agreement.

Generally, the rent is agreed in advance, and landowners will have the option of either index-linked or turnover-based rental agreements. With some solar leases, the rent payment is the larger figure of the two options. In this case, the developer is required to provide the landowner with meter readings and independent turnover figures[25].

Essentially, when entering into a commercial contract with a developer, it is very important to research the basic terms which will provide a valuable starting point in commencing negotiations. Clearly, the degree of saturation of the local grid and the location of the land in question are key factors impacting upon a farmer's ability to negotiate favourable terms.

## Right to Renew? Absolutely Not

A clause allowing the developer to extend the term of the lease is not unusual. However, from the landowner's perspective, the developer should not be given an automatic right of renewal. If at all possible, the developer should be obliged to re-negotiate with the landowner.

However, it is perhaps arguable that a wind turbine or a solar panel is a "building" and so the demised premises may satisfy the definition of a "tenement" for the purpose of s 5 of the Landlord and Tenant (Amendment) Act 1980, and so carry with it a right to renewal of the lease after 5 years' business use, unless the tenant renounces that right under s 17. Relief is provided to lessees by allowing them claim renewal of the lease at market value, where the property being leased consists predominantly of buildings, and where the land attached to those buildings is considered to be "subsidiary and ancillary" to the building, as per s 5 of the 1980 Act. This is discussed in more detail in the Leasing chapter. What constitutes a building is a question of fact.

---

[25] Farming Independent "Getting ready for the solar gold rush" Barry Casli, Teagasc; Edel Traynor from Barry Healy & Co Solicitors and Adam Hogg from Mason, Hayes & Curran 16 February 2016.

A concrete well for a petrol storage tank was held to be a building in the case of *Mason v Leavy*.[26] In that case, Black J applied the test that: "it could not be removed without disintegration of its own substance".[27] It appears to follow that something that can be picked up and carried away is not a "building" for the purpose of the Act.

In *Terry v Stokes*,[28] it was held that sheds built without foundations used for the installation and repair of radiators for motor vehicles were held to be "buildings".

In *Dursley v Watters*,[29] a cage used for the protection of the applicant's equipment, a small lock-up shed or hut, a pit or holding tank to catch water as it drained away from the cars as they were washed, and a self-assembled office shed, were held to be "buildings".[30]

It would be prudent that, along with removing any clause in the lease whereby a developer is given an automatic right of renewal, the developer would also sign a Deed of Renunciation, renouncing any automatic right to renewal of the lease, and obtain independent legal advice in advance of signing same.

Most leases will include a voluntary termination clause in favour of the developer, on furnishing of written notice. The landowner should seek as lengthy a termination notice period as possible, for example, 6 to 12 months, and it should be coupled with a termination payment.

## Title

A developer will always conduct comprehensive due diligence enquiries in respect of the property, and the landowner's title must be fully investigated. The landowner must produce evidence of good and marketable title. If there is a charge over the title, the landowner must obtain the written consent of the owner of the charge, usually a bank, before a lease can be signed.

---

[26] *Mason v Leavy* [1952] 1 IR 40.

[27] ibid, at 50.

[28] *Terry v Stokes* [1993] 1 IR 204.

[29] *Dursley v Watters* [1993] 1 IR 224.

[30] ibid, at 228.

## Choosing the Right Developer

It is important for landowners to research previous projects completed by the developer, and to investigate his or her track record. Ideally, the developer would have experience in this area of activity, and be familiar with the complexities of such transactions. The developer should be credible, have a proven track record, be of good financial standing, and have already obtained access to funds to finance the proposed development.

The largest offer might not be the best one in the long-term. There is no guarantee that the energy company will be successful in developing a solar or wind project. Time may see the less experienced companies leaving the marketplace.

## Tax Implications

The taxation implications of entering into a solar farm or wind farm contract are as varied as the individual contracts themselves, so it is advisable that each individual's circumstances be examined in order to establish the particular tax consequences involved and, more importantly, to avail of any potential tax planning opportunities.

In general, most solar farm and wind farm agreements follow a standard lease arrangement. As already discussed, a landowner enters into a long term lease agreement (typically for a period of 25 years or more) with the solar farm or wind farm operator.

### Income Tax

Under general tax law, a landowner can potentially avail of an exemption from income tax on the long term leasing of farmland, where certain criteria are satisfied. One of those criteria is that the land constitutes farmland and is let to an individual or company for the purposes of farming.[31] The Revenue Commissioners have clarified, in Tax Briefing 53/16,[32] that the leasing of farmland to a solar energy company is not considered as a trade of farming by that operator and, as such, the exemption from income

---

[31] Tax Consolidation Act 1997, s 664(1)(a).

[32] Revenue, 'Revenue eBrief No 53/16' (2016) <www.revenue.ie/en/practitioner/ebrief/2016/no-532016.html> accessed 17 July 2016.

tax in respect of the lease of farmland to a solar energy company will not generally be available. On a practical basis, some solar farm constructions involve the mounting of solar panels on frames, which can facilitate the grazing of sheep and other small mammals underneath. Where a land-owner leases land to a solar energy company and, as part of the agreement, is permitted to have his or her animals graze those lands, the Revenue Commissioners have confirmed that such arrangements will, unfortu-nately, not facilitate the claiming of an exemption from income tax, pre-sumably on the basis that the lease income is substantially derived from operation of solar panels rather than from sheep grazing.[33] In the case of wind energy companies, in many cases the lease is for the area immedi-ately around a wind turbine as opposed to the larger quantity of land occupied by solar panels. Similarly, the leasing of land to a wind energy company would not constitute income-tax free lettings.

The letting of farmland to a solar energy company or a wind farm com-pany will constitute rental income for the landowner, subject to USC, income tax and PRSI, in the normal way. There are fewer opportunities to shelter rental income from taxation than in the case of trading income, for example, only certain expenses are allowable as a deduction against rental income. This is in contrast to a wider scope for deduction of expenses against trading income.

## Capital Gains Tax[34]
Under the law as it stands, a business owner can avail of certain exemp-tions from Capital Gains Tax (CGT) where they dispose of the business,[35] either by way of sale or transfer, where a landowner, who is over 55 years of age,[36] has owned[37] and operated that business[38] for a minimum period

---

[33] Revenue eBrief No. 53/16 Leases of Farmland for Solar Energy Development 23 May 2016 Part 2.1.

[34] Taxes Consolidation Act 1997, ch 3. See also Revenue, 'Guide to Capital Gains Tax' (2015) <www.revenue.ie/en/tax/cgt/leaflets/cgt1.pdf> accessed 17 July 2016, and 'Guide to Farming Taxation Measures in Finance Act 2014' (2014) <www.revenue.ie/en/tax/cat/leaflets/guide-farming-taxation-measures-fa2014.pdf> accessed 17 July 2016.

[35] Taxes Consolidation Act, 1997 s 598 and s 599.

[36] Taxes Consolidation Act, 1997 s 598(2)(a).

[37] Taxes Consolidation Act, 1997 s 598(1)(a).

[38] Taxes Consolidation Act, 1997 s 598(1)(a).

of 10 years up to the point of disposal[39]. From a Capital Gains Tax perspective, the letting of farmland may impede a landowner's capacity to avail of the "retirement relief" exemption from Capital Gains Tax on the subsequent sale or transfer of land, as, by granting a long-term lease of the lands, they effectively have ceased to operate their business of farming prior to its sale or transfer.[40]

However, in the case of farmland, certain exemptions allow landowners to let or lease their land and continue to benefit from the Capital Gains Tax reliefs where a disposal or sale occurs within a pre-defined period. Under changes implemented by the Finance Act 2014, a farmer who satisfies certain criteria, including having owned and farmed their land for a minimum period of ten years prior to first letting, can subsequently let or lease their land and continue to avail of an exemption from Capital Gains Tax on a subsequent sale or disposal, where that sale or disposal occurs within a 25-year period.[41] In the case of disposals to third parties, one of the fundamental criteria to be satisfied is that the land is let to a person for the "purposes of farming".[42]

In these cases, because of the strict requirement that the land be used for the "purposes of farming", there is considerable doubt about the possibility of availing of retirement relief under the Capital Gains Tax legislation for the obvious reason that using land as a location for solar panels or wind turbines is unlikely to be classified as land used for the "purposes of farming". Thus, it is vitally important that any person who is considering using some or all of his or her farmland for either or both of these purposes take expert tax advice in advance of entering into any binding agreement. It is also worth noting at this point that Capital Gains Tax legislation differentiates between the criteria applicable to, on the one hand, sales or transfers to children (and persons deemed under Irish law, equivalent to children), and, on the other hand, sales or transfers to other persons. This is another reason why a high degree of planning should be exercised in order to determine how, and in what manner, the land will be disposed of, and the likely taxation consequences.

---

[39] Taxes Consolidation Act 1997, s 598(1)(a).
[40] Taxes Consolidation Act 1997, s 598(1)(a).
[41] Finance Act 2014, s 50.
[42] Finance Act 1997, s 50(1)(a).

Where a landowner receives payments in respect of option agreements, such payments can be considered as being the disposal of an asset in its own right, with resulting Capital Gains Tax implications. From a taxation perspective, there may be alternative taxation strategies worth exploring such as a sale of land with the option available to the farmer to repurchase the land at the end of the proposed production period.

## Capital Acquisitions Tax (Gift Tax)[43]

At present, uncertainty exists as to whether land used as a location for solar panels and wind farms can be classified as agricultural land and thus allow any person inheriting it, or taking it as a gift, claiming agricultural relief. This is hugely significant because, as discussed in the chapters dealing with Transferring the Family Farm and Wills, Administering an Estate and Enduring Powers of Attorney, agricultural relief, when available, can greatly reduce, or even eliminate, any liability to CAT. Agricultural relief, where available, can reduce the market value of agricultural property by 90%. From a taxation perspective, agricultural relief currently applies, subject to certain conditions and criteria, in the case of land that is transferred to a successor who farms it him/herself or leases it to someone who farms it for a minimum period of six years.

Though there has been no clear and definite ruling on the matter, considerable doubt exists as to whether agricultural relief can be claimed in respect of land used as a solar or wind farm. It is possible that agricultural relief could be claimed in respect of the part of the land not actually used for the solar panels, or wind turbines as the case may be. In other words, there would have to be separate treatment for inheritance or gift tax purposes of, on the one hand, the part of the land still used for ordinary agricultural purposes, and, on the other hand, the part devoted to solar panels and/or wind turbines. The doubt is in relation to whether land occupied by solar panels or wind turbines still constitutes agricultural property, where the land remains agricultural land (presumably at a minimum having capacity to produce agricultural produce). Even if the individual can show that the property is considered "agricultural land", the question remains whether or not the individual, or a lessor as the case may be is actually carrying on farming activities on a commercial basis where the land is

---

[43] Capital Acquisitions Tax Consolidation Act (CATCA) 2003.

occupied by wind turbines or a solar energy installation. This could create huge challenges as there could, among other matters, be great difficulty in negotiating with the Revenue Commissioners, regarding the apportionment of valuations between the two uses. Pending such clarification by the Revenue Commissioners, any person who is considering the construction of solar panels or wind turbines on his or her land should take expert tax advice before entering into any binding agreement.

## Conclusion

It is nearly always advantageous for a landowner to consider any alternative enterprises which will improve his or her quality of life, and the income that can be earned from his or her land. However, before entering into any alternative enterprise, such as solar farms or wind farms, it is critical that advice be sought from professionals with specific experience in these matters. This is a highly specialised area of law, involving potentially complex taxation issues which require careful consideration. As with all commercial agreements, the devil is in the detail. Essentially, the agreements involved attempt to strike a balance between the rights of the landowner, on the one hand, and the needs of the development company, on the other. It can be a difficult balance to achieve and a landowner should never rush into signing such agreements without careful thought and professional advice.

# CHAPTER EIGHT

# Animals and the Law

Animals have always played an important part in the lives of Irish farmers and, in many cases, the very livelihood of farmers has depended entirely on the production of animals, such as cattle, sheep, and pigs. For that reason, much of the focus of this chapter is on issues relating to animals. Under the law as it has developed, farmers now have considerable responsibilities with regard to their animals. As result, it is more important than ever that they protect themselves by becoming familiar with those laws, by complying fully with them, and by putting in place safeguards so as to reduce the likelihood of a breach. They should also endeavour to prevent any accident occurring which could give rise to a civil claim.

A basic understanding of the general law of torts,[1] and especially the more common torts, such as negligence, nuisance and trespass, is required in order to have a full appreciation of the issues raised in this chapter and a brief outline of these is included below. The chapter is divided into two main parts, the first dealing with civil liability and the second dealing with criminal liability. It also addresses the general rules of tort. This chapter outlines some of the more important obligations owed by a landowner to members of the public, and his or her potential liability to persons who suffer injury, death, or damage to property, resulting from an accident arising from the negligence of the farmer in connection with his or her animals. It outlines some of a landowner's legal obligations in relation to such activities, and lists a number of possible defences available to a farmer, should a claim be made. The latter part of the chapter, which focuses on criminal matters, outlines some of the responsibilities owed by a farmer to his or her animals, together with the main criminal offences, and the penalties that can be imposed.

---

[1] A 'tort' is a civil wrong (other than a breach of contract or breach of trust) for which the normal remedy is an action for unliquidated damages. *Secretary of State for War v Studdert* [1902] 1 IR 375 (HL) affg [1902] 1 IR 240 (CA).

## Civil Liability

The issue of liability arising from injury or damage caused by animals is an important feature of the law for everyone involved in agriculture. For that reason, it is essential to examine the special rules pertaining to liability for animals, as well as the general rules applicable under the general law of torts. As already stated, it is appropriate, in the first instance, to consider the general rules of tort, before moving to examine the special rules (including the principle of scienter, discussed later in this chapter). A basic understanding of both is necessary.

In all cases involving animals causing injury to a person, or causing damage to property, the first step is to examine the special rules which apply to animals, in order to establish if the facts of the case are compatible with the principles laid down therein.

However, if the special rules are not applicable, then recourse should be sought from the general tort rules, such as those of negligence, nuisance, trespass and the rule in *Rylands v Fletcher*,[2] as the non-applicability of special rules does not preclude the bringing of such claims.

### General Laws of Tort

#### A. Negligence

The tort of negligence is significant in terms of establishing liability in civil litigation. Negligence is a very broad concept and the tort of negligence includes a huge variety of activities. In order for a plaintiff to succeed in an action for negligence, a number of elements must be established:

#### (i) Duty of Care

The concept 'duty of care' is significant, as it acts as a control device which enables the court to limit the range of liability.[3] To make a successful claim, an injured party must establish that the person who is being sued did in fact owe a duty of care. The development of the concept of a duty of care

---

[2] *Rylands v Fletcher* (1868) LR 3 HL 330.

[3] McMahon & Binchy, *Law of Torts* (4th edn, Bloomsbury 2013) para 6.01.

was first found in the decision in the leading case of *Donoghue v Stevenson*,[4] where the court stated:

> You must take reasonable care to avoid acts or omissions which you can reasonably foresee would be likely to injure your neighbour. Who then, in law, is my neighbour? The answer seems to be-persons who are so closely and directly affected by my act that I ought reasonably to have them in contemplation as being so affected when I am directing my mind to the acts or omissions which are called in question.[5]

Essentially, a person owes a duty to anyone they can reasonably foresee that they could injure, either by their acts or by their omissions.

The duty of care test was further developed in the case of *Anns v Merton London Borough Council*,[6] by the formulation of the following two-tier test:

> First, one has to establish whether, as between the alleged wrongdoer and the person who has suffered damage, there is a sufficient relationship of proximity or neighbourhood such that, in the reasonable contemplation of the former, carelessness on his part may be likely to cause damage to the latter, in which case a prima facie duty of care arises. Secondly, if the first question is answered affirmatively, it is necessary to consider whether there are any considerations which ought to negative, or to reduce or limit the scope of the duty or the class of person to whom it is owed or the damages to which a breach of it may give rise...[7]

In Ireland, the Supreme Court decision in *Glencar Exploration plc v Mayo County Council*[8] re-formulated the test applicable to the duty of care developed previously in the *Donoghue*[9] and *Anns*[10] cases.

Keane CJ stated, in his judgment, that where there was injury or damage to a property, in establishing the existence of a duty of care, the court must have regard to the following:

(a) The proximity of the relationship;
(b) Any public policy considerations; and
(c) Whether the imposition of the duty is just and reasonable.[11]

---

[4] *Donoghue v Stevenson* [1932] AC 562.

[5] ibid at 580.

[6] *Anns v Merton London Borough Council* [1978] AC 728.

[7] ibid at 751.

[8] *Glencar Exploration plc v Mayo County Council* [2002] 1 IR 84.

[9] [1932] AC 562.

[10] [1978] AC 728.

[11] *Glencar Exploration plc v Mayo County Council* [2002] 1 IR 84 at 8.

## (ii) Standard of Care

The second element of negligence is to show that the defendant falls below the standard of the "reasonably careful man".[12] This standard was described in the case of *Kirby v Burke & Holloway*.[13] The plaintiff in this case purchased a pot of rhubarb and ginger jam from the defendant. The product was defective, and, as a consequence, the plaintiff and those of his family who consumed the product suffered from gastroenteritis. In this judgment, Gavan Duffy J stated

> ... the foundation of liability at common law is blameworthiness as deter-
> mined by the existing average standards of the community; a man fails at
> his peril to conform to those standards. Therefore, while loss from accident
> generally lies where it falls, a defendant cannot plead accident if, treated as
> a man of ordinary intelligence and foresight, he ought to have foreseen the
> danger which caused injury to his plaintiff.[14]

Essentially, in order to establish the appropriate standard of care, a court must have regard to both the nature and the capacity of the litigants.

Over time, the courts have made several attempts at describing the standard of the reasonable person. It is now clear that it is not sufficient to do your best, if your best does not meet the standard of the reasonable person.[15]

## (iii) Causation

In order for a plaintiff to succeed in an action in negligence, the plaintiff must show that the defendant "caused" the injury complained of. The plaintiff must also demonstrate that the injury complained of is not so far removed from the alleged act of the defendant that he/she cannot be held liable for it.

In the case of *Howard v Bergin, O'Connor & Co*,[16] a number of cattle, which were being unloaded at a railway station escaped, causing injury and damage. The Supreme Court held that the defendants were liable in negligence

---

[12] *McComiskey v McDermott* [1974] IR 75, 89.

[13] *Kirby v Burke & Holloway* [1944] IR 207.

[14] [1944] IR 207, 214.

[15] Cf *Vaughen v Menlove* (1837) 132 ER 490, 493, as cited per McMahon and Binchy, *Law of Torts* (4th edn, Bloomsbury 2013), para 7.04.

[16] *Howard v Bergin, O'Connor & Co* [1925] 2 IR 110.

on the basis that they did not use the platform provided for unloading animals; they had left a gate open during the loading operation, and they had left the cattle unattended during the loading operations, which amounted to causation.

## B. Nuisance

The tort of nuisance is also an important consideration in respect of animals and of civil liability generally. Nuisance concerns the wrongful interference with a public right or with another person's reasonable use or enjoyment of his or her property. The decision of *Connolly v South of Ireland Asphalt Co*[17] describes nuisance in the following terms:

> It has been said that actionable nuisance is incapable of exact definition. The term nuisance contemplates an act or omission, which amounts to an unreasonable interference with, disturbance of, or annoyance to, another person in the exercise of his rights. If the rights so interfered with belong to the person as a member of the public, the act or omission is a public nuisance. If these rights relate to the ownership of land, or of some easement, profit or other right enjoyed in connection with land, then the acts or omissions amount to a private nuisance.[18]

In essence, in order for the tort of nuisance to be established, there must be some form of interference, and it must be unreasonable. For example, a farmer will be held liable if his or her animals stray from his or her property and wrongfully interfere with another landowner's reasonable use or enjoyment of his or her property.

A landowner may also be held liable for private nuisance if animals are kept in unreasonable numbers, thereby causing, for example, noise or an unpleasant smell, and, as a consequence, interfere with a property owner's reasonable use or enjoyment of his or her property. In *O'Gorman v O'Gorman*,[19] the manner and place in which bees were kept went beyond the lawful use of their owner's land in relation to their neighbour. The landowner had 20 beehives near the plaintiff's haggard and was held liable when the bees swarmed and attacked the plaintiff's horse.

---

[17] *Connolly v South of Ireland Asphalt Co* [1977] IR 99.

[18] ibid at 103.

[19] *O'Gorman v O'Gorman* [1903] 2 IR 573.

## C. Trespass

Very simply, the tort of trespass arises when someone intentionally or negligently enters, remains, or causes something to placed, on another person's land without lawful authority.[20] In the context of animals, if the defendant drives cattle onto another person's land, then the defendant is committing the tort of trespass. On the other hand, if the cattle decide to stray onto another person's land of their own volition, then the rule of 'scienter' will be applicable. This is dealt with later.

## D. Rylands v Fletcher

A landowner may also face the imposition of liability for the dangerous use of a property. This tort arose out of the decision in the case of *Rylands v Fletcher*,[21] which concerned two mining companies that were carrying out mining operations on properties adjoining each other.

The defendant built a reservoir on his land in order to supply water to a mill. However, the independent contractors carrying out the construction on behalf of the defendant, failed to discover that there was a disused mine shaft underneath the reservoir. As a consequence, substantial quantities of water escaped and damaged the plaintiff's property. The plaintiff sued in nuisance, negligence, and trespass, but the court failed to find liability against the defendant on the aforementioned grounds. However, the court took the view that the defendant should nonetheless be held liable. In finding against the defendant in a landmark decision, Blackburn J stated:

> We think that the true rule of law is that the person who, for his own purposes, brings on his lands and collects and keeps there anything likely to do mischief if it escapes, must keep it in at his peril, and, if he does not do so, is prima facie answerable for all the damage which is the natural consequence of its escape.[22]

In order for a plaintiff to succeed in an action under the rule in *Rylands v Fletcher*, therefore:

a) The defendant's use of the land must be a non-natural use;
b) The defendant must have brought the source of danger onto property; and
c) An item must have escaped from the defendant's property.

---

[20] McMahon & Binchy, *Law of Torts* (4th edn, Bloomsbury 2013) para 23.01.
[21] *Rylands v Fletcher* (1868) LR 3 HL 330.
[22] (1868) LR 3 HL 330, 339-40.

## Scienter

Earlier in this chapter it was noted that there are special rules addressing liability arising from injuries or damage caused by animals. The principle laid down by 'scienter' is that, in the context of liability, there is a distinction to be drawn between wild animals and domestic animals.[23]

A landowner keeps wild animals, such as elephants, tigers, or bears, at his or her own peril, and, where any damage is caused by those animals, the owner is strictly liable.[24]

On the other hand, if the landowner keeps domestic animals,[25] the owner is only liable if he or she knows that the animal has a "mischievous propensity" to cause damage of the kind of which the complaint was made[26]. In order to demonstrate a "mischievous propensity", it must be shown that the animal has a "vicious, mischievous or fierce" tendency.[27] The decision in the case of *Quinn v Quinn*[28] is useful in clarifying the concept of "mischievous propensity". Here, the plaintiff's cow was killed by one of the defendant's sows. In order to succeed in his case, the plaintiff had to establish that the defendant's sow had a "mischievous propensity". The plaintiff advanced proof that, to the defendant's knowledge, the sow had previously attacked and killed fowl, and this was sufficient to hold the defendant liable. It is not necessary for the plaintiff to prove that the defendant had first-hand knowledge of the propensity. It is sufficient that the owner has simply heard about the mischievous tendency in order to be held liable.

An action under scienter can sometimes be problematic, as it may be difficult to establish that the owner had knowledge that his animal had a mischievous propensity.

---

[23] McMahon & Binchy, *Law of Torts* (4th edn, Bloomsbury 2013) para 27.15.

[24] McMahon & Binchy, *Law of Torts* (4th edn, Bloomsbury 2013) para 27.16.

[25] Domestic animals include cats, dogs, cattle, horses, pheasants, and partridge and bees, McMahon & Binchy, *Law of Torts* (4th edn, Bloomsbury 2013) para 27.23.

[26] McMahon & Binchy, *Law of Torts* (4th edn, Bloomsbury 2013) para 27.15.

[27] *Fitzgerald v ED & AD Cooke Bourne (Farms) Ltd.* [1964] 1 QB 249 at 270.

[28] *Quinn v Quinn* [1905] 39 ILTR 163.

In the alternative, if a plaintiff fails in establishing scienter, he or she is not precluded from bringing a claim under the general principles of tort such as negligence.

## Dogs

The Control of Dogs Act 1986 (hereafter 'the 1986 Act') provides special statutory provisions pertaining to damage caused by dogs. The 1986 Act provides that dogs, whether working dogs or pets, must always be under the control of a person when they are in a public place. The Control of Dogs Regulations 1998[29] lists some categories of dogs which must be muzzled in public, must bear the name and address of their owner, and must be kept on a short leash by a person over the age of 16 years, who is capable of controlling them. The following dogs are listed:

- American pit bull terrier;
- English bull terrier;
- Staffordshire bull terrier;
- Bull mastiff;
- Doberman pinscher;
- German shepherd (Alsatian);
- Rhodesian ridgeback;
- Rottweiler;
- Japanese akita;
- Japanese tosa;
- Bandog.

Section 21 of the 1986 Act abolished an old maxim which had applied in law, namely that 'every dog is entitled to his first bite'. Whether the dog owner knew or ought to have known that a dog had a mischievous propensity is no longer relevant to the imposition of liability in respect of injury or damage caused by the dog under the 1986 Act.

Under s 21, strict liability is imposed on the owner of the offending dog, for any damage caused by an attack on a person, or any injury caused by it to any livestock. 'Strict liability' means that the plaintiff need only prove that the incident occurred, and that the defendant's dog was responsible. Under the 1986 Act, the injured plaintiff need not prove negligence on the part of the dog owner.

---

[29] Control of Dogs Regulations 1998, SI No 442 of 1998.

The section provides as follows:

(1) The owner of a dog shall be liable in damages for damage caused in an attack on any person by the dog and for injury done by it to any livestock; and it shall not be necessary for the person seeking such damages to show a previous mischievous propensity in the dog, or owner's knowledge of such propensity, or to show that such injury or damage was attributable to neglect on the part of the owner;

(2) Where livestock are injured by a dog on land on to which they had strayed, and either the dog belonged to the occupier of the land or its presence on the land was authorised by the occupier, a person shall not be liable under this section in respect of injury done to the livestock, unless the person caused the dog to attack the livestock;

(3) A person is liable in damages for any damage caused by the dog kept on any premises or structure to a person trespassing thereon only in accordance with the rules of law relating to liability for negligence.

Where a person enters on to a dog owner's land without invitation, express or implied, that person is known as a trespasser. Section 21(3) of the 1986 Act states that a trespasser cannot rely on strict liability, as afforded by the 1986 Act, and thus the trespasser's claim can only be founded in negligence. This may be difficult for a trespasser to prove.

## Cattle Trespass

A special rule known as "cattle trespass" has developed which specifically addresses the situation whereby cattle stray on to another person's land. In this situation, the animal owner will be liable for any damage caused, irrespective of negligence. It is important to reiterate that liability under the cattle trespass rule only arises where the cattle stray on to another person's property on their own volition.[30] Case law in this area also suggests that 'cattle' includes horses, sheep, goats, pigs, asses, domestic fowl, and domesticated deer.[31]

In the converse situation, if cattle are driven on to another property, then the rule in cattle trespass does not apply, and liability will be founded in trespass. However, if cattle cause damage while they are being driven on the public road, the owner will be liable only for the damage caused if he

---

[30] *Brady v Warren* [1900] 2 IR 632; *Ryan v Glover* [1939] Ir Jur 65.

[31] McMahon & Binchy, *Law of Torts* (4th edn, Bloomsbury 2013) para 27.43.

is, in some way, negligent in the course of driving the cattle.[32] Examples of how negligence might arise in this instance may include, driving too many cattle at once, or failing to have adequate assistance to control the animals.

## Control of Horses

The Control of Horses Act 1996 (hereafter the '1996 Act') was introduced for the purpose of protecting people and their property against the dangers of wandering horses. Section 45 of the 1996 Act states:

(1) The owner, keeper, or person in charge, or in control of, a horse who wilfully or recklessly permits the horse to pose a danger to a person or property or to cause injury to a person or damage to any property, shall be guilty of an offence;

(2) A person who wilfully or recklessly causes a horse to pose a danger to a person or property or to injure a person or damage any property shall be guilty of an offence.

Section 45 of the 1996 Act, on the face of it, would appear to be a criminal offence in nature as it is headed "criminal liability". However, the wording would suggest that it confers a civil right of action. According to McMahon & Binchy, s 45 does, in fact, confer a civil right of action on the basis that it attempts to protect a relatively narrow class of potential victims, rather than the public as a whole.[33]

## Farm Animals on Public Roads

The law in this area no longer makes a landowner strictly liable for his or her animals that cause damage or injury on the highway. Instead, the wrongdoer is subjected to the normal rules of negligence and nuisance.

Section 2 of the Animals Act 1985 (hereafter 'the 1985 Act') states that a farmer has a duty to prevent damage by animals straying on to a public road. A farmer must show that he or she exercised reasonable care in ensuring that his or her animals did not escape on to the public road. Furthermore, s 2(2)(a) of the 1985 Act also states that

...where damage is caused by an animal straying from unfenced land on to a public road, a person who placed the animal on the land shall not be

---

[32] McMahon & Binchy, *Law of Torts* (4th edn, Bloomsbury 2013) para 27.42.

[33] McMahon & Binchy, *Law of Torts* (4th edn, Bloomsbury 2013) para 27.65.

regarded as having committed a breach of duty to take care by reason only of placing it there if –

> i. the land is situated in an area where fencing is not customary, and
> ii. he had a right to place an animal on that land.

Connemara provides many examples of land where fencing is not customary, and it is commonplace to see sheep grazing at the side of the road, with no fencing surrounding them.

In the case of *O'Shea v Tilman Anhold and Horse Holiday Farm Ltd*,[34] the plaintiff was driving along a public road when a horse that had escaped from an adjoining field landed on the plaintiff's car, causing him serious injuries. The horse had somehow escaped from a field which was adequately fenced and which had a gate with an automatic locking mechanism. The High Court found the second named defendant negligent, but this decision was overturned on appeal to the Supreme Court.

In the Supreme Court, Keane J took the view that the defendants were not liable in negligence in the circumstances, as they had taken all the precautions which a reasonable person would take to prevent the particular animals, a stable of horses, from straying on to the road. The decision is important, as it emphasises that landowners are not subject to strict liability[35] for any animal that escapes from a property. However, the landowner should take due care to ensure that animals do not escape on to the highway through the predictable or foreseeable carelessness of others.

A farmer must be in a position to show that he took reasonable care by having adequate fencing and a locked gate (if the circumstances require). The landowner is not required to prove how the animals came to be on the road, and the fact that the animals succeeded in escaping on to the road is not, of itself, proof of any negligence on the landowner's behalf.

Farmers should minimise the risk of liability by ensuring that they have a written document in place which outlines the procedure for carrying out stock movement in a safe, controlled, and responsible manner. Such a document would help to prove that reasonable steps were in place at all

---

[34] *O'Shea v Tilman Anhold and Horse Holiday Farm Ltd* (unreported, 23 October 1996) SC.
[35] Strict liability is liability on a party without a finding of fault.

times so as to ensure that livestock were secure and that proper procedures were in place, should a claim arise. Stock-proof fencing is recommended. Landowners should ensure that livestock have sufficient water and grass available to them at all times, so that they will not stray because of thirst or hunger. It would also be prudent for the farmer to adopt a procedure which ensures that all gates leading on to a public road are padlocked.

Farmers have a higher duty of care in respect of dangerous animals, such as bulls. Farmers must have regard to the animal's nature, type, species, breed, development and environment. Bulls are, naturally, regarded as being more dangerous than lambs, for example. Thus, greater precautions and a higher degree of care must be exercised in relation to bulls. It is not advisable for a farmer to place a bull on land near a public roadway, or on land over which there is a right of way, or where members of the public are known to congregate.

Naturally, every situation, circumstance, and animal is unique, but the following are some practical precautions which should be put in place:

- Ensuring that a padlocked gate is in place near public roads;
- Having due and adequate regard to the animal's nature, type, species, breed, development and environment. For example, the measures required to prevent a bull from straying will differ greatly from the measures required to prevent a lamb from straying;
- Ensuring the stock is well cared for and fed so as to obviate a need or desire for them to stray;
- Ensuring that the fencing is properly maintained, in good condition, and is stock proof. The condition of the fencing and gates leading into a farmer's premises are always carefully considered in any action to determine whether or not the defendant landowner had exercised reasonable care in maintaining his or her fences in a stock proof condition, and had taken all reasonable steps to ensure that his or her stock did not stray on to the public road; and
- Having a written document or record available to indicate that there is a system in place for checking fences and gates regularly.

As noted clearly above, a farmer who exercises reasonable care in ensuring that his or her property is adequately fenced in accordance with his or her duty of care should not be held liable if one of his or her animals escapes from the land.[36]

---

[36] The Animals Act 1985 did not impose strict liability.

## General Defences

At this point it is appropriate to expand upon defences that may be available to a farmer who is sued for damages for injuries sustained through his own actions or the actions of his or her animals. Very often, these cases involve cattle trespass. The defences are:

- (a) An Act of God;
- (b) Fault entirely on the part of the plaintiff;
- (c) Inevitable accident; and
- (d) Contributory negligence

### (a) An Act of God

An Act of God is defined as any accident or event not influenced by man. They are accidents caused by nature. Hurricanes, tsunamis, wildfires, earthquakes and tornados are all considered Acts of God. Generally, these Acts of God eliminate or limit liability for injuries or other losses that result from them.

### (b) Fault Entirely on the Part of the Plaintiff

A defendant cannot be held liable for a loss that was entirely the plaintiff's own fault. This is illustrated in the case of *Ponting v Noakes*.[37]

The plaintiff's horse died after it reached over the defendant's fence and ate some leaves from a poisonous yew tree. The defendant was not liable as the yew tree was entirely within the confines of the defendant's land.

Charles, J said:

> I do not see that they can be made responsible for the eating of these Yew leaves by an animal which, in order to reach them, had come upon his land. The hurt which the animal received was due to his wrongful intrusion. He had no right to be there and the owner therefore has no right to complain.[38]

### (c) Inevitable Accident

An inevitable accident occurs when the consequences complained of as a wrong were not intended by the defendant and could not have been foreseen and avoided by the exercise of reasonable care and skill.

---

[37] *Ponting v Noakes* (1894) 2 QB 281.
[38] ibid at 286.

This is illustrated in *Stanley v Powell*.[39] In this case a bullet ricocheted off of a tree and injured the plaintiff. The injury was held to have been an inevitable accident. A person will not be liable for an event over which he or she had no control, and could not have avoided, using even the highest skill and care.

### (d) Contributory Negligence

Contributory negligence arises where the plaintiff is himself found to be in some way responsible for what has befallen him. It essentially involves a lack of reasonable care for one's own safety[40] or the safety of one's property.[41]

The court has power to apportion blame, on a percentage basis, between the plaintiff and the defendant, under the Civil Liability Act 1961.[42]

## Criminal Liability

This part of the chapter deals with criminal, as opposed to civil liability, meaning that the wrong committed may lead to a criminal prosecution, separate from any civil claim that may be brought by an injured party.

### Microchipping of Dogs

Under the Microchipping of Dogs Regulations 2015[43] (hereafter 'the 2015 Regulations'), a programme of microchipping has been introduced which makes it obligatory for all dogs to be microchipped. A microchip is a tiny device, about the size of a grain of rice, inserted, using a sterile needle, under the skin between the shoulder blades of the dog. Microchips contain a unique 15-digit numerical code which must be registered alongside the owner's details on an authorised database.[44]

A microchip can be implanted in a dog of any age. Regulation 3(2)(a) of the 2015 Regulations state that dogs must be chipped by the time they are

---

[39] *Stanley v Powell* (1891) 1 QB 86.

[40] *Murphy v O' Brien* 6 ILT (ns) 75 (CC).

[41] *Cody v Player & Wills* (Ir) Ltd (1975) 109 ILTR 32 (CC).

[42] Civil Liability Act 1961, ch 3.

[43] Microchipping of Dogs Regulations 2015, SI No 63 of 2015.

[44] https://www.agriculture.gov.ie/media/migration/animalhealthwelfare/dogmicrochipping/FAQdogmicrochipping040516.pdf.

12 weeks old, but they can be chipped earlier than that. Most chips should last far longer than the lifetime of the animal into which they have been implanted.

All dogs must be: (i) microchipped; and (ii) registered with an authorised database.[45] Compliance with the legislation requires completion of both steps. The registration should be contemporaneous with the microchipping. Dog owners whose dogs are currently chipped should check that their details are up to date and correct.[46]

Currently approved databases which meet the requirements of the 2015 Regulations are:

- Animark;
- Fido;
- Irish Coursing Club;
- Irish Kennel Club.

An up-to-date list is maintained by the Department of Agriculture.[47]

A person who contravenes or fails to comply with a provision of the 2015 Regulations commits an offence and is liable on summary conviction to a class A fine or to imprisonment of up to 6 months or to both, or on indictment, to a fine not exceeding €250,000 or to a term of imprisonment not exceeding 5 years, or both.[48]

### Animal Health and Welfare

The Animal Health and Welfare Act 2013 (hereafter 'the 2013 Act') outlines further responsibilities of those who own an animal. It applies, not just to farmers, but to all animal owners, or persons in control or in possession of animals. The 2013 Act includes provision for increased powers for authorised officers to investigate complaints of animal cruelty, and

---

[45] Microchipping of Dogs Regulations 2015, SI No 63 of 2015, reg 3.

[46] Microchipping of Dogs Regulations 2015, SI No 63 of 2015, reg 4.

[47] Department of Agriculture, Food and the Marine, 'Microchipping Databases' <www.agriculture.gov.ie/media/migration/animalhealthwelfare/dogmicrochipping/Microchippingdatabases210416.pdf> accessed 7 July 2016.

[48] Microchipping of Dogs Regulations 2015, SI No 63 of 2015, reg 13.

it makes provision for stricter penalties upon conviction. This particular part of the chapter focuses on animal health and welfare in light of the 2013 Act.

Section 2 of the 2013 Act defines 'protected animal' as an animal kept for farming, recreational, domestic or sporting purposes in the State, when it is in the possession or under the control of a human being whether permanently or on a temporary basis, or that is not living in a wild state.

The following are some of the obligations that are imposed under the 2013 Act:

Section 11(1) of the 2013 Act states:

> A person who has a protected animal in his or her possession or under his or her control shall, having regard to the animal's nature, type, species, breed, development, adaptation, domestication, physiological and behavioural needs and environment, and in accordance with established experience and scientific knowledge, take all necessary steps to ensure that
>
> i. the animal is kept and treated in a manner that;
>   (i) safeguards the health and welfare of the animal, and
>   (ii) does not threaten the health or welfare of the animal or another animal, and
>   (iii) all buildings, gates, fences, hedges, boundary walls and other structures used to contain the animal are constructed and maintained in a manner so that they do not cause injury or unnecessary suffering to the animal.

Section 12(1) of the 2013 Act states that:

> a person shall not
>
>   a) do, or fail to do, anything or cause or permit anything to be done to an animal that causes unnecessary suffering to, or endanger the health or welfare of, an animal, or
>   b) neglect, or be reckless, regarding the health or welfare of an animal.

Where a person has been convicted of an offence under this section, the court may, in addition to any penalty it imposes,[49] order the person to

---

[49] Animal Health and Welfare Act 2013, s 52(1).

make a contribution towards veterinary expenses.[50] The court, in making a decision, will have regard to a number of factors, such as whether:

- the suffering could have been avoided, terminated or reduced, and whether;
- the suffering was caused for a legitimate purpose, such as benefiting the health and welfare of an animal or protecting a person, property or another animal.

Section 13 of the 2013 Act states that a person who has a protected animal in his or her possession or under his or her control, or transports such an animal, shall provide and supply to the animal a sufficient quantity of wholesome and uncontaminated drinking water or other suitable liquid appropriate to its physiological or behavioural needs which satisfies the animal's fluid intake requirements,[51] and a quantity of suitable and wholesome food sufficient to satisfy the reasonable requirements of the animal.[52]

Section 14(1) of the 2013 Act makes it an offence for a person who has in his or her possession or control a protected animal, to abandon an animal. It is important to note that if he or she does abandon the animal, he or she is not relieved of responsibility for the animal.

Section 21(1) of the 2013 Act states that:

A person who has in his or her possession or under his or her control a protected animal for sale or supply shall ensure that;

(a) the animal is kept at all times in accommodation that is suitable as respects the size, temperature, lighting, ventilation, cleanliness of the accommodation,

(b) the animal is supplied with, and has ready access to, a sufficient quantity of suitable food and drink…

(c) the animal is not sold or supplied where, having regard to—
  (i) the age of the animal, and
  (ii) the animal's nature, type, species, breed and degree of development, its adaptation and domestication and its physiological and behavioural needs in accordance with established experience and scientific knowledge,

---

[50] Animal Health and Welfare Act 2013, s 12(3).

[51] Animal Health and Welfare Act 2013, s 13(1)(a).

[52] Animal Health and Welfare Act 2013, s 13(1)(b).

the sale or supply of the animal at that age causes, or is likely to cause, avoidable or unnecessary suffering to the animal,

(d) all reasonable precautions are taken to prevent the spread of disease or a disease agent among animals or to human beings, and

(e) the animal is safeguarded against fire, environmental or other hazards.

An authorised officer may serve an animal health and welfare notice on the owner, occupier or person in charge of the land or premises, or person in control or possession of the animal requiring the person on whom it is served to take action as specified in the notice.[53]

A person who commits an offence under ss 11, 13, 14 and 21 of the 2013 Act is liable, on summary conviction, to a class A fine or imprisonment for a term not exceeding 6 months, or to both, or on conviction on indictment, to a fine not exceeding €250,000 or imprisonment for a term not exceeding 5 years, or to both.[54] On a conviction for some offences, the court has the power, in addition to the penalty imposed, to order that the person be disqualified from owning an animal and working with animals for a period, including, where appropriate, for the life of the person, as the court considers appropriate.[55]

The gravity with which the courts view breaches of the 2013 Act is illustrated by a 2015 Circuit Court decision. A pig farmer admitted to five charges of animal cruelty.[56] The charges to which he pleaded guilty included that, on 25 July 2011, he caused unnecessary suffering to a pig by failing to treat or euthanise it after it was found, having been partly eaten alive by other pigs at his farm. The court heard that the farmer starved his pigs and failed to give them proper supplies of water. He failed to comply with a welfare notice that had been served upon him. Ó Donnabháin J imposed a custodial sentence of 18 months on the farmer, having referred to the mistreatment of the animals in question as 'cruelty on an industrial scale'.

---

[53] Animal Health and Welfare Act 2013, s 42(1).

[54] Animal Health and Welfare Act 2013, s 52(2).

[55] Animal Health and Welfare Act 2013, s 58(1).

[56] *DPP v Rory O' Brien* (2011) and "Farmer jailed for 18 months after pigs ate each other" (*Irish Times*, Barry Roche, 12 February 2015).

The 2013 Act also deals with destruction of animals,[57] prevention and control of animal disease,[58] and animal health levies,[59] which are not dealt with in detail in this chapter but it is important to be aware of such legislation.

Part 5 of the 2013 Act is concerned with animal health levies and is based on the Bovine Diseases (Levies) Acts 1979 and 1996. There is provision to allow the charging of animal health levies on a wide range of species and diseases, where levies are only paid in respect of cattle and milk and are intended for the control of TB and brucellosis.[60]

Part 6 of the 2013 Act deals with the destruction and disposal of animals. This Part provides for the slaughter of animals for disease control purposes, and for consequent compensation, with the overall aim of making the compensation provisions more explicit. There is an independent valuation and arbitration system to ensure that, where this is done, owners are treated fairly.[61]

Part 7 of the 2013 Act deals with measures to prevent the risk of spread of disease, the control or eradication of disease, and matters relating to animal welfare, animal transport and identification.[62]

## Conclusion

Animals will always be a central feature of farming in Ireland. The farm dog is never far from his master's side. Animals provide a livelihood and companionship to farmers. Owning animals is a privilege, and with privilege comes responsibility.

It is understandable that many farmers who keep animals fear potential civil claims being taken against them. Such fears may be allayed by ensuring that good practice is observed. The farmer who takes all reasonable steps in ensuring the welfare, control and safety of his or her animals minimises his or her exposure to criminal and civil liability.

---

[57] Animal Health and Welfare Act 2013, Part 6.
[58] Animal Health and Welfare Act 2013, Part 2.
[59] Animal Health and Welfare Act 2013, Part 5.
[60] Animal Health and Welfare Act 2013, s 28.
[61] ibid.
[62] ibid.

However, a cautionary note must be sounded, as the 2013 Act carries potentially grave consequences for a farmer who is found to be in breach of its provisions. The courts now have the power to impose custodial sentences,[63] and, in addition, to disqualify a person from owning or keeping an animal for the duration of his or her lifetime.[64] It is important that an animal owner behaves in a responsible manner at all times. Once a farmer takes all necessary steps to ensure that an animal is kept and treated in a manner which safeguards its health and welfare, and the animal is kept in an environment that does not threaten that health and welfare, he or she will not have to worry when, or if, an Animal Health and Welfare officer attends on his or her farm to carry out an inspection.

---

[63] Animal Health and Welfare Act 2013, s 52(2).

[64] Animal Health and Welfare Act 2013, s 58(1).

# The Law on Shrubs, Trees, Hedges, Drainage and Public Roads

Section 70 of the Roads Act 1993 (hereafter 'the 1993 Act') provides that the owner or occupier must take reasonable steps to ensure that any structure on the land is not a hazard, or a potential hazard, to persons using the public road.

## Trees and Shrubs

In an agricultural environment, overgrowing shrubs and trees can sometimes impinge on public roads, and regular maintenance must be carried out in order to ensure that they do not pose a hazard to road safety. The obligations of landowners and occupiers are laid out in the 1993 Act.

Section 70(2) of the 1993 Act states:

(a) The owner or occupier of land shall take all reasonable steps to ensure that a tree, shrub, hedge or other vegetation on the land is not a hazard or potential hazard to persons using a public road and that it does not obstruct or interfere with the safe use of a public road or the maintenance of a public road.

(b) Where a tree, shrub, hedge or other vegetation is a hazard or potential hazard to persons using a public road or where it obstructs or interferes with the safe use of a public road or with the maintenance of a public road, a road authority may serve a notice in writing on the owner or occupier of the land on which such tree, shrub, hedge or other vegetation is situated requiring the preservation, felling, cutting, lopping, trimming or removal of such tree, shrub, hedge or other vegetation within the period stated in the notice.

This section makes it clear that the owner or occupier of land must take all reasonable steps to ensure that any such trees or shrubs do not interfere with the safe use of a public road. Thus, hedge growth maintenance along a road is the responsibility of the owner or occupier of the land.

It is also worth noting that, by virtue of s 17 of the Forestry Act 2014 (hereafter 'the 2014 Act'), it is illegal to uproot any tree over 10 years old, or cut down any tree of any age, including trees which form part of a hedgerow, without a licence. A felling licence may be obtained from the Felling Section of the Forest Service of the Department.[1] The licence may contain conditions which can include environmental and replanting conditions.

Section 19 of the 2014 Act states that the requirement for a felling licence for the uprooting or cutting down of trees does not apply in some circumstances; for example

- The tree in question is an apple, plum, damson or pear tree
- The tree is less than five years of age that came about through natural regeneration and removed from a field as part of the normal maintenance of agricultural land (but not where the tree is standing in a hedgerow); or
- Within 30 metres of a building (other than a wall or temporary structure, but excluding any building built after the trees were planted).

Section 44(1) of the Land and Conveyancing Law Reform Act 2009 (hereafter 'the 2009 Act') provides landowners with a right to carry out works on boundaries between two neighbouring properties, such as clearing or filling in ditches or cutting or replacing hedges.

In practical terms, the person wishing to carry out the works should obtain, in advance, the consent of the adjoining landowners, setting out what work is to be done, when it is intended to do the work, and why it needs to be done.

However, in the event of a dispute in exercising those rights, s 44(4) of the 2009 Act states that the person wishing to carry out the works can apply to court for an order authorising the carrying out of those works.

---

[1] For further information, see Department of Agriculture, Food and the Marine website, 'Felling' <www.agriculture.gov.ie/forestservice/treefelling/treefelling/>, email <forestry-info@agriculture.gov.ie>, or telephone 1890 200 509 / 053 91 63400. For written enquiries, contact Felling Section, Forest Service, Department of Agriculture, Food and the Marine, Johnstown Castle, Wexford.

# Hedges

Section 40 of the Wildlife Act 1976, as amended by s 46 of the Wildlife (Amendment) Act 2000, forbids cutting or removal of hedgerows or other vegetation during the bird nesting season, from 1 March to 31 August each year.

An exception is made for farmers who destroy, in the ordinary course of agriculture or forestry, any vegetation growing on or in any hedge or ditch, as well as the cutting or grubbing of isolated bushes or clumps of gorse, furze, or whin, or the mowing of isolated growths of fern in the ordinary course of business.

# Drainage and Public Roads

The matter of drainage is dealt with under s 76 of the 1993 Act and makes provision for the owners or occupiers of land adjacent to a public road. Section 76(5) of the 1993 Act provides that:

> The owner or occupier of any land adjacent to a public road shall take all reasonable steps to ensure that:
>
> (a) Water is not prevented, obstructed or impeded from draining into, onto, under, through or to his land from a public road;
> (b) Water, soil or other material is prevented from flowing or falling onto a public road from his land.

Section 76(3) of the 1993 Act states that where there is 'an immediate and serious hazard to persons using a public road', the road authority can take immediate action and enter the lands where the hazard exists, taking such steps as are necessary. As a consequence of having to take such action, the road authority is entitled to recover the cost, as a simple contract debt, from the landowner or occupier.

# Enforcement Notices and Penalties

## Enforcement Notices

Section 70(2) of the 1993 Act states that, where hedges are a hazard or potential hazard to persons using a public road, the road authority may serve a notice on the owner or occupier of the land requiring the felling, cutting, or trimming of the hedge within a period stated in the notice.

Where the owner or occupier of land fails to comply with such a notice, he or she will be guilty of an offence. The road authority may take the action specified in the notice and then recover any reasonable cost incurred by it from the owner or occupier of the land.

A relevant road authority may serve a notice on the relevant owner or occupier of the lands in question where there has been an infringement of the foregoing sections.

If a landowner or occupier receives such a notice, and is unhappy with his or her obligations under it, he or she can appeal this notice to the District Court within 14 days from the date of service[2], on any of the following grounds:

(i)   He or she is not the owner or occupier of the structure[3];
(ii)  He or she is not the owner or occupier of the land on which the structure, tree, shrub, hedge or other vegetation is situated[4];
(iii) The structure, tree, shrub, hedge or other vegetation is not a hazard to persons using a public road or does not obstruct or interfere with the safety or maintenance of a public road[5];
(iv)  Compliance with the requirements of the notice would involve unreasonable expense[6]; or
(v)   The notice specified an unreasonably short time for compliance.[7]

It is important to highlight the fact that the road authority must be put on notice of the appeal as it is entitled to appear, be heard, and adduce evidence on the hearing of the appeal.

It is to be noted that any notice served by the road authority should also make it clear to the landowner or occupier that it is an offence not to comply with the notice.

---

[2] Roads Act 1993, s 70(3)(a).
[3] Roads Act 1993, s 70(3)(a)(i).
[4] Roads Act 1993, s 70(3)(a)(ii).
[5] Roads Act 1993, s 70(3)(a)(iii).
[6] Roads Act 1993, s 70(3)(a)(iv).
[7] Roads Act 1993, s 70(3)(a)(v).

Section 81 of the 1993 Act states that a person guilty of an offence shall be liable, on summary conviction, to a fine not exceeding €5,000.

## Conclusion

It is clear that all owners or occupiers of land must and should take all reasonable steps to ensure that any trees or shrubs on their lands do not interfere adversely with users of a public road and are not a potential hazard or allowed to become a hazard. All owners and occupiers of land should inspect their land regularly to ensure that overgrowing shrubs, trees and hedges, and drainage do not pose a hazard to road safety.

# CHAPTER TEN

# Collaborative Farming

In practice, farmer collaboration has existed in Ireland for generations. Historic examples are threshing and coring. One of the major challenges facing Irish farming is how best to mobilise resources into productive agriculture. These resources include land, labour and capital. Access to land is a critical constraint on many progressive farms. Access to skilled labour and work/life balance also become constraints as scale increases. Collaborative farming arrangements offer a potential route to gaining access to a broad range of resources. These include land, facilities, skills, labour efficiency, superior lifestyle, companionship, economies of scale and the potential for higher profits.

This chapter considers registered farm partnerships, contract-rearing of replacement heifers, share farming and cow-leasing.[1] The law which forms the basis of contract-rearing of heifers, share farming and cow-leasing is contract law. Registered farm partnerships are governed by the Partnership Act 1890 (hereafter 'the 1890 Act') and case law. The 1890 Act applies to all types of partnerships, not just those involving farming enterprises. It is advisable to consult a Teagasc advisor, private consultant, solicitor and accountant in advance of entering into a collaborative farming arrangement.

## Farm Partnerships

A farm partnership arises where two or more farmers combine their farming operations into one business. The partners share, on agreed terms, the profit which the enterprise makes. Partnerships allow farmers to combine their resources, such as land, labour, facilities, machinery etc. for the mutual

---

[1] For more detailed information, see Thomas Curran, 'Collaborative Farming: A Suite of Options to Improve the Structures of Irish Dairy Farming' (2015) <www.teagasc.ie/media/website/rural-economy/farm-management/Moorepark-Open-Day-July2015.pdf> accessed 18 July 2016.

benefit of all the parties involved.[2] Some of the benefits include improved lifestyle, increased economies of scale and greater labour availability.

However, one of the main benefits is the use of a partnership as a transitional arrangement to steer the farm family through the succession process until a full farm transfer to a son or daughter takes place at a later date. Partnership allows for a gradual introduction of the successor, in a formal way, into the farming business over the lifetime of the arrangement. This is facilitated through the on-farm agreement.

Partnership may also be used as an intermediate structure by farm families where there is no identified successor. An example of this would be where an existing farmer, with no apparent successor, enters into partnership with a young trained farmer who is not from a farming background, has insufficient land of his own, or who has no prospect of inheriting a farm. Partnership arrangements are suitable for all of the main farming enterprises, including dairying, beef, tillage, sheep and other enterprises, such as horticulture.

In addition, the Revenue Commissioners and the Department of Agriculture[3] have taken a favourable approach towards registered farm partnerships, the key issue being that each farmer in the arrangement should be treated no less favourably than a farmer farming on his or her own. All qualifying farmers in a registered partnership are treated as individuals for tax purposes and EU and government support schemes.

### The Importance of a Well-Written Partnership Agreement

In cases where there is no partnership agreement, or where the agreement is found to be null and void, the partnership will be governed by the 1890 Act. That Act sets out the basic terms of the partnership, which will apply to every partnership agreement unless they are modified by agreement of the partners, or a valid written agreement is put in place. It is a matter of critical importance to have a well-drafted partnership agreement,

---

[2] Teagasc 'New opportunities for farmer collaboration in Ireland' Thomas Curran Farm Structures Specialist' https://www.teagasc.ie/media/website/rural-economy/farm-management/Collaborative-Farming-2014.pdf.

[3] Department of Agriculture, Food and the Marine.

which clarifies precisely how the partnership will be formed, operated and dissolved.

In the natural lifetime of a partnership, the arrangement can change for a variety of reasons and it is vital that the partnership agreement be updated on an on-going basis to reflect any changes that take place. This ensures that, when the arrangement is to be dissolved, the agreement is up-to-date and deals effectively with dissolution.

Farmers entering partnership must be mindful of the possibility of dissolution of the agreement at any stage during the lifetime of the agreement. This is especially important in relation to plans for expansion or new capital investment by the partnership. Expansion typically requires capital investment in facilities and infrastructure. In advance of any capital being invested, the partners must agree on how this investment is to be treated on dissolution, and adjust the written agreement accordingly.

The agreement must be signed by all partners, and each signature should be witnessed by a suitably qualified person. The agreement that is signed should, of course, be the final document, and not an earlier draft form. It is also critical that both parties are independently advised prior to signing the agreement.

Section 1 of the 1890 Act defines a "partnership" as "the relation which subsists between persons carrying on a business in common with a view of profit".

Some of the provisions in the 1890 Act, as outlined, demonstrate why it is important to have a written partnership agreement in place, as otherwise, the provisions of the 1890 Act automatically apply. In essence, in the absence of a partnership agreement, the 1890 Act offers a default, if imperfect, partnership agreement.

Section 25 of the 1890 Act states, "No majority of the partners can expel any partner unless a power to do so has been conferred by express agreement between the partners".

As a result, there is no right of expulsion of a partner, no matter how inappropriate the conduct. This must be addressed in a partnership agreement.

Section 26 of the 1890 Act states, "where no fixed term has been agreed upon for the duration of the partnership, any partner may determine the partnership at any time on giving notice of his intention so to do to all the other partners".

It should be noted that a partner can effectively dissolve the partnership at any time without notice, for example in the event of a family dispute.

Section 33 of the 1890 Act states "subject to any agreement between the partners, every partnership is dissolved as regards all the partners by the death or bankruptcy of any partner".

This means that, if one partner dies or is declared bankrupt, the partnership is automatically dissolved.

Having a well-drafted, written partnership agreement is critical. There is always potential, with family partnerships in particular, for disputes to get out of control.

### *Joint and Several Liability*

A farm partnership has unlimited liability. This is another reason why a well-written partnership agreement is important.

Section 9 of the 1890 Act states:

> Every partner in a firm is liable jointly with the other partners, and in Scotland severally so, for all debts and obligations of the firm incurred while he is a partner; and after his death his estate is also severally liable in a due course of administration for such debts and obligations, so far as they remain unsatisfied, but subject in England or Ireland to the prior payment of his separate debts.

When two or more partners have joint and several liability, a person who has been harmed or wronged, including a financial institution, can effectively sue all of the partners and seek to recover damages and collect the amount of such damages from one, or several of, or all of the parties. Each partner may be liable for all of the damages.

It is important to note that a partnership that operates as one business cannot function effectively without joint and several liability. One can seek to limit joint and several liability in a partnership agreement. This is discussed later.

Section 6 of the 1890 Act states "an act or instrument relating to the business of the firm done or executed in the firm-name, or in any other manner showing an intention to bind the firm, by any person thereto authorised, whether a partner or not, is binding on the firm and all the partners".

The 1890 Act details the types of actions carried out by a partner which will result in liability for the partnership:

- An act which constitutes the carrying on in the usual way of business of a kind carried on by the business[4];
- An act or instrument which relates to the business of the partnership[5];
- A wrongful act or omission, which is within the ordinary course of business of the business[6];
- Misapplying money or property which is within the scope of a partner's apparent authority[7];
- Money or property which is misapplied in the course of its business[8];
- An admission or representation which is made in the ordinary course of its business[9]; or
- Any act which is necessary to wind up the affairs of the partnership.[10]

Because of the principle of joint and several liability, the difficulty is that, if the farm business is found liable for the acts of one partner, then all the partners are liable for the acts of that one partner. The key factor in determining a partnership's liability is determining whether the acts of a partner are within the partnership's ordinary course of business.

## Example

A farm partnership would be liable if one of its partners purchased cattle at the mart, as that partner was acting within the ordinary course of the farm business. However, if the partner ordered a sports car for

---

[4] Partnership Act 1890, s 5.
[5] Partnership Act 1890, s 6.
[6] Partnership Act 1890, s 10.
[7] Partnership Act 1890, s 11(a).
[8] Partnership Act 1890, s 11(b).
[9] Partnership Act 1890, s 15.
[10] Partnership Act 1890, s 38.

the partnership, the contract would not be binding on the partnership, as ordering sports cars falls outside the ordinary course of the farm business.

Section 8 of the 1890 Act states that,

> if it has been agreed between the partners that any restriction shall be placed on the power of any one or more of them to bind the firm, no act done in contravention of the agreement is binding on the firm with respect to persons having notice of the agreement.

If two parties are entering into a farm partnership, they can insert clauses into the agreement to limit their joint and several liability. For example, they can agree that no partners shall be liable for any acts done, or omissions, prior to entering into the partnership agreement. In the event that there is no partnership agreement, or clauses are omitted from the partnership agreement, and the agreement is silent in relation to the limitation of joint and several liability, the question of liability will be determined according to the provisions of 1890 Act.

In the absence of recognition of limited liability partnerships in relation to farm partnerships in Ireland at the time of writing, the best practical advice that can be given is that the partnership agreement should include a clause that obliges each partner to take out fully comprehensive insurance in relation to the acts or omissions of each partner, and that all partners would be entitled to ask the other partners for a copy of their up-to-date insurance policy at any time during the term of the partnership agreement. Provision should also be made to allow one partner to terminate the agreement in the event that the other partner(s) failed to maintain such a policy.

### Important Provisions to Insert into a Partnership Agreement
Partnerships can be adapted to meet differing needs, thus offering versatility and flexibility. It is advisable that any agreement be both clear and comprehensive. A template agreement has been developed by Teagasc.[11]

---

[11] http://www.agriculture.gov.ie/farmingsectors/newfarmpartnershipregister/.

This is the most commonly used agreement in the formation of farm partnerships, and it is updated as necessary.

The following are some provisions that should be included in the partnership agreement:

- Definition of the activities to be included in (and excluded from) the partnership[12];
- Names and addresses of the parties to the partnership[13];
- Definition of the roles, responsibilities and limits of the activities of each party[14];
- Definition of profit sharing ratios[15];
- The percentage of the ownership of each partner[16];
- The allocation of profits and losses between partners[17];
- Clauses in relation to the death or retirement of a partner. It is common practice that the partnership agreement would include a provision to the effect that a payment would be made to the estate of a deceased partner. However, if there is no such provision, the partnership has no obligation to pay anything to the estate of the deceased partner[18];
- Procedures for resolving disputes. A partnership agreement should always deal with how disputes will be resolved, and in what order, from mediation, arbitration or the expensive option of litigation[19];
- Details as to who can bind the partnership in legal agreements and contracts[20];
- The duration of the agreement[21];
- Details identifying resources and capital being provided by all parties[22];
- Details establishing bank accounts[23] and the herd number[24];

---

[12] Teagasc Specimen 'Farm Partnership Agreement', p 5.

[13] Teagasc Specimen 'Farm Partnership Agreement', p 1.

[14] Teagasc Specimen 'Farm Partnership Agreement', pp 8, 9 and 10.

[15] Teagasc Specimen 'Farm Partnership Agreement', p 22.

[16] Teagasc Specimen 'Farm Partnership Agreement', p 22.

[17] Teagasc Specimen 'Farm Partnership Agreement', pp 7 and 8.

[18] Teagasc Specimen 'Farm Partnership Agreement', pp 10 and 11.

[19] Teagasc Specimen 'Farm Partnership Agreement', pp 12 and 13.

[20] Teagasc Specimen 'Farm Partnership Agreement', pp 9 and 10.

[21] Teagasc Specimen 'Farm Partnership Agreement', p 5.

[22] Teagasc Specimen 'Farm Partnership Agreement', pp 5 and 6.

[23] Teagasc Specimen 'Farm Partnership Agreement', pp 6 and 7.

[24] Teagasc Specimen 'Farm Partnership Agreement', p 1.

- Details on how accounts are to be prepared and the make-up of the capital account[25]; and
- Details on repayment of capital – the 1890 Act states that partners are not entitled to interest on the capital they contributed to the partnership unless the partnership agreement provides for such payment.[26] A well-drafted partnership agreement should cover the return of any capital invested and any interest to be paid. Considerable difficulty can arise if a retiring partner demands immediate withdrawal of all the capital he or she invested in the partnership. The agreement can specify timescales and terms of phased payment over a certain time period.

This is not meant to be an all-inclusive list, and a solicitor should always be consulted in advance of entering into a partnership or signing a partnership agreement.

## Types of Partnerships

There are two types of registered farm partnerships. These are:

1. Intra-Family Partnerships – these involve both spouses in a partnership, or a parent and child, or uncle and nephew or niece or variations of this; such partnerships usually involve only one farm.
2. Inter-Family Partnerships – these are partnerships between farmers outside of each other's immediate family and involve the owners immediate family and involve the owners of at least two farms coming together to form a partnership agreement.

### Intra-Family Farm Partnerships

Intra-family partnerships are more common in Ireland, and often arise in advance of a full transfer of the farm from the owner to a son or daughter. Transferring the family farm to the next generation can be a difficult and protracted process, with many concerns to be addressed. It is often complex, and therefore needs early and careful planning. A registered family partnership is one possible option to consider as part of the succession planning process. Parents may have different reasons for delaying the transfer of the farm to a son or daughter and these reasons often revolve around concerns such as family farm income and security for the parents and other family members, who still have to be provided for. These

---

[25] Teagasc Specimen 'Farm Partnership Agreement', pp 6 and 7.

[26] Partnership Act 1890, s 24(4).

concerns may be alleviated by the formation of a registered partnership between the parents and the son or daughter as an interim step, before considering a full farm transfer. There are very considerable advantages to forming a partnership, for both the parents and the son or daughter.[27]

In a registered partnership, the parents do not give up control of the farm; they share it with their son or daughter. They retain ownership of assets such as land, buildings, and entitlements. These assets are licensed for use by the partnership, but only for the duration of the partnership. Assets such as stock and machinery are transferred to the partnership and, as a result, they become partnership assets. The financial value of these assets is recorded in a capital account created by the accountant for each partner at the beginning of the arrangement. The capital account is updated each year during the lifetime of the agreement. These capital accounts become a key mechanism for the dissolution of the agreement at a later date.

A partnership also allows parents the opportunity to see how their son or daughter will adapt to the partnership, to utilise their agricultural training and knowledge on the farm, while working on the farm with shared decision-making and management. It also allows the parents to retain some control over the farm and to share their experience and knowledge with their future successor. A profit sharing ratio is agreed between the parents and the son or daughter.

## Succession Farm Partnerships (Pending)
As part of Budget 2016, the government proposed a scheme for a new farm succession transfer model partnership.[28] The relief is subject to state aid rule approval[29] and thus will come into operation once commenced.

The purpose of this proposed scheme is to encourage older farmers to form partnerships with young trained farmers and to transfer ownership of the

---

[27] For more detailed information, see Thomas Curran, 'Collaborative Farming: A Suite of Options to Improve the Structures of Irish Dairy Farming' (2015). <www.teagasc.ie/media/website/rural-economy/farm-management/Moorepark-Open-Day-July2015.pdf> accessed 18 July 2016.

[28] http://www.budget.gov.ie/Budgets/2016/2016.aspx A6.

[29] http://www.budget.gov.ie/Budgets/2016/2016.aspx A6.

farm, within three to ten years,[30] to that young trained farmer. It allows for both intra-farm partnerships and inter-farm partnerships.

The partners are entitled to an annual €5,000 tax credit divided between them in accordance with the profit-sharing ratio specified in the agreement.[31] The credit can be claimed for a maximum of 5 years from the date on which the partnership is registered.[32] The credit is not available in the year where the successor has reached 40 years of age.[33]

In order to be registered, and to avail of the tax credits and grants available, the partnership must comply with all of the following conditions[34]:

1.  The farm partnership must have at least 2 members, each of whom is a natural person,[35] which means they cannot be a limited company;
2.  Of the members of the farm partnership:
    a)  At least one partner (i.e. the farmer) must have been farming on at least 3 hectares for a minimum of 2 years immediately before the formation of the partnership[36];
    b)  Of the others, each partner (i.e. the successor) must have an agricultural qualification (the 'Green Cert' or its equivalent), be entitled to at least 20% of the profits of the partnership, and should not have reached 40 years before registration[37];
3.  Approval must be obtained from the Minister for Agriculture for the business plan of the farm partnership before an application for registration is made[38];
4.  The farmer must enter into an agreement with the successor to transfer at least 80% of the farm assets to the successor within 10 years of the commencement of the partnership.[39] The transfer can begin after year 3;

---

[30] Taxes Consolidation Act 1997, s 667(D)(2)(d).
[31] Taxes Consolidation Act 1997, s 667(D)(6)(a).
[32] ibid.
[33] Taxes Consolidation Act 1997, s 667(D)(6)(b).
[34] Taxes Consolidation Act 1997, s 667(D)(2).
[35] Taxes Consolidation Act 1997, s 667(D)(2)(a).
[36] Taxes Consolidation Act 1997, s 667(D)(2)(b)(i).
[37] Taxes Consolidation Act 1997, s 667(D)(2)(b)(ii).
[38] Taxes Consolidation Act 1997, s 667(D)(2)(c).
[39] Taxes Consolidation Act 1997, s 667(D)(2)(d).

5. The terms of the partnership agreement shall include:
   a) The farm assets of the partnership on the day of application for registration[40];
   b) Any conditions to which the transfer will be subject[41];
   c) The year in which the proposed transfer may take place[42]; and
   d) Any other terms agreed between the farmer and successor, such as the conduct of the farming trade or creation of any rights of residence in dwellings on the land.[43]

If at least 80% of the farm assets are not transferred within the 10-year deadline, there will be a claw-back of the tax credits claimed.[44]

## Registered Partnerships

The registration of farm partnerships is governed by the Registration of Farm Partnerships Regulations 2015.[45] Registered farm partnerships are available to both intra-farm partnerships and inter-farm partnerships.

Regulation 4 requires the following:

a) The partnership is engaged in the trade of farming;
b) The partnership consists of at least 2 persons but not more than 10 persons;
c) At least one partner in the farm partnership shall be a person who has been engaged in the trade of farming on land owned or leased by that person consisting of at least 3 hectares of useable farmland, for at least 2 years immediately preceding the date of formation of the partnership;
d) Where only one partner satisfies the requirement referred to at (c) above, at least one other partner has an agricultural qualification listed in the Schedule to the Regulations, or a qualification determined by Teagasc on behalf of the Minister for Agriculture as being equivalent to those listed in the Schedule to the Regulations, and hold an entitlement to at least 20% of the profits in the farm partnership profit sharing arrangement;
e) The partnership agreement is in writing;
f) The partnership agreement operates in accordance with the 1890 Act;

---

[40] Taxes Consolidation Act 1997, s 667(D)(2)(e)(i).
[41] Taxes Consolidation Act 1997, s 667(D)(2)(e)(ii).
[42] Taxes Consolidation Act 1997, s 667(D)(2)(e)(iii).
[43] Taxes Consolidation Act 1997, s 667(D)(2)(e)(ii).
[44] Taxes Consolidation Act 1997, s 667(D)(6)(c).
[45] Registration of Farm Partnerships Regulations 2015, SI No 247 of 2015.

g) The partnership commits to a period for operation of the partnership agreement of not less than 5 years;

h) Unless otherwise approved by the Minister for Agriculture in writing, no partner is in occupation of farmland outside the farm partnership at any time during the period of registration;

i) Unless otherwise approved by the Minister for Agriculture in writing, all payments to the partners arising from the trade of farming shall be paid to the farm partnership. The partnership agrees to co-operate with inspections and provide such information as the Minister for Agriculture may reasonably require at any time during the period of registration to ensure compliance with registration;

j) Farmland of partners in occupation of such land shall not be more than 50 kilometres from the farmland of another partner; and

k) The partnership agrees to notify the Minister for Agriculture within 21 days of any material change to the farm partnership or its activities.

Regulation 8 states that the Minister for Agriculture shall grant registration for a period not exceeding 5 years and shall issue a certification of registration and a unique identifier number to the partnership.

Further information on registered farm partnerships, such as information on setting up partnership bank accounts, a checklist for setting up a registered farm partnership and the application form for registering a partnership are available from Teagasc.[46]

### Tax Implications of Partnerships

Apart from the succession farm partnership tax credit (outlined above), there are a variety of tax implications that follow on from engaging in a farm partnership. First, each individual partner must be registered for income tax in order that their share of the partnership income can be declared to the Revenue Commissioners. The partnership itself will also need to register for income tax (Form TR1), and this should be done at the point at which the partnership commences trading. One set of financial statements or "accounts" is usually prepared for the partnership, with the profits declared on a partnership tax return (Form 1). Each individual partner must separately declare their share of the partnership profits on his/her own individual income tax return (Form 11). In many instances, a partnership business involves the evolution

---

[46] Please see https://www.teagasc.ie/rural-economy/farm-management/collaborative-farming/ registered-farm-partnerships/ or call to your local Teagasc office.

from a sole trader business as a result of the inclusion of another person in the running of the business. For example, a farmer may decide to include their spouse's name on the accounts to reflect a jointly-run business. Similarly, a farmer may choose to involve a successor in his or her farming trade by inclusion as a partner, rather than a salaried employee. Where a farmer intends to commence a partnership, it is important to ensure, not only that a smooth transition occurs, but rather that the transition actually takes place.

On a practical basis, partners should consider some or all of the following:

i)   Whether the partnership has its own bank account;
ii)  Whether the herd number is changed over to reflect the name of the partnership; and
iii) Whether suppliers and customers have been adequately informed.

A clear break from any previous sole trader income is important in accurately calculating the profits of the sole trader business and distinguishing them from those of the newly formed partnership.

On commencement of a partnership, one of the partners must be nominated as the precedent acting partner. This is a responsible position, and the individual concerned must be aware that the obligation for submitting correct and full returns for the partnership to the Revenue Commissioners rests with him or her.[47] There are also specific rules, whereby a person carrying on a sole trade which evolves into a partnership, is deemed to have ceased his/her sole trader activity and commenced a new trade under the partnership.[48] The tax implications of this can be onerous. In particular, a farmer who has had his/her profits assessed under income averaging will be deemed to have opted out of this scheme, with the potential for a clawback arising in respect of the previous four years' tax assessments (prior to the final year in averaging). However, special provisions were given to registered farm partnerships under s 15 of the Finance Act 2008, whereby the permanent discontinuation of another trade of farming and the commencement of the partnership trade shall be treated as a continuation of that other trade.[49] Ceasing to trade as a sole trader can also result in a "balancing

---

[47] Taxes Consolidation Act 1997, s 1007(1).
[48] Taxes Consolidation Act 1997, s 69.
[49] Taxes Consolidation Act 1997, s 657(10)(A).

charge" event, meaning that income tax could become payable on the difference between the book value and the market value of plant, equipment and farm machinery. Similarly, an income tax charge can arise on cessation of a sole trade, where stock have a higher market value than their book value at the date of cessation. From an income tax perspective, a planned approach to setting up a partnership and ceasing a sole trader business can potentially result in the avoidance of these difficulties by choosing an optimal time to convert to partnership, and by ensuring relevant elections, exemptions and reliefs are claimed. It is advisable to begin a partnership at the end of the previous tax year. This negates the impact of cessation and commencement rules on the farmers beginning a partnership, as it coincides with the normal preparation of annual farm accounts. The exception to this is where two farmers with different tax years (e.g. January and April) enter into a farm partnership. In this case, one farmer will have to complete a short tax year in order to align the tax years of both partners.

There are multiple tax benefits of partnerships. These include:

i)   The potential to use otherwise unused additional tax bands and tax credits of the new partners. This can reduce the overall exposure to taxes by the business;

ii)  The potential for partners to make PRSI contributions[50] (and obtain relevant social welfare benefits in the future as a result);

iii) The capacity to benefit from higher Capital Gains Tax retirement relief[51] thresholds as a result of additional partners being involved in running the business; and

iv)  Partnerships may avail of enhanced 50% stock relief.[52] A simple example is that of a husband farming in his own right, and who has a spouse with no source of income. On a practical basis, where the spouse is actively involved in the running of the business, it would be possible to register a farm partnership under both spouses' names and avail of the above mentioned tax benefits. If a person who is not actively involved in the business is included in the partnership trade as a partner, then, on investigation by the Revenue Commissioners, that person may be deemed to be a passive partner, resulting in a variety of restrictions on tax relief.[53]

---

[50] Social Welfare Consolidation Act 2005, Chapter 3 Part II.
[51] Taxes Consolidation Act 1997, s 598 and s 599.
[52] Taxes Consolidation Act 1997, s 667C.
[53] Taxes Consolidation Act 1997, s 381C.

In deciding whether partnership is an appropriate step to take, it is worthwhile weighing up the tax implications of all alternatives (such as employing a spouse or child, as opposed to including them as a partner).

## Contract Rearing of Replacement Heifers

Contract rearing of heifers is an arrangement which involves a dairy farmer entering into a contractual agreement with another farmer and rearing replacement stock on the other farmer's holding. The farmer enters into a contract where he or she is paid to rear heifers for a dairy farmer.

Essentially, the rearing period can be broken down into five stages as follows:

1. Calf-rearing;
2. First grazing season;
3. First winter;
4. Second grazing season; and
5. Second winter.[54]

The important issue for the rearer is to cover costs and receive adequate payment for his or her labour. The heifers must reach their target weights at housing after the first grazing season, at mating and approaching calving after the second grazing season. It is critical to the dairy farmer that the heifers reach these weights. The rearer must be aware of the average starting weight for the group of heifers and have realistic expectations for weight gain during the rearing period. Regular weighing of heifers is recommended in order to monitor the progress of the animals.

### Written Contract

An agreement for the contract-rearing of heifers is a written legal agreement between a dairy farmer and the rearer. The dairy farmer is the person who owns the heifers and wishes to contract out the rearing of them to another. The rearer is the person who rears the heifers on his or her land,

---

[54] Teagasc, 'A Guide to Transferring the Family Farm' (2015) 40. <www.teagasc.ie/media/website/publications/2014/3300/A_Guide_to_Transferring_the_Family_Farm.pdf> accessed 18 July 2016.

with a view to returning them to the dairy farmer at a specified time. If the arrangement is successful, it can be continued on a yearly basis.

Before a dairy farmer, or a rearer, enters into a contract rearing of heifers agreement, there are some practical tips of which he or she should take note and implement:

- Seek a rearer or dairy farmer with a good reputation and a good track record;
- The rearer and dairy farmer should walk each other's farms;
- Be satisfied that the standard of animal management is good on either farm;
- Check with the Department of Agriculture that the two previous herd test results have been clear;
- Check the general disease status on both farms, compliance with vaccination programmes etc.;
- Observe animal rearing practices on both farms;
- Note the condition and security of the boundaries and fences; and
- Ensure the dairy farmer and the rearer are of good financial standing and have a good financial track record.

### Benefits of a Written Contract

In all cases, it is strongly advised that there be a written agreement. Having no contract, a badly drafted contract, or an incomplete contract, can lead to ambiguity and disputes. The giving of instructions for the drafting of a contract also helps both parties to focus their minds on the issues and practicalities involved in advance of animals being transferred. This will allow potential problems to be addressed at an early stage. The effort involved in putting a written contract in place will take time and incur expense, but it is important to put the expectations and responsibilities of both parties in writing before any arrangement commences.

### Terms to Insert into a Written Contract

Contracts should include:

1. Confirmation of the duration of the agreement[55]. The normal rearing period is for approximately nineteen months, usually beginning in late April or early May;

---

[55] Teagasc Specimen 'Dairy Heifer Rearing Agreement Flat Rate Contract' p 9.

2. The responsibilities, obligations and expectations of both parties[56];
3. Confirmation that the dairy farmer's animals come from herds that are TB free.[57] The dairy farmer must have had a clear test within the previous twelve months. Evidence of this should be produced to the rearer in advance of entering into the agreement. The animals subject to the contract rearing arrangement should be kept separate from any other animals owned or contract reared by the rearer. If desired, this should be stated in the agreement at the beginning of the arrangement;
4. Where a vaccination programme is in place for the heifers, the dairy farmer normally supplies the vaccines and the rearer administers the vaccines. This process must be clearly set out in the written agreement to provide clarity[58];
5. Targets in terms of weight gain should be specifically defined.[59] These should outline if the heifers are to be weighed, and, if so, by whom, and at what stage. There are two types of contracts: a flat rate contract and a weight bonus contract. The flat rate contract is the most common. In a flat rate contract, the payment is based on a per head per day rate that is negotiated at the beginning of the contract. In a weight bonus contract, a base level payment is agreed, with a bonus paid on an agreed percentage of the animals reaching the required target weights;
6. The contract must clearly state how and with what frequency payment is to be made.[60] This must be negotiated between the respective parties. The rearing periods need to be borne in mind when planning a rate of payment. Rearing the calves to twelve weeks of age and keeping the animals over the winter periods are generally the most expensive. The grazing seasons are by far the least expensive rearing periods. In setting up these arrangements, the parties should agree the start and finish dates of the term of rearing. If the rearer is to receive a bonus for reaching target weights, this should be detailed in the agreement. Details of what happens when targets are not met should also be inserted.[61] Agreement must be reached regarding the costs that are to be incurred by each party. This will determine the rate of payment per head per day. A recording system must be used to monitor costs. This can be done very simply by

---

56 Teagasc Specimen 'Dairy Heifer Rearing Agreement Flat Rate Contract', pp 14–15.
57 Teagasc Specimen 'Dairy Heifer Rearing Agreement Flat Rate Contract', pp 10–11.
58 Teagasc Specimen 'Dairy Heifer Rearing Agreement Flat Rate Contract', p 11.
59 Teagasc Specimen 'Dairy Heifer Rearing Agreement Weight Bonus Contract', pp 12–13.
60 Teagasc Specimen 'Dairy Heifer Rearing Agreement Flat Rate Contract', pp 12.
61 Teagasc Specimen 'Dairy Heifer Rearing Agreement Weight Bonus Contract', pp 12–13.

using a written system, or through computers using programmes such as the Teagasc Cost Control Planner[62];

7. The protocol for breeding and the costs associated with it must be clearly set out in the agreement at the beginning of the arrangement.[63] The dairy farmer is normally responsible for the choice of AI bulls used, AI costs, and the provision of stock bulls to clean up. Depending on the skills of the rearer, he or she may be responsible for heat detection and pregnancy diagnosis costs. When heat detection skills are poor, or the rearer does not want this responsibility, the parties normally agree on a synchronisation protocol. The agreement may provide that the rearer must notify the dairy farmer, should any heifers not be in calf following scanning;

8. Provisions in relation to the death of any of the animals need to be considered, together with the cost of disposal of the dead animals.[64] Normal thresholds of between 2 and 5% are taken into consideration in the template agreement. It should be detailed, and make reference to whether or not the rearer receives payment for rearing the heifer up to the date of death, or whether the rearing costs should be refunded in the case of such a death. Knackery charges are usually the responsibility of the rearer. The dairy farmer should be notified, at the latest, within one day of the death of a heifer. If losses of more than 5% of a herd occur, the rearer should refund, in full, any fees paid[65];

9. Tagging and de-horning is important. All stock should be tagged and de-horned on delivery to the rearer, with the rearer then being responsible for replacing any damaged or lost tags;

10. Responsibility for veterinary costs should be identified and included in the agreement at the beginning of the arrangement. Routine veterinary practices, such as dosing and TB testing, are normally the responsibility of the rearer. The protocol around provision and administration of vaccines must be outlined in the agreement. However, vaccinations are normally provided by the dairy farmer and administered by the rearer;

11. Details outlining who is responsible for the transportation of the animals must be provided in the agreement. Normally, it is the dairy farmer who bears the cost of both delivery and return;

12. A farmer cannot insure animals he or she does not own. Therefore, it is advisable that the dairy farmer continues to insure the animals against injury or death on the rearer's lands. The rearer must also

---

[62] https://www.teagasc.ie/media/website/rural-economy/farm management/HeiferRearing CostCalculatorGuidelines.pdf.

[63] Teagasc Specimen 'Dairy Heifer Rearing Agreement Flat Rate Contract', pp 13–15.

[64] ibid

[65] ibid.

seek the advice of his or her insurance company in respect of the animals, subject to the contract rearing agreement;

13. Clauses in relation to disputes should always be included.[66] An agreement should have a facilitation, conciliation and arbitration clause. An arbitration clause obliges the parties to resolve their disputes through an arbitration process, thus avoiding a lengthy court process. The parties to a dispute refer it to arbitration by one or more persons and agree to be bound by the arbitrator's decision. It is more cost and time effective than going to court;

14. Dates of arrival and planned removal of animals[67];

15. Details of payment methods; and

16. Details of how often the dairy farmer will visit the rearer's farm to check the heifers.

Good communication and trust are essential to the success of any rearing contract, or indeed any other collaborative arrangement. The parties involved should be in regular contact to discuss the progress of the heifers and make key decisions on issues such as breeding and health.[68]

The above list is not exhaustive. Every situation is unique and each contract will depend on the facts, circumstances and desires of each party. The success or failure of a contract heifer rearing enterprise can depend on the quality of the contract between the rearer and the owner.

For further information, see the Teagasc website (www.teagasc.ie), which contains some more detailed guidelines, providing target live weights, guideline costings, and advice on the risks involved, as well as disease control.[69] Teagasc have developed two specimen heifer rearing contracts[70] and a heifer rearing cost calculator, both of which are available on its website.[71]

---

[66] Teagasc Specimen 'Dairy Heifer Rearing Agreement Flat Rate Contract', pp 15–17.

[67] Teagasc Specimen 'Dairy Heifer Rearing Agreement Flat Rate Contract', pp 10.

[68] Teagasc, 'A Guide to Transferring the Family Farm' (2014) 41 <www.teagasc.ie/media/website/publications/2014/3300/A_Guide_to_Transferring_the_Family_Farm.pdf> accessed 18 July 2016.

[69] See also, Teagasc, 'Guidelines for the Contract Rearing of Replacement Heifers' (2013) <www.teagasc.ie/publications/2013/1912/GuidelinesContractRearingReplacementHeifers.pdf> accessed 18 July 2016.

[70] <www.teagasc.ie/collaborativearrangements/specimen_agreements.asp>.

[71] <www.teagasc.ie/collaborativearrangements/contract_rearing_of_heifers.asp>.

## Share Farming

Share farming is an arrangement between two parties, whereby the landowner and share farmer carry on separate farming businesses on the same area of land, without forming a partnership or company. It operates on the principle that the share farmer and landowner, although farming the same land as individual businesses, have separate incomes and separate expenses from which to calculate their individual profits. Share farming allows for a new way of accessing land, something which can increase scale in a controlled manner.

In setting up a share farming agreement, it is crucial that the parties do not entertain any sort of profit or partial profit-sharing arrangement. This includes the setting up of joint merchant accounts or bank accounts in joint names. Where this occurs, the arrangement may be judged to be a partnership rather than share farming. The key feature of share farming which distinguishes it from a partnership is that two completely separate farming businesses operate on one area of land.

For the landowner, the agreement offers the opportunity to participate in the farm and to reap the rewards of the enterprise. The price to be paid for this is that the landowner must also participate in the risk of growing the crop or rearing the livestock. Both parties must contribute some costs to grow the crop or rear the livestock. The proportion which each party takes depends on the agreement. The output from the crop or the livestock will also be shared between both parties. Share farming can be fully compliant with EU and government support schemes. Both parties maintain their separate tax affairs as normal.[72]

### The Importance of a Written Agreement

It is important to ensure that a written agreement is put in place. The form of agreement is critical. It is essential for all parties to be aware that the existence of a written share farming agreement is not, in itself, sufficient evidence of an actual share farming arrangement being in place.

---

[72] Revenue, 'Share Farming' (2010) (12) Tax Briefs <www.revenue.ie/en/practitioner/tax-briefing/archive/2010/no-122010.html> accessed 21 July 2016.

Unless appropriate legal advice is taken, a partnership, a lease or a letting arrangement can unintentionally arise in law. The carrying on of the arrangement on a day to day basis must comply with the principles of share farming and reflect the written agreement in place. The written agreement should not be an attempt to hide the fact that an arrangement is a de facto conacre system[73] or a retirement mechanism for landowners. A share farming arrangement does not exist where the relationship between the parties is that of landlord and tenant, employer and employee, or partners.

It is important that the agreement be implemented on the terms as agreed and with all parties adopting a practical approach. Each party makes separate contributions to the arrangement, for example, land, machinery, labour and expertise, and takes a share in the output. Each party is responsible for their own costs of production, as otherwise, parties run the risk of unintentionally entering into a partnership. Each party keeps their own accounts and calculates their individual profits as separate and independent businesses, notwithstanding that each business is closely linked to the other. Each party, the landowner and share farmer, is free to sell his/her shares of produce as he/she sees fit. No rent is paid for the land, as otherwise the structure may be construed as a letting. The share farmer is not paid for his or her labour. A contractor hire cost is not paid to the share farmer for the use of his or her machinery.

An arrangement that is found to operate as something other than share farming will be taxed on the basis of the actual arrangement that is in place. This may have income tax, Capital Gains Tax (CGT), Pay-As-You-Earn (PAYE), Value Added Tax (VAT) and Stamp Duty implications for the participants.

Trust between the parties is an essential element that must be present before they consider entering into such an agreement. It is important that the agreement be in place before the commencement of share farming. It is advisable that the parties seek advice from professionals on all aspects of the proposal, including the relevant legal, financial and taxation implications.

---

[73] Conacre is the right to sow and harvest crops on another's land.

### Issues to be Covered in the Share Farming Agreement

A full discussion on all elements of the agreement is essential before commencing operations.

The following are some of the issues to be covered in a share farming agreement:

- The duration of the agreement;
- An exact description of the lands to be provided by the landowner;
- How produce is to be stored, marketed and sold;
- Procedures for resolving disputes;
- Who is to provide livestock;
- Who is to provide machinery;
- The basis for division of costs and produce;
- Insurance; and
- Procedures to apply in the event of dispute, death or termination of the agreement.

It is also important to ensure that all parties named on the title to the lands are party to the agreement, for example, a spouse. In addition, the previous cropping history and the fertility status of the land should be set out.

In practice, it is the preparation of the schedules to the agreement that often prompt the most thought in relation to major aspects of the agreement.

Where livestock are involved, each party must warrant that their animals are free from infection and have been vaccinated. Machinery should be in good order at the start. Fences should be inspected and put in repair and good order before the commencement of the agreement. This helps to prevent disputes. If they are not in order, a schedule of dilapidations should be prepared and agreed.

It is always advisable to insert a period of notice of termination into the agreement, as this will allow the parties to plan ahead for their respective farming businesses.

Clauses should be inserted into the agreement to allow for the dissolution of the arrangement in a methodical way in the event of the share farming agreement breaking down due to major or persistent breaches by either party.

As in the case of the contract rearing of heifers agreements, the above list is not exhaustive. Every situation is unique and each agreement will depend on the facts, circumstances and aspirations of each party.

For further information, see the Teagasc website (www.teagasc.ie), which contains some more detailed guidelines on share farming, including specimen dairy share farming agreement and tillage share farming agreements, and a crop share calculator.[74]

## Cow Leasing

Cow leasing is a collaborative arrangement, where a farmer, with cows that are surplus to his or her requirements, leases those cows to another farmer.[75] Cow leases are business relationships that require a significant level of trust. The two farmers involved in the agreement must work towards building up a good working relationship.

### Cow Leasing Agreements

Cow leasing agreements should be in writing, with the written contract clearly identifying all the agreed terms. The document should set out the responsibilities and obligations of each party. A properly written lease also provides protection to both parties in the event of the death of one or other of them, and encourages detailed thought and joint decision-making. The task of giving instructions for the preparation of the lease serves as a reminder of the terms agreed upon, and successors will find the agreement invaluable in determining the nature of the relationship.

The lessor is the owner of the cows. The lessee is the person who leases the cows from the lessor.

Provisions that should be inserted into the agreement include:

1. Personal details of the parties, including their names, addresses and tax reference numbers;
2. Commencement date of the agreement;

---

[74] <www.teagasc.ie/collaborativearrangements/share_farming/agreement.asp>.

[75] Teagasc "Cow Leasing: A New Collaborative Arrangement" Page 1 - https://www.teagasc.ie/media/website/rural-economy/farm-management/Cow-Leasing-Feb2015.pdf.

3. Duration of the agreement. The lease can be short-term, one to two years for example, or for a longer term of, perhaps, four to five years. In general, cows on a short term arrangement will return to the owner, whereas those on a long term lease generally will not. The criteria for the replacement of animals must be set out and agreed at the start of the arrangement. These include lactation number, age, disease status etc. Cows leased out for four to five years are generally replaced with an equivalent group of cows at the end of the agreement. The profile of the leased cows should be noted at the start of the agreement, and the group of cows that are returned must be, at a minimum, equivalent in terms of age, lactation, and disease status, and superior in terms of economic breeding index (EBI) status.[76] These criteria should be agreed between the parties at the beginning of the agreement and noted in writing. Calves born out of the leased cows are the property of the lessee and this allows him or her to build up a stock of replacements for the herd, and also to cover the return of the cows as part of the lease agreement[77];

4. A detailed payment schedule and method of payment should be agreed and documented in the agreement. The two parties should agree an average value per cow at the outset of the agreement, and this should be included in writing. They must also arrive at a leasing cost that is fair to both parties and there should be an agreed method of payment included in the written agreement;

5. Animal identity and value clauses should be inserted. The identity of the animals to be leased is clearly a critical part of the agreement. The bovine tuberculosis eradication (BTE) tag numbers can be entered into the tables provided in the standard agreement;

6. Facilitation clauses must be inserted. The document becomes a written record of what is agreed between the parties before the start of the lease period. In the event of any difficulties arising, the agreement may be viewed by the parties to resolve the issue and, in cases where a disagreement cannot be resolved, there is a facilitation process provided to resolve disputes.

In advance of entering into a cow leasing arrangement, it is vitally important that both parties consult their own veterinary surgeons regarding how best to deal with any potential disease risk.

---

[76] *Agriland "What to consider before leasing cows – Teagasc"* By Thomas Curran Farm Structures Specialist, 5 March 2015 – *http://www.agriland.ie/farming-news/what-to-consider-before-leasing-cows-teagasc/*

[77] Thomas Curran, 'What to consider before leasing cows' (2015) <www.teagasc.ie/publications/2015/3515/TodaysFarm_MarApr2015.pdf> accessed 21 July 2016.

The lease must also include a signed undertaking by both parties that the cows will not be moved into, or out of, either party's holding, unless they have passed tuberculosis/brucellosis tests in accordance with the animal health regulations in force at the time.

The fully completed form and lease must be presented to the local District Veterinary Office for noting in advance of the start date of the arrangement.

Only those cow lease arrangements which meet all of the conditions set out above are deemed to be acceptable to the Department of Agriculture. A copy of the Animal Health and Movement (AIM) Certificate of Compliance, which de facto confirms the disease status of the herds, must be presented to the lessee's milk purchaser in advance, and the milk purchaser must notify the Department of Agriculture of the arrangement, so that an inspection may be carried out.

For further information, see the Teagasc website (www.teagasc.ie), which contains some more detailed guidelines, including a specimen cow leasing agreement and information on the tax treatment of cow leasing arrangements.[78]

## Conclusion

Collaborative arrangements offer a great opportunity for farmers to come together with others to achieve economies of scale, share facilities, become involved in a new and alternative farm enterprise and as a result, enjoy an improved lifestyle. The Irish government and EU Commission is actively encouraging the uptake of collaborative farming in Irish agriculture, with the introduction of polices in relation to income tax and Common Agricultural Policy (CAP) schemes. For farmers, there are now more options than ever before, with a variety of structures under which they can farm. However, to reap the benefits of such arrangements, it is vital to have a well-prepared, written agreement in place to safeguard the interests of all parties before the arrangement commences. The agreement must be reviewed and updated on an annual basis to ensure its continued relevance.

---

[78] <www.teagasc.ie/collaborativearrangements/Draft-Cow-Lease-Long-Term-2013.pdf>.

# CHAPTER ELEVEN

# Family Law and the Farm

Marital breakdown in rural Ireland is now a reality. One of the biggest issues that arises when it comes to divorce cases involving farmers is the physical structure of the traditional family farm. The family home is often at the centre of a block of land, surrounded by the farm buildings and other infrastructure essential to the running of the business. Divorce was enacted into law in Ireland in 1996.[1] In the 20 years since, the Irish courts have granted over 100,000 divorces.[2] When a marriage breaks down, knowledge of one's options and rights is particularly important. People have preconceived ideas and thoughts on marital breakdown, which often are not reflective of reality, and they may even serve to worsen already poor relations between the parties.

This chapter deals with the resolution of marital breakdown without resort to the courts, separation agreements, judicial separation, divorce, custody and access to children, maintenance, nullity, pre-nuptial agreements and co-habitants' rights arising from relationship breakdown. It also explores emerging trends in decisions taken by the courts in divorce cases. It concludes by addressing the tax implications arising from the disposal of assets on foot of marital breakdown.

The law in relation to family law and divorce in Ireland is predominantly contained in the Judicial Separation and Family Law Reform Act 1989 (hereafter 'the 1989 Act'), the Family Law Act, 1995 (hereafter 'the 1995 Act') and the Family Law (Divorce) Act 1996 (hereafter 'the 1996 Act').

---

[1] Family Law (Divorce) Act 1996.

[2] K Fox, 'Divorce in Ireland' (RTÉ Investigations Unit 2016) <www.rte.ie/iu/divorce/> accessed 22 July 2016.

## Marital Breakdown – Avoiding Court Proceedings

When a marriage ends, it can be devastating for both parties, and the children, if any. If at all possible, it is best to keep the relationship on amicable terms, maintaining open lines of communication between the parties, especially if there are children involved.

Alternative dispute resolution (ADR) such as mediation and collaboration, should be explored.

### Mediation

Mediation is a service to help couples who have decided to separate or divorce, or who have already separated. It helps parties to negotiate their own settlement terms, while addressing the needs of all involved. A mediator encourages cooperation between the separating couple with the aim of reaching an agreement.[3] Mediation in the Family Mediation Service is free of charge.

If a couple arrive at a mediated agreement, they will be advised to attend separate solicitors to obtain independent legal advice on the proposed agreement. The purpose of this is to ensure that the agreement is fair to both parties. Once this advice has been obtained, the agreement can then be signed. If the parties so wish, it can be made a rule of court. This means that a judge can be asked to receive the document and make orders where appropriate. Some issues, such as pensions, cannot be dealt with in a binding manner by way of mediated agreement only, and orders must be made to ensure enforceability.

### Collaborative Law

Collaboration is another approach which can help to resolve disputes. The aim of collaborative law is to find a fair and sustainable solution for people who are in dispute. Collaborative practice is a structured, creative and principled process aimed at helping parties reach the best possible agreement for them at the time. The approach addresses the needs of the whole family. Resolution is achieved through the meeting of both parties at the same table, often with the help of professionals, including solicitors,

---

[3] http://www.amen.ie/q_and_a.html.

accountants and child specialists.[4] If the process is unsuccessful, then the professionals who have been involved must cease to act and the parties should retain different legal teams if the matter proceeds to a court room setting.

## Separation Agreements

Separation agreements result in both parties reaching a formal agreement in relation to matters such as maintenance, access to children, the family home, farm and the division of the assets. A separation agreement can be concluded by mutual agreement through the parties' solicitors, or by a mediator, as set out above. A separation agreement is a legal document which sets out the future rights and duties of a married couple to each other. Separation agreements are signed by both parties and witnessed. It is essential that both parties receive independent legal advice.

Both parties must consent to the terms of separation. It is essential that both parties swear an affidavit of means, which is a document setting out a person's income, assets, liabilities and expenses, prior to entering into a deed of separation.

A separation agreement (like a mediated agreement) cannot deal with matters in respect of a pension, and an application must be made to court for any pension adjustment order. Such an order, which is binding, requires that a proportion of the pension benefits of a spouse be transferred to the other spouse. An application for a pension adjustment order can be made to the court under s 12 of the 1995 Act and s 17 of the 1996 Act.

## Judicial Separation

Where spouses cannot agree the terms of the separation, or where only one spouse seeks a separation, an application for a decree of judicial separation can be made to court by virtue of s 2 of the 1989 Act. The spouse seeking the separation in court is known as the applicant and the spouse from whom separation is sought is known as the respondent. The division of assets such as farmland and finances, as well as the maintenance and custody of children, is decided by the court.

---

[4] http://www.acp.ie/index.php/does-it-take-long?id=133:faqs&catid=31:general.

Section 2 of the 1989 Act sets out the grounds for a decree of judicial separation, which may be any one or more of the following:

- Adultery committed by the respondent;
- Behaviour by the respondent, which makes it unreasonable to expect the applicant to live with that person;
- Desertion for a continuous period of one year up to the time of the application;
- The spouses have lived apart for a continuous period of up to one year at the time of the application and the respondent consents to a judicial separation;
- The spouses have lived apart for a continuous period of up to three years prior to the application. In this case, the consent of the respondent is not required; or
- The court is satisfied that there has not been a normal marital relationship between the spouses for at least one year before the application.

The welfare of the child is paramount in family law. Section 3(2) of the 1989 Act states that a court shall not grant a decree of judicial separation until provision has been made for any children of the family or will be made by an order, on the granting of the decree of judicial separation.

The court, when granting a decree of judicial separation, can make a number of orders dealing with property, maintenance, the family home, farmlands, pensions and children. The court, under s 8 of the 1995 Act, can make the following orders in relation to maintenance and lump sums:

1. A periodical payments order, which is an order that either spouse shall make to the other spouse such periodical payments of such amount, and at such times, as may be specified in the order, or an order that either spouse shall make periodical payments to such person for the benefit of a dependent child of the family;
2. A secured periodical payments order, which is an order that either spouse shall secure to the other spouse to the satisfaction of the court, such periodical payments as may be so specified; or an order that a spouse shall secure periodical payments for the benefit of such dependent child of the family;
3. A lump sum order.

A pension adjustment order, as mentioned earlier, can be applied for under s 12 of the 1995 Act.

By virtue of s 9 and s 15 of the 1995 Act, a court can make various orders in relation to property on foot of an application for judicial separation, such as:

1. An order extinguishing or reducing one spouse's interest in a property[5];
2. An order for the transfer by one spouse of a property to the other spouse, or a dependent child[6];
3. An order allowing one spouse to remain in the family home for their lifetime or for a specific period to the exclusion of the other spouse[7]; and
4. An order for the sale of the family home[8] and farmland.[9]

## Divorce

A decree of divorce dissolves a marriage and allows both parties to remarry.

Section 5 of the 1996 Act states:

Where, on application to it in that behalf by either of the spouses concerned, the court is satisfied that—

(a) at the date of the institution of the proceedings, the spouses have lived apart from one another for a period of, or periods amounting to, at least four years during the previous five years,[10]
(b) there is no reasonable prospect of a reconciliation between the spouses, and
(c) such provision as the court considers proper having regard to the circumstances exists or will be made for the spouses and any dependent members of the family,

the court may, in exercise of the jurisdiction conferred by Art 41.3.2° of the Constitution, grant a decree of divorce in respect of the marriage concerned.

---

[5] Family Law Act 1995, s 9(1)(d).

[6] ibid, s 9(1)(a).

[7] ibid, s 10(1)(a)(i).

[8] ibid, s 10(1)(a)(ii).

[9] ibid, s 15(1).

[10] A Thirty Fifth Amendment of the Constitution (Divorce) Bill 2016 has been proposed to the Houses of the Oireacthas to reduce the time period of 4 years to 2 years in relation to the grant of a divorce.

The court, upon granting the decree of divorce, may give such directions as it considers proper regarding the welfare, or custody of, or right of access to, any dependant member of the family.

Parties need not be living apart, if they can demonstrate to the court that they are living separate lives.[11]

## Case

In the case of *McA v McA*,[12] a husband had returned to the family home, agreeing to pay rent of £750 a month, and later increasing it to £1,000. The applicant in this case sought a judicial separation and the husband counterclaimed, seeking a divorce. The applicant challenged the husband's counterclaim on the basis that he could not satisfy the living apart requirement, as he shared the family home with the applicant. The court held that, although the husband lived in the same house as the applicant, it was not activated by a desire to restart the marriage. McCracken J stated that, "I do not think one can look solely at where the parties physically reside, or at their mental or intellectual attitude to the marriage. Both of these elements must be considered, and in conjunction with each other."[13]

In the present economic climate, this has relevance where a separated couple might not have alternative accommodation to revert to upon a breakdown of their marriage. Thus, a couple could reside in the same property and still be considered living separately for the purposes of family law relief in either a judicial separation or a divorce. The courts normally consider whether the parties have behaved as a couple during the period in question. Amongst the considerations for the court are the following:

- Did the couple have an intimate relationship (sexual or otherwise) during the period in question?
- Did the couple holiday together or present themselves to the world as a married couple during the period in question?
- Did the couple perform the normal incidents of married life for each other, such as cooking, cleaning etc.?

---

[11] *McA v McA* [2000] 1 IR 457.
[12] ibid.
[13] ibid, p 463.

By virtue of s 20(1) of the 1996 Act,

> the court shall ensure that such provision as the court considers proper having regard to the circumstances exists or will be made for the spouses and any dependent member of the family concerned.

When deciding on "proper provision" the court shall, in particular, have regard to the following matters:

- The length of the marriage[14];
- The contribution both parties made to the marriage, financial or otherwise[15];
- The current and likely future income[16];
- The earning capacity and assets of each party[17];
- The current and future financial needs and obligations of each party[18];
- The standard of living of the family before the marital breakdown[19];
- The age of each party[20];
- The accommodation needs of each party[21];
- The input which each spouse has made and is likely to make to the welfare of the family[22];
- The degree to which the marriage affected the ability of each party to earn[23]; and
- The conduct of each party.[24]

This is a general guide, rather than an exhaustive list. It will be discussed in further detail later in the chapter. Divorce in Ireland does not take fault into account in most circumstances. The role of the court is to divide assets in order to provide financial support for spouses and children, and to reach agreements in relation to custody. Its role is not to punish either party.

---

[14] Family Law (Divorce) Act 1996, s 20(2)(d).

[15] ibid, s (20)(2)(f).

[16] ibid, s 20(2)(a).

[17] ibid.

[18] Family Law (Divorce) Act 1996 s 20(2)(b) as amended by s (157) of the Civil Partnership and Certain Rights and Obligations of Cohabitants Act 2010.

[19] ibid, s 20(2)(c).

[20] ibid, s 20(2)(d).

[21] ibid, s 20(2)(j).

[22] ibid, s 20(2)(f).

[23] ibid, s 20(2)(g).

[24] ibid, s 20(2)(i).

## Duty to Provide Full and Proper Financial Disclosure

It is critical that both parties give an accurate account of their assets and finances to their respective solicitors. The parties should also ensure that an auctioneer who is experienced and knowledgeable in relation to the value of farm stock, basic payment entitlements, and farm machinery, is instructed to carry out valuations for court. Realistic valuation of assets should always be obtained. Full financial disclosure from both parties is crucial. The subsequent discovery of an asset, not disclosed by one spouse at the time of judicial separation or divorce, provides an opportunity to re-open legal proceedings at a later date.

### Case

In the case of *SN v PO'D*,[25] the husband submitted that the wife had not fully disclosed details in relation to her companies prior to the settlement, and that she had subsequently sold her companies for a large sum. The husband was awarded a further €500,000 for what the judge called an "information deficit loss", which meant that the judge found that she had not intentionally withheld the information but that it had, nonetheless, not been made available to the husband and, accordingly, impacted on the settlement. The decision was appealed by the wife to the Supreme Court and that Court substantially increased the overall payment to the husband. This is one of the few examples of where the court penalised a party to matrimonial proceedings for failure to make full and proper financial disclosure.

## Guardianship, Access and Custody

One of the main causes of conflict in divorce or marital breakdown is in the area of access, custody, and ensuring children are looked after.

Access refers to the right of the parent with whom the child does not reside to spend time with the child. It can include the right to have the child stay overnight, either occasionally, on alternate weekends, or during school holidays, and the right of parent and child to go on holidays together.

Custody is the right to the physical care and control of a child. It involves the daily care, residency, and upbringing of the child. In cases of judicial

---

[25] *SN v PO'D* [2009] IESC 61.

separation or divorce, an order is often made for joint custody, but providing that the children reside permanently with one parent. The parent with whom the children reside permanently has de facto custody, and the other parent is granted custody of the children at agreed times, which can include overnight access.

The parents may agree informally between themselves the arrangements for custody of, and access to, the child.

In the event that agreement cannot be reached, either parent may make an application to the District Court under s 11 of the Guardianship of Infants Act 1964 (hereafter 'the 1964 Act') to decide on issues in relation to custody of, and access to, children. An application can also be made during judicial separation or divorce proceedings.

### How Does the Court Decide with Whom the Children Should Reside?

Section 3 of the 1964 Act, in deciding that question, states, that the court shall regard "the best interests of the child as the paramount consideration." Welfare comprises "the religious and moral, intellectual, physical and social welfare of the infant."[26]

It is a child's right to see both parents, and access by the non-custodial parent will only be denied if the court believes that it is not in the best interest of the child. The court can set out the time, place, and duration of access visits, and can order supervised access where another adult is present during visits if it considers it appropriate.[27]

## Succession Rights

Section 14 of the 1995 Act allows a court to grant an application extinguishing the share to which either spouse would be entitled in the estate of the other spouse as a legal right, provided that adequate and reasonable provision of a permanent nature has been made to provide for the future security of the spouse whose succession rights are in question.

---

[26] Guardianship of Infants Act 1964, s 2.

[27] ibid, s 11(2)(a) substituted by s 53 of the Children and Family Relationships Act 2010.

Where a couple are divorced, they are no longer spouses and so the terms of the Succession Act 1965 do not apply. However, it is possible to make an application for a share of a former spouse's estate under the terms of the 1996 Act. To enable parties to achieve finality in respect of succession, s 18(10) of the 1996 Act allows the court to make an order extinguishing either party's right to apply to court for a share of the other's estate upon death.

It is very important, when a relationship breaks down, that both parties make a will or review their existing will, in light of their new circumstances.

## Maintenance

Maintenance is governed by the Family Law (Maintenance of Spouses and Children) Act 1976 (hereafter 'the 1976 Act'). A voluntary maintenance agreement can be reached between the parties, but, if not, an application may be made to court under s 5 of the 1976 Act. This application can be made in the District, Circuit or High Court.

At present, the District Court and Circuit Court can award any amount up to €500 per week for a spouse, and €150 per week for each child.[28] Where the parties have very significant assets, the application may be brought in the High Court. It is, however, increasingly unusual for maintenance applications to be brought in the High Court as opposed to the Circuit Court. Even where there are very significant assets, parties often commence in the Circuit Court, as it is a speedier and less costly process.

In order to obtain a maintenance order, the applicant must prove that the respondent has failed to provide maintenance as is proper in the circumstances.

Section 5(4) of the 1976 Act states the following:

> The Court, in deciding whether to make a maintenance order and, if it decides to do so, in determining the amount of any payment, shall have regard to all the circumstances of the case and, in particular, to the following matters—

---

[28] Family Law (Maintenance of Spouses and Children) Act 1976, s 23(2)(a) as amended by s 20 of the Courts and Courts Officers Act 2002.

The income, earning capacity (if any), property and other financial resources of the spouses and of any dependent children of the family, including income or benefits to which either spouse or any such children are entitled by or under statute, and

The financial and other responsibilities of the spouses towards each other and towards any dependent children of the family and the needs of any such dependent children, including the need for care and attention.

It is important to note that the standard of living of a child must be maintained to the best of the parents' ability following a separation. Paying maintenance does not in itself give a parent right of access or guardianship rights. The paying of maintenance usually involves the parent who does not have custody paying maintenance to the parent who has the day to day care and control of the child. There are costs associated with maintaining a child's standard of living which he or she enjoyed before the separation. Often the parent who has custody is left to bear these costs. Thus, it is therefore important for courts to issue maintenance orders.

Maintenance payments are determined by the court, based on the needs of the spouse and the ability of the other spouse to pay maintenance.

Maintenance can also be dealt with upon application for a judicial separation or divorce.

## Division of Property

### The Family Home

The "family home" is defined according to s 2(1) of the Family Home Protection Act 1976 as "primarily, a dwelling in which a married couple ordinarily reside".

The family home cannot be sold without the consent of both spouses. The fact that the family home is in the name of one spouse does not negate the fact that the consent of the non-owning spouse is required for a sale. Section 3(1) of the 1976 Act states:

Where a spouse, without the prior consent in writing of the other spouse, purports to convey any interest in the family home to any person except the other spouse, then, subject to [subsections (2), (3) and (8)] and section 4, the purported conveyance shall be void

The family home in farming situations is unique, due to the fact that it is usually in close proximity to the farmyard and lands. The farmer, also due to the nature of farming, needs to be located near the farm, as his or her presence can be required on the farm at a moment's notice. Where a spouse is departing the family home because it is not reasonable or practical to remain, the court will usually award an amount to be given to provide alternative accommodation, provided that the remaining spouse has sufficient assets and income to provide this lump sum.

The court can make a number of property adjustment orders and sale orders in relation to the family home, as per s 9 and s 15 of the 1995 Act and s 14 and s 19 of the 1996 Act, such as:

1. Transfer of the family home, which is in the name of one spouse, to the non-owning spouse;
2. Extinguishment or removal of the interest of a spouse in the family home; or
3. Sale of the family home.

The transfer of property can be made whether or not one spouse has made a financial contribution to the purchase of property.

## Case

In *C v C*,[29] the applicant husband had a strong claim to the family home that he had previously inherited. His wife had not contributed to the property, either directly or indirectly. The court took the view that the division of assets was not appropriate in this case, in circumstances where proper provision was still made for the wife by providing her with a new house and maintenance for the children and herself.

However, it should be noted that the facts of every case are different and there are no strict rules to determine how assets should be dealt with in these types of proceedings.

In the case of *C O'C v D O'C*,[30] Dunne J found that the needs of the family as a whole must be considered. The family home was the only property to retain

---

[29] *C v C* [2005] IEHC 276.
[30] *C O'C v D O'C* [2009] IEHC 248.

any realistic equity given the precarious nature of the husband's financial circumstances. The needs of the wife and the dependent children were most closely met by transferring the entire interest in the family home to the wife.

## The Family Farm

The family farm is unique, and it differs from most other businesses for a number of reasons. Farms are often inherited and sometimes the ownership can be shared with parents or siblings. Farming is primarily a way of life, rather than merely a business. The value of farmland is usually very substantial compared to the income generated from it. Dividing the farm is rarely an option unless the holding is significant. A smaller holding will not usually be viable and capable of providing an income. Attention must be given to the seasonal nature of farming and the fact that EU farm subsidies form a significant portion of many farm incomes.

The court has power to make a number of property adjustment orders and sale orders in relation to the family farm as per s 9 and s 15 of the 1995 Act and s 14 and s 19 of the 1996 Act, some of which are as follows:

1. Transfer of the family farm, which is in one spouse's name, to the non-owning spouse;
2. Extinguishment or removal of a spouse's interest in the family farm; or
3. Sale of the family farm.

A spouse can often claim to have contributed in some way to the value of land. This contribution could be financial or physical. If the court is satisfied that the claim is valid, it can make a property adjustment order in relation to the farm. Even if a spouse has not contributed to the running of a farm or to the acquisition of lands, property adjustment orders can still be made by the court.

In reality, a divorce does not automatically mean that the spouse is entitled to half the farm; the court must ensure that proper provision is made for both parties and children. Some options that may be available to ensure that proper provision is made, would be giving a spouse a lump sum payment and/or the family home, giving a spouse an investment property or giving a spouse pension funds, shares, or a site.

In order to achieve "proper provision" for a spouse and children, the only option may be that the lands are sold in order to raise capital for the purchase of an alternative home. In the current climate, where finance is extremely difficult to secure due to the tightening of credit facilities, a farmer may not be in a position to raise the requisite finance, and the next step may, unfortunately, be an order for sale of a portion of the land or, in certain circumstances, the entire land holding.

However, courts are generally reluctant to force a sale of the farm unless there are no other assets, especially if the farm is viable. Where there are children involved, the courts will, at all times, ensure that the best interest of the children is the basis on which the decision is made.

In practical terms, it is very important to be in a position to give the court options. This means that preliminary work must be done by anyone wishing to hold on to a farm, or a large portion thereof. Enquiries should be made to see whether or not a mortgage can be raised. Alternatively, enquiries should be made as to whether a portion of the lands can be sold without affecting the operation of the farm to an excessive extent. Enquiries can also be made of the planning authorities to determine whether planning permission would be granted for building sites. The more work that is done by the parties in advance of the court hearing, the greater the number of options available to the court. Where the parties arrive expecting the court to solve the problem, it is more likely that there will be an order for sale of a portion of the lands, as this tends to be regarded by the courts as a fall-back position.

## What Constitutes "Proper Provision"?

The term "proper provision" has been considered by the courts since the enactment of family law legislation.

The term "proper provision" was examined in the case of *YG v NG*.[31] Here, the parties had already judicially separated and orders had been made. The applicant returned to the court at the time of divorce, seeking further redistribution of assets in her favour. In that case, the Supreme Court held that the term "proper provision" does not mean that there has to be a provision of assets or a redistribution of wealth, as such. Rather, the court conducts a judicial exercise, examining the family circumstances

---

[31] *YG v NG* [2011] 3 IR 717.

as a whole, and decides, based on factors set down in the 1989 Act and the 1996 Act, what constitutes proper provision. Factors such as earning capacity, income, property and the financial resources of each of the parties, their ages, their dependents and obligations, their standard of living, their lifestyle arrangements prior to separation, the contribution made by each party toward the marriage, their accommodation needs going forward, and such like considerations must be taken into account by the court in order to determine what is proper provision in each case. From a practical point of view, this means that both spouses will not necessarily walk away with equal assets or income. It depends on how the assets were acquired, how long the parties were married, what each brought to the marriage and what responsibilities and dependents each of them has going forward, and whether or not that would be a fair result.

## Earning Capacity of Spouses

One factor that is taken into account when deciding on "proper provision" is the earning capacity of both spouses. While the court will have regard to the economic climate where it affects a woman's re-entry into the workplace, they will also have regard to the same climate in respect of a man's ability to provide an income in the long term.

In the case of *H v D*,[32] Irvine J stated:

> It is undoubtedly the case that the respondent is now very well qualified. However, she has had practically no work experience over the past ten years, and again, having regard to the economic climate, I cannot assume that she could walk into a job tomorrow even if she decided it was feasible as a single parent. Further, any such employment would generate significant childcare costs on a daily basis with even greater costs whilst the children are on holiday from school.[33]

The option to pay maintenance for a number of years to enable the wife to return to work, having regard to the ages of the children, might have been a worthy proposal in the circumstances. Neither spouse can take the view that there is no need for them to return to work regardless of previous circumstances. Clearly, the older a woman is, the longer she is out of the

---

[32] *H v D* [2011] IEHC 233.
[33] ibid.

workforce and the longer the marriage, the less likely that the courts will anticipate a return to work.

## Change in Circumstances

Another factor to be considered by courts in determining what constitutes "proper provision" is a change in circumstances since the making of an earlier order. In the case of *NF v EF*,[34] Abbott J ordered a property to be sold in divorce proceedings, notwithstanding the presence of a full and final clause in a previous settlement, on the basis that the wife had acquired Parkinson's disease. A significant change in property values may also be considered by courts to be a change in circumstances.

## Inherited Assets

The legislation does not specifically deal with the issue of how an inheritance should be treated. However, it does allow a judge to take inherited assets into account in determining proper provision for both spouses following a separation, and a judge has enormous discretion in this regard.

The leading Irish case in this area is the case of *C v C*.[35] The main asset here was a landed estate which had been inherited by the husband, and which had been in his family for generations. The gross value of the assets was over €30 million and the wife sought to have the manor house transferred to her. The court refused to transfer the house to the wife, finding:

> The Applicant (husband) has a strong claim to the house. Firstly he is the sole owner. Secondly he has family connections with it for a very long time. Thirdly the Respondent (wife) did not contribute either directly or indirectly to its acquisition as the house was inherited.[36]

The husband in this case had an after tax income of €750,000 and the judge awarded the wife a lump sum of €3.3 million to purchase a family home for herself and the children, together with maintenance of €320,000 per annum for herself and the children. Therefore, in cases involving substantial assets, the court is unlikely to give a spouse a significant proportion of the inherited assets of the other spouse, particularly if the inheritance was quite recent.

---

[34] *NF v EF* [2011] 2 IR 100.
[35] [2005] IEHC 276
[36] ibid at 39.

In the case of YG v NG, the Supreme Court made a general observation regarding inherited assets and their relevance to cases before the courts, stating:

> Assets which are inherited will not be treated as assets obtained by both parties in a marriage. The distinction in the event of separation or divorce will all depend on circumstances. In one case, where a couple has worked a farm together, which the husband had inherited, the wife on separation sought 50%, however, the order given by a court was 75% to the husband and 25% to the wife. This is a precedent to illustrate an approach, but the circumstances of each case should be considered specifically.[37]

A court must take account of the judgment in *YG v NG*,[38] however, if there are insufficient assets to provide proper provision, the court is more likely to take inherited assets into account when deciding what is proper provision for each party.

## Nullity

Nullity of marriage is a declaration by a court that a supposed marriage is null and void, and that no valid marriage exists between the parties. In other words, it is a declaration that the apparent marriage never existed and the parties are single again.[39]

Nullity (or annulment) is not the same as divorce. Divorce is a declaration ending a valid marriage. Nullity is a declaration that a valid marriage never existed.[40]

A decree of nullity can only be made if one of the parties to the marriage applies to the court for an annulment. If the court decides that a marriage is voidable, it will then declare that the marriage was invalid from the start.[41]

---

[37] [2011] 3 IR 717, 732.

[38] [2011] 3 IR 717.

[39] Law Society of Ireland: A report by the Law Reform Committee 'Nullity of Marriage: The case for reform", p 42.

[40] ibid.

[41] ibid.

The court may grant nullity in situations such as the following:

- The couple were not capable of marrying each other, for example, one person was already married, with marriage being 'the union of one man and one woman to the exclusion of all others'[42];
- One party did not give a full, free and informed consent to the marriage[43];
- One of the parties is unable to perform the complete sexual act with the other party[44]; or
- There is an inability to form and sustain a normal marital relationship, for example, one party may be suffering with a personality disorder, unknown to the other person at the time of the marriage.[45]

## Case

In *ST (formerly J) v J*,[46] the defendant, who was biologically female, underwent a partial female-to-male sex change. Sometime later, the defendant entered into a relationship with the plaintiff, which culminated in a marriage ceremony. The plaintiff remained unaware of the defendant's gender at birth until, in the course of later divorce proceedings, the birth certificate of the defendant was submitted. The plaintiff applied for annulment and was successful.

In order to obtain an annulment of an alleged marriage, an application must be made to the Circuit Court or High Court.

## Pre-Nuptial Agreements

In a study conducted in 2015 by the Irish Examiner and ICMSA, it was revealed that 73% of Irish farmers were in favour of pre-nuptial agreements.[47] Figures from the Central Statistics Office, released in 2015, show that the average age of a groom is now 35 years, while the average age for brides is 33.[48] As the average age of parties entering into first

---

[42] Per Lord Penzance in *Hyde v Hyde* (1866) L.R. 1 P & D 130 at 133.

[43] *N (orse K.) v K* [1986] ILRM 75.

[44] *LC v BC*, Unreported, HC, 1 November 1985.

[45] *D v C* [1984] ILRM 173.

[46] *ST (formerly J) v J* [1998] 1 All ER 431.

[47] http://banda.ie/wp-content/uploads/Irish-Examiner-ICMSA.pdf, p 22.

[48] http://www.cso.ie/en/releasesandpublications/er/mcp/marriagesandcivilpartnerships 2015/.

time marriages continues to increase, people tend to have accumulated more wealth.

Nowadays, people have more assets of their own before they get married and, very often, they do not want to risk losing those assets if they end up getting divorced. In many cases, prior to getting married, one party will have taken over or inherited the family business or farm, that has been in the family for generations.

A pre-nuptial agreement is a formal agreement which may be drawn up between parties to a future marriage. It sets out how they would like to divide their assets in the event of a future divorce. The agreement can serve as a snapshot inventory of assets owned and debts owed by each spouse prior to their marriage. It can also contain an agreement to convey property between the parties or dictate that neither spouse will acquire an interest in the other's property.

Any asset, no matter how big or small, can be included in a pre-nuptial agreement, including savings, property, income, or even pensions, all of which could be split if a person gets divorced. Only financial and property matters can be dealt with within the agreement. It cannot be used to make arrangements for children.

The pre-nuptial agreement may state that the property owned by each party prior to marriage will remain theirs should the relationship end. It also sets out how property acquired during the relationship should be treated. A statement that neither party should have a financial claim on the other, should the relationship end, is also common.

While a pre-nuptial agreement is not, at present, recognised under Irish law, this does not mean that it is a pointless exercise to enter into such an agreement. Each case, of course, will depend on the individual facts and circumstances. In a divorce situation if there is a properly drafted pre-nuptial agreement in place, the court will often take it into consideration in deciding how the marital assets should be divided. There is nothing to prevent the court taking a well drafted pre-nuptial agreement into account in the event of a divorce.

In the UK case of *Radmacher v Granatino*,[49] the court outlined factors to be taken into consideration in determining the appropriate weight to be given to a pre-nuptial agreement. The court listed five factors:

- The period of time parties lived together;
- The financial contribution of each party;
- The dependency of the spouse;
- The contribution of work of either party in the home; and
- Whether or not there are any children from the marriage.

An Irish court is also likely to take these considerations into account before recognising an agreement.

A couple contemplating a pre-nuptial agreement should discuss it in detail at least six months in advance of the anticipated wedding. It is critical that each party receives independent legal advice in order to avoid either party claiming that they were misled, did not understand, or were not fully informed, when signing. It is also essential that both parties provide each other with full and fair disclosure of their financial circumstances, including all debts. Both parties must enter into the agreement under their own free will.

It is also important that both parties have adequate time to read, review, and contemplate the agreement prior to signature. It is essential to review the agreement periodically, especially after children have been born.

## Co-Habitant Rights on Relationship Breakdown

The Civil Partnership and Certain Rights and Obligations of Cohabitants Act 2010 (hereafter 'the 2010 Act') provides for the rights and duties of cohabiting couples, whether same sex or opposite sex.

Cohabitants are defined in s 172(1) of the 2010 Act as

> "one of 2 adults (whether of the same or the opposite sex) who live together as a couple in an intimate and committed relationship and who are not related to each other within the prohibited degrees of relationship or married to each other or civil partners of each other".

---

[49] *Radmacher v Granatino* [2010] UKSC 42.

Co-habitants can range from young couples living together, to older couples, where one or both may be separated or divorced and do not wish to or are unable to enter into marriage.

Section 172(5) of the 2010 Act confirms that a cohabiting couple must have lived together in an intimate and committed relationship for five years, or two years if the parties have children together, and the person applying to the court must be financially dependent on the other person.[50]

Section 173 of the 2010 Act allows qualified cohabitants, in the event of a relationship ending, to apply to the courts for various financial reliefs, such as:

- Property adjustment orders[51];
- Compensatory maintenance orders—both periodical payments and lump sum payments[52];
- Pension adjustment orders[53]; or
- Application for provision from the estate of a deceased cohabitant.[54]

The court may make redress orders if it is satisfied that one party is financially dependent on the other, and that such dependency arose because of the relationship or the ending of the relationship. Section 173 of the 2010 Act states that the court must consider a range of factors, including:

- The financial circumstances, needs and obligations of each qualified cohabitant;
- The rights and entitlements of any spouse, civil partner or former spouse or civil partner;
- The rights and entitlements of any dependent child or any child of a previous relationship of either cohabitant;
- The duration of the relationship, the basis on which the parties entered the relationship and the degree of commitment of the parties to one another;

---

[50] Civil Partnership and Certain Rights and Obligations of Cohabitants Act 2010, s 173(2).
[51] Civil Partnership and Certain Rights and Obligations of Cohabitants Act 2010, s 174.
[52] Civil Partnership and Certain Rights and Obligations of Cohabitants Act 2010, s 175.
[53] Civil Partnership and Certain Rights and Obligations of Cohabitants Act 2010, s 187.
[54] Civil Partnership and Certain Rights and Obligations of Cohabitants Act 2010, s 194.

- Any contributions made by either cohabitant to the relationship, whether financial or otherwise;
- The effect on the earning capacity of each of the cohabitants of the relationship;
- Any mental or physical disability; and
- The conduct of each of the cohabitants, if it would be unjust to disregard such conduct.

Cohabiting couples do not have automatic rights; the court will decide each case based on its own circumstances and merits. A cohabitant must first prove "financial dependence" on the other cohabitant, either during the relationship or as a result of its ending. The courts will not make financial orders in favour of a financially independent cohabitant.

## Case

A High Court decision by Baker J, in the case of *DC v DR*,[55] is likely to provide some clarity to cohabitants in deciding whether or not to bring claims before the court, in particular, the rights of a cohabitant in applying for financial provision from the estate of their deceased cohabitant.[56]

In that case, the plaintiff, the surviving cohabitant, claimed to be in an intimate cohabiting relationship with the deceased, who died intestate (i.e she did not leave a valid will). He had been in a previous marriage, which was annulled, and he had no children. The deceased never married and had no children. The plaintiff sought provision from the estate of the deceased upon her death. The defendant was a brother of the deceased. The plaintiff was 64 years of age. The deceased was 69 years of age when she died. They met in 1994. They became intimate in 1995, and entered into a committed relationship soon after the deceased's mother passed away. The deceased inherited land which was sold in 2005 and she received €3.1 million. For approximately 8 years from that point, he lived with the deceased a few nights a week at her home. In 2004, he moved in with the deceased and lived with the deceased until she passed away. Evidence was given by the plaintiff that they shared common interests, shared a double bed, ate their meals together and attended 40 weddings together. The deceased was

---

[55] *DC v DR* [2015] IEHC 309.

[56] Civil Partnership and Certain Rights and Obligations of Cohabitants Act 2010, s 194(1).

diagnosed with cancer. The surviving cohabitant looked after her throughout her illness.

The claimant had to prove that he had lived together with his cohabitant in an "intimate and committed relationship".[57] The court took into account the criteria set out in s 172(2) of the 2010 Act which sets out factors such as the duration of the relationship, the degree of financial dependence if one of the adults cared for and supported the children of the other and the basis on which the couple lived together.

This involved a number of interconnected elements such as the degree of shared activities that persons enjoy, such as shared meals, especially evening meals and breakfast, shared activities, shared division of household chores and shared holidays. Baker J held that, although the couple were not financially dependent for the basics of life, the plaintiff clearly had a degree of financial dependence on his deceased cohabitant.

The court went on to say that:

> Inherited property, and property and financial resources acquired before the relationship commenced and independently of any direct or indirect contribution from the other, must in my view be treated as somewhat different from property acquired in the course of a cohabiting relationship, whether that property was acquired in joint names or in the sole name of either of the parties to that relationship.[58]

The court, however, emphasised also that inherited assets were not automatically excluded from the application for redress under the 2010 Act.

The judge took into account what the plaintiff might have obtained if they had been married or in a civil partnership and the other cohabitant had died without making a will, and the extent to which any claim or any amount which the plaintiff would receive would displace the interest of any other beneficiary.

The court also took into account that the plaintiff did not have sufficient financial resources for his own needs and that there were no other persons

---

[57] Civil Partnership and Certain Rights and Obligations of Cohabitants Act 2010, s 172(1).
[58] *DC v DR* [2015] IEHC 309, para. 118.

in respect of whom the deceased had any obligations to provide financially. The plaintiff did have a small farm, which did not have residential accommodation.

The court ordered that the surviving cohabitant be granted provision of approximately 45% of the deceased cohabitant's share. This case demonstrates the degree to which a plaintiff, in bringing these types of claims, must prove, a number of factors to the court, including that there was an intimate and committed relationship, that the parties enjoyed activities together, that they presented as a couple and that there was some financial dependency between the parties.

Some couples have decided to opt out of the 2010 Act by entering into a cohabitation agreement, which sets out, in advance, how they intend to deal with their financial affairs, should the relationship fail. Co-habitation agreements are similar to pre-nuptial agreements for married couples. Both parties should receive independent legal advice prior to signing.

## Tax Issues on Marital Breakdown

Each of the taxes mentioned below are principally governed by the Capital Acquisitions Tax Consolidation Act (CATCA) 2003, Taxes Consolidation Act 1997, and Stamp Duties Consolidation Act 1999, as updated to the Finance Act 2015.

It should be noted that this section outlines the basic principles and effects on tax in the context of a separation and/or divorce, and it is very important to seek advice in relation to one's particular set of circumstances at the earliest possible point in time.

### Income Tax[59]

A married couple is, by default, taxed under joint assessment, where both incomes are jointly assessed for income taxes.[60] A married couple[61] or civil partners[62] can, where a relevant election is made, opt for separate

---

[59] Taxes Consolidation Act 1997, Part 44 Chapter 1.
[60] Taxes Consolidation Act 1997, s 1018(4)(a).
[61] Taxes Consolidation Act 1997, s 1023.
[62] Taxes Consolidation Act 1997, s 1031H.

assessment or separate treatment. Separate assessment involves the Revenue Commissioners raising assessments on each spouse or civil partner. However, unused tax bands and unused tax credits can still be shared between spouses or civil partners,[63] and, as such, the tax outcome with separate assessment mirrors that achieved by joint assessment. Separate treatment involves totally individualised assessments, with no sharing of tax bands or tax credits[64]. A couple is considered separated for tax purposes if the separation is likely to be permanent or it has been made legal.[65] At this point, it is important to explain the concept of an "assessable spouse". A married couples' or civil partners'[66] income is, as mentioned previously, by default, taxed jointly, but the Revenue Commissioners must issue an assessment addressed to one individual. On a practical basis, this allows the Revenue Commissioners to hold one of the persons responsible for the return and payment of taxes. The Revenue Commissioners would have huge difficulty in pursuing the payment of taxation where neither spouse took responsibility for their tax return and payment of taxes. To overcome this obstacle, tax legislation dictates that, by default, a husband is the "assessable spouse/civil partner", allowing the Revenue Commissioners to hold this individual responsible for the filing of tax returns and the payment of taxes.[67] However, a couple can jointly elect to nominate the wife as the assessable spouse.[68] This can also arise where the wife has higher income than her husband and no election is made to the Revenue Commissioners, or where a wife is self-employed pre-marriage, while the husband remains a PAYE worker. A married couple/civil partners will therefore have one assessable spouse/civil partner and one non-assessable spouse/civil partner.

In the year of permanent separation, the assessable spouse/civil partner is taxed on his or her own income for the entire year, and the income of his or her spouse/civil partner up until the date of separation.[69] The assessable

---

[63] Taxes Consolidation Act 1997, s 1023(2).

[64] Taxes Consolidation Act 1997, s 1023 and s 1031H.

[65] Taxes Consolidation Act 1997, s 1015(2)(a) and (b).

[66] Finance (No 3) Act 2011 applies the same tax treatment to civil partners as to married couples.

[67] Taxes Consolidation Act 1997, s 1018(4).

[68] Taxes Consolidation Act 1997, s 1018(1).

[69] Irish Tax Institute Irish Tax Series 2014/2015, Chapter 25, p 527 25.6.1.

spouse/civil partner benefits from the standard tax band and tax credits available to a married couple/civil partnership.[70] Meanwhile the non-assessable spouse/civil partner is taxed as a single person based on his or her income from the date of separation to the end of the tax year.[71] Based on these particular rules, the tax outcome for a couple in the year of separation can actually work out more favourably than for a couple who remain married for the entire year. In the case of a couple who had previously opted for separate treatment, both individuals are assessed individually in the year of separation, as would have been the case had they remained married.

### Taxation Following Separation

Following the year of separation, each individual is responsible for filing their own tax return, where relevant. In the normal course of events, a separated spouse with no source of non-PAYE income and not registered for income tax will not be required to file a return.[72] On a practical basis, both spouses should contact the Revenue Commissioners to ensure that they have been made aware of the separation, to update correspondence addresses, and to ensure that each spouse is satisfied as regards his or her future tax filing obligations. Special rules allow separated or divorced couples to continue to elect to be assessed under joint assessment where legally enforceable maintenance payments are paid between the parties (see below).[73]

### Maintenance Payments

In the case of maintenance payments, a variety of circumstances can arise. First, maintenance payments, whether of a voluntary nature or of the legally enforceable kind, for the benefit of children, are ignored for tax purposes.[74] For voluntary maintenance payments or non-legally enforceable payments towards an estranged spouse, no income tax deduction for

---

[70] ibid.

[71] ibid.

[72] Taxes Consolidation Act 1997, s 959B(1).

[73] Taxes Consolidation Act 1997, s 1026 (spouses) and s 1031K (civil partners) inserted by s1(1) Finance (No 3) Act 2011.

[74] Taxes Consolidation Act 1997, s 1025(4) and s 1031J.

the payer is due.[75] The Revenue Commissioners will, by concession, grant the payer the benefit of the married tax credit (currently worth an extra €1,650 above the standard single person tax credit) only in the case where the voluntary payments are sufficient to wholly or mainly maintain the spouse.[76] The receiving spouse is not liable to income tax on such payments, and is taxed on his or her own other income under the standard provisions applicable to single persons.

## Legally Enforceable Maintenance Payments

Legally enforceable maintenance payments are made without deduction of tax. The spouse who makes the payments is entitled to a deduction from the income chargeable to tax and Universal Social Charge (USC) in respect of the maintenance payments made for the other spouse or former spouse's benefit,[77] but only where such payments are annual or periodical. The spouse who receives the maintenance is liable to tax on the payments as income.[78] Special rules allow separated or divorced couples to continue to elect to be assessed under joint assessment where legally enforceable maintenance payments are paid between the parties, both persons remain resident in the State, and neither party has remarried or entered into a civil partnership. In such cases, the spouse making the payments does not get a tax deduction for them and the spouse who receives the payments is not taxable on them.[79] On a practical basis, there may be an advantage to electing for joint assessment, particularly where one spouse has a relatively high income, with the other spouse having little or no income. In such circumstances, the couple can benefit from otherwise unused tax bands and unused married tax credits. In practice, it is almost unheard of for couples to make such an election. In any event, where one spouse has relatively high income with the other spouse having little or no income, the payment of the maintenance payments will generate a tax deduction for the payer.[80] It should be noted that parties to a separation or divorce should consider the proposed maintenance order from a tax perspective. Although there may be a high degree of animosity

---

[75] Irish Tax Institute Irish Tax Series 2014/2015 Chapter 25 25.6.3, p 530
[76] Taxes Consolidation Act 1997, s 461(a)(ii).
[77] Taxes Consolidation Act 1997, s 1025(3) and s 1031(J)(3).
[78] Taxes Consolidation Act 1997, sch D, Case IV.
[79] Taxes Consolidation Act 1997, s 1026 and s 103K.
[80] Taxes Consolidation Act 1997, s 461(a)(ii).

between spouses, it can be more tax efficient to structure a settlement as in the form of maintenance payments towards a spouse (as opposed to directed towards the children, which would not be tax deductible for the payer). In strict interpretation of the legislation, legally enforceable maintenance payments are only deductible where payments are either annual or periodical. As such, once-off lump sum payments would not be regarded as tax deductible.[81]

## Tax Credits Following Separation

An additional credit may be available to a separated or divorced parent. The single person child carer credit (SPCCC) is a tax credit that is available to a single person who is a parent of a child, or who has custody of and maintains a child who is living with him or her.[82] The credit is, by default, granted to the primary claimant being an individual with whom a qualifying child resides for the whole or greater part of the year. A qualifying child is a child:

- Who is born in the tax year; or
- Who is under 18 years of age at the start of the tax year; or
- Who is over 18 years of age at the start of the tax year but in receipt of full-time instruction; or
- Who is over 18 years of age at the start of the tax year but is permanently incapacitated and was incapacitated before the age of 21 years or, if the incapacity happened after age 21, it occurred while he or she was in receipt of full-time instruction.[83]

The primary claimant may give up his or her entitlement to the credit in favour of a secondary claimant provided that the child resides with that person for a period of not less than 100 days on aggregate in the year. The primary claimant can withdraw his or her entitlement to the credit.[84] On a practical basis, an individual who is a main stay-at-home carer for a child or children may have little taxable income and the sharing of the otherwise unused SPCCC can offer a significant tax boost for the other spouse. The SPCCC is currently worth €1,650 per annum, with only one

[81] Taxes Consolidation Act 1997, s 1025(2)(a).
[82] Taxes Consolidation Act 1997, s 462(2)(b).
[83] Revenue, 'Taxes Consolidation Act 1997 Notes for Guidance (Finance Act 2015 Edition)' (2015) Part 15, 7-8.
[84] Revenue, 'Taxes Consolidation Act 1997 Notes for Guidance (Finance Act 2015 Edition)' (2015) Part 15, 8.

such credit available regardless of the number of children.[85] Importantly, the credit is not available where the claimant cohabitates, remarries, or enters into a civil partnership.

## Capital Gains Tax (CGT)[86]

Capital Gains Tax (CGT) is a tax on the increase in value of assets, such as land and buildings, from the date on which the transferor acquired the assets to the date on which he or she disposes of them. The current tax rate is 33%.

Transfers of assets between spouses or civil partners are exempt from CGT. Similarly, transfers of assets between spouses or civil partners who are separated are exempt from CGT if they are made under a separation agreement or a court order.[87] Transfers of assets between spouses or civil partners on foot of a court order in a decree of divorce or dissolution are exempt from CGT,[88] but transfers of assets after the granting of the decree that are not ordered by the court are not. On a practical basis spouses who separate and who, for example, agree on an amicable basis to continue to own assets jointly for the future benefit of their children can arrive at difficult tax outcomes where a subsequent decision is made to divide the ownership of the assets amongst themselves. Similarly, complications can arise where one spouse benefits from retirement relief while the other spouse does not. The capacity to restructure tax affairs by transferring property into the sole name of one spouse before the ultimate transfer to a successor is no longer tax efficient in the case of separated or divorced spouses.

## Capital Acquisitions Tax (CAT)[89]

A married couple can transfer assets between each other entirely exempted from Capital Acquisitions Tax (CAT), otherwise known as gift tax.[90] Separation does not affect this exemption but divorce or dissolution does. Property transferred as a result of a court order also benefits from the

---

[85] Taxes Consolidation Act 1997, s 462(3).

[86] Taxes Consolidation Act 1997.

[87] Taxes Consolidation Act 1997, s 1030(2).

[88] Taxes Consolidation Act 1997, s 1031(2).

[89] Capital Acquisitions Tax Consolidation Act (CATCA) 2003.

[90] Capital Acquisitions Tax Consolidation Act (CATCA) 2003, s 70 (gifts) and s 71 (inheritances).

exemption from CAT,[91] but any transfers of assets not covered by a court order are treated as taxable transfers between strangers.

### Stamp Duty[92]

An exemption enables the transfer of property between spouses or civil partners to be free from stamp duty.[93] Similarly, transfers of property on foot of a court order between separated or divorced spouses[94] or civil partners are also exempted from stamp duty.[95] The transfer of assets after the granting of the decree that is not ordered by the court is not exempt from stamp duty.

Given the complexity of the taxation system, separating or divorcing parties should always seek independent specialist tax advice in relation to all potential taxation implications.

## Conclusion

Farmers, more so than any other business owners, rely heavily on land remaining intact so as to generate an income, whether it is dairy farming or crop farming. In contrast to other businesses, where an alternative business property can be sourced if required, farmers are dependent on the land to produce an income and alternative land is not as easily sourced due to the current high cost of agricultural land, and a lack of property available adjacent to existing enterprises.

Farmers are therefore understandably fearful of the prospect of a divorce in the family. Whilst it is no doubt a very difficult and traumatic time in a farmer's life, remaining on amicable terms with his or her spouse, communicating clearly and respectfully, and being practical, and realistic, will ensure that the process runs smoother than he or she may have initially envisaged. It is a highly specialised area of family law and it is important to seek specialist legal advice at the outset.

---

[91] Capital Acquisitions Tax Consolidation Act (CATCA) 2003, s 88.
[92] Stamp Duties Consolidation Act 1999.
[93] Stamp Duties Consolidation Act 1999, s 96.
[94] Stamp Duties Consolidation Act 1999, s 97.
[95] Stamp Duties Consolidation Act 1999, s 97(A).

# CHAPTER TWELVE

# Planning Law

The planning system in Ireland is administered by local planning authorities in each county, with some larger counties, including Dublin and Cork, having more than one such authority. All appeals, regardless of which authority granted or refused the original application, are dealt with by An Bord Pleanála, based in Dublin. Planning permission is required for any "development", as defined in the various Planning Acts, and in regulations made under those Acts. The Planning Acts and Regulations also contain a comprehensive list of "exempted developments", which are developments that do not require planning permission.

This chapter provides an overview of planning law in Ireland, with specific reference to its relevance to, and impact upon, the agricultural sector. It discusses the concepts of development, unauthorised development, and exempted development, under the law as it currently stands. It goes on to deal with the regularising of an unauthorised development by means of an application for retention permission. This chapter explores some common breaches of planning law, which may lead to prosecution, as well as possible defences to prosecution, and the penalties which can be imposed. It also deals with enforcement notices issued by a planning authority. This chapter outlines the process of appealing a planning decision to An Bord Pleanála, and of judicial review of a planning decision in the High Court.

The Planning and Development Act 2000 (hereafter 'the 2000 Act') was introduced for the purpose of modifying existing planning law and consolidating it into a single Act. The 2000 Act is the main statute dealing with planning and development law in this country.

## Development

The main objective of the 2000 Act is to ensure that there is a proper level of control over all development. A substantial proportion of the material in this chapter is devoted to the concept of what amounts to "development" under the 2000 Act, which is of primary importance in planning law. There is also an emphasis on the exemptions from planning permission, as these may provide significant advantages to farmers and other landowners.

Part III of the 2000 Act deals with the control of development and the making of planning applications. Section 3(1) of the 2000 Act defines "*development*" as "except, where the context otherwise requires, the carrying out of any works on, in, over or under land or the making of any material change in the use of any structures or other lands".

Clearly, this is a very wide definition and, broadly speaking, there are two categories of development. First, the "carrying out of any works", with "*works*" defined in s 2 of the 2000 Act, as

> ...any act or operation of construction, excavation, demolition, extension, alteration, repair or renewal, and, in relation to a protected structure or proposed protected structure, includes any act or operation involving the application or removal of plaster, paint, wallpaper, tiles or other material to or from the surfaces of the interior or exterior of a structure.

The second category of development is the making of a material change in use of land. In *Westmeath County Council v Quirke & Sons*,[1] Budd J held that:

> Many alterations in the activities carried out on land constitute a change of use; however, not all alterations will be material. Whether such changes amount to a material change in use is a question of fact.... Consideration of the materiality of a change in use means assessing not only the use itself, but also its effects.

The change of the use to the lands has to be material to amount to development, and a change of use that is merely a very minor change will not amount to development.

## Carrying Out an Unauthorised Development

"*Unauthorised development*" is the carrying out of unauthorised works, such as the construction, erection, or making of any unauthorised structure. A typical example would be the construction of a large shed or extension without

---

[1] *Westmeath County Council v Quirke & Sons* (unreported, 23 May 1996) HC (Budd J).

planning permission. Furthermore, the definition of unauthorised development also includes any unauthorised use of lands, such as quarrying.[2]

An interesting case, in the context of carrying out an unauthorised development, is that of *Wicklow County Council v Kinsella and Anor*.[3] Here, Wicklow County Council applied to the High Court under the 2000 Act for an order to compel the first respondent to remove an unauthorised development in the form of a chalet, which was the family home of the respondent. The decision in this case marks a departure from a previous High Court decision,[4] which had taken the view that the inviolability of the dwelling operated as a factor in its own right, so as to preclude the demolition of an unauthorised development.[5]

Kearns P, in the *Wicklow County Council* case, considered the underlying basis for planning laws in Ireland, stating:

> I believe in this case one must commence by considering why we have planning laws and why they must be enforced. In one sense the reason is obvious: without effective planning laws and adequate enforcement procedures to ensure compliance with them, anarchy would rule the roost with regard to all sorts of developments. Dangerous, unsuitable and haphazard developments would be likely, some of which might be constructed or established in locations where a single citizen could inconvenience neighbours, destroy areas of natural beauty, disrupt traffic and even undermine the capacity of the community to engage in normal social function and activities. In short, there would be nothing to stop a 'free for all' development culture from running riot. Take an extreme example: might an individual create a structure overnight outside the GPO, bring in sleeping and cooking facilities, and claim thereafter that he is immune from removal as his 'dwelling' is 'inviolable' under Article 40.5 of the Constitution? I offer this example merely to highlight the levels of absurdity that may arise when the property rights of the individual, even when acting unlawfully, are seen in every instance to trump those of a democratic society which can only function when its constituent members are equally bound by rules which regulate matters such as planning and development.

---

[2] Planning and Development Act 2000, s 2.
[3] *Wicklow County Council v Kinsella and Anor* [2015] IEHC 229.
[4] *Wicklow County Council v Fortune* [2012] IEHC 406.
[5] *Council of Wicklow v Fortune* [2012] IEHC 406 , 12 Paragraph 41.

A person can be prosecuted in the District Court for carrying out an unauthorised development and, if convicted, may be liable to a fine not exceeding €5,000 or, at the discretion of the court, to imprisonment for a term not exceeding six months, or both.[6] If prosecuted and convicted in the Circuit Court, a person may be liable to imprisonment for up to two years and/or a fine of €12,697,380.78.[7]

## Exempted Development

The 2000 Act provides for developments that are exempt from planning permission. Essentially, exempted development involves minor or immaterial works which do not require planning permission. The following is not an exhaustive list of activities exempted under s 4 of the 2000 Act, but rather it notes some of the exemptions that are relevant to the agricultural sector, such as:

(a) use of land and any building occupied for agriculture[8];

(b) the carrying out of works for the maintenance, improvement or alteration of any structure, which affect only the interior of the structure or do not materially affect the external appearance of the structure[9];

(c) the thinning, felling or replanting of trees, forests or woodlands, except for the replacement of broadleaf high forest by conifer[10];

(d) the construction, maintenance or improvement of a non-public road or works ancillary to that development, where the road serves forests and woodlands[11];

(e) use of any structure or land within the curtilage of a house for any purpose incidental to the enjoyment of the house[12]; or

(f) development consisting of the carrying out of any of the works referred to in the Land Reclamation Act 1949, such as field drainage, but not including the fencing or enclosure of land which has been open to, or used by, the public within the ten years preceding the date on which the works are commenced, or works consisting of land reclamation or reclamation of estuarine marsh land and of callows.[13]

---

[6] Planning and Development Act 2000, s 156(1)(b) as amended by s 46(a) of the Planning and Development (Amendment) Act 2000.

[7] Planning and Development Act 2000, s 156(1)(a).

[8] Planning and Development Act 2000, s 4(1)(a).

[9] Planning and Development Act 2000, s 4(1)(h).

[10] Planning and Development Act 2000, s 4(1)(i).

[11] Planning and Development Act 2000, s 4(1)(i).

[12] Planning and Development Act 2000, s 4(1)(j).

[13] Planning and Development Act 2000, s 4(1)(l).

## Agricultural Developments

Section 4(1)(a) of the 2000 Act defines *"agricultural development"* as "development consisting of the use of any land for the purposes of agriculture and development consisting of the use for that purpose of any building occupied together with land so used".

Section 2 of the 2000 Act defines the term *"agriculture"* as including

> ... horticulture, fruit growing, seed growing, dairy farming, the breeding and keeping of livestock (including any creature kept for the production of food, wool, skins or fur, or for the purposes of its use in the farming of land), the training of horses and the rearing of bloodstock, use of land as grazing land, meadow land, osier land, market gardens and nursery grounds ...

It is important to understand the implications of exempted development and how they apply to agricultural developments. The use of land for agriculture is exempted, but not the carrying out of works for those purposes. This view was confirmed in the recent High Court decision of *Cunningham v An Bord Pleanála*.[14] In this case, the applicant farmer erected a tractor shed and the question arose as to whether this development constituted an exempted development. Hogan J, in that case, confirmed that this exemption applies only to development (in the more limited sense of that term) that consists of the *use* of a structure for agricultural purposes. It does not apply to the *construction* of such a structure.

## Planning and Development Regulations 2001

The Planning and Development Regulations 2001 (hereafter the '2001 Regulations'), as amended, as well as Schedules 1 and 2 thereto, provide for exempted development.[15] The scope of the regulations provides for exemption where a development involves minor or immaterial works which do not necessitate planning permission.

---

[14] *Cunningham v An Bord Pleanála* [2013] IEHC 234.
[15] For an exhaustive list, see the Planning and Development Regulations 2001, SI No 600 of 2001, sch 2, pt 3.

The exemptions relating to agricultural works are contained in the 2001 Regulations and, more specifically, in part 3 of Schedule 2. The following is a summary of the activities exempted in rural areas[16];

(a) temporary use of land for any tent, campervan or caravan, or for the mooring of any boat, barge or other vessel used for the purpose of camping, subject to conditions and limitations;

(b) temporary use of land for any scout camp not exceeding 30 days in any year;

(c) construction or maintenance of any gully, drain, pond, trough, pit or culvert, the widening or deepening of watercourses, the removal of obstructions from any watercourse and the making or repairing of embankments in connection with any of the foregoing works;

(d) the construction, erection or maintenance of any fence that does not exceed 2 metres in height or, in the case of deer farming, not exceed 3 metres;

(e) roofed structure for the housing of cattle, sheep, goats, donkeys, horses, deer or rabbits, having a gross floor space not exceeding 200 square metres and it must be for agricultural purposes only;

(f) roofed structure for the housing of pigs, mink or poultry, having a gross floor space not exceeding 75 square metres;

(g) roofless cubicles, open loose yards, self-feed silo or silage areas, feeding aprons, assembly yards, milking parlours or structures for the making or storage of silage or any other structures of a similar character or description, having an aggregate gross floor space not exceeding 200 square metres;

(h) provision of any store, barn, shed, glass-house or other structure not exceeding 300 metres gross floor space;

(i) development consisting of the carrying out of drainage and/or reclamation of wetlands;

A number of restrictions are imposed by the 2001 Regulations[17] and, where there is a contravention, then the relevant exemption can be de-exempted if it would, inter alia:

(a) contravene a condition or any specified use of planning permission;

(b) present a traffic hazard to road users;

---

[16] For an exhaustive list of limitations and conditions attached to each class of exemption, see the Planning and Development Regulations 2001, SI No 600 of 2001.

[17] Arts 6 and 9 of the Planning and Development Regulations 2001, as amended, provide a list of the restrictions on the exempted development provisions in regulations. For proper analysis, one should consider consulting a specialist text in the area of planning law.

(c) comprise the construction, erection, extension or renewal of a building on any street so as to bring forward any part of the building beyond the front wall of the building on either side or beyond the building line as determined in the development plan or draft variation or draft development plan for the area;

(d) interfere with the character of the landscape or a view or prospect of special amenity value or special interest;

(e) consist of or comprise the extension, alteration, repair or renewal of an unauthorised structure, or a structure the use of which is unauthorised;

(f) consist of the demolition or alteration of a building or structure which would preclude or restrict the continuance of an existing use of a building or structure where it is an objective of the planning authority to ensure that the building or structure would remain available for use; or

(g) obstruct a public right of way.

## Regularising an Unauthorised Development

There are limited circumstances in which it is possible to bring an unauthorised development within the planning laws and have it regularised retrospectively. This can be done by applying to the planning authority for retention permission.[18] However, it should be pointed out that the planning authority will refuse to accept an application for retention permission in any development that would require:

- Environmental Impact Assessment (EIA)[19];
- A determination as to whether EIA was required (i.e. screening for EIA)[20]; or
- An appropriate assessment under the Habitats Directive (since such an assessment is also required prior to permission for a proposed development).[21]

It is also important to note that the lodging of an application for planning retention for a development that is already the subject of enforcement action, does not diminish any offence committed.

---

[18] Planning and Development Act 2000, s 31(1)(b).

[19] This is the process by which the anticipated effects on the environment of a proposed development or project are measured. For further information, see <www.epa.ie/monitoringassessment/assessment/eia>.

[20] ibid.

[21] Directive 2011/92/EU.

## Summary Offences

The following is a list of the more common offences prosecuted in the District Court.

### Failure to Remove or Alter a Structure

The planning authority can serve a notice under s 46 of the 2000 Act, requiring a landowner to remove or alter a structure, or discontinue the use of the structure. This often arises where a landowner has failed to demolish an unauthorised building.

If a notice of this nature is served, any person who fails to comply with such a notice, can be prosecuted in the District Court and, if convicted, is liable to fine not exceeding €5,000 or, at the discretion of the court, to imprisonment for a term not exceeding six months, or both.[22]

### Damaging a Protected Structure

Where the owner or occupier of land has an interest in a protected structure, they must ensure that the protected structure is not endangered. Section 58(1) of the Planning and Development Act 2000 provides that:

> Each owner and each occupier shall, to the extent consistent with the rights and obligations arising out of their respective interests in a protected structure, or a proposed protected structure, ensure that the structure, or any element of it which contributes to its special architectural, historical, archaeological, artistic, cultural, scientific, social or technical interest, is not endangered.

A protected structure is a structure that a planning authority considers to be of special interest from an architectural, historical, archaeological, artistic, cultural, scientific, social or technical point of view. A structure must be listed on the planning authority's Record of Protected Structures (RPS) to qualify for protected status.[23] Essentially, this means that the structure must not be exposed to harm, decay or damage, whether immediately, or over a period of time, through neglect. However, this duty only arises after a person has been notified that the structure has been proposed for protection.

---

[22] Planning and Development Act 2000, s 156(4), as amended.
[23] Planning and Development Act 2000, s 51.

A person who actively damages a protected structure, or a proposed protected structure, is guilty of an offence punishable in the Circuit Court by up to two years' imprisonment and/or a fine of €12,697,380.78.[24] It should be noted that this indictable offence[25] can also be tried in the District Court and, upon summary conviction, that person shall be liable to a fine not exceeding €5,000 or to imprisonment for a term not exceeding six months, or both.[26]

## Failure to Prevent a Structure Becoming Endangered

Where a structure is likely to become endangered, a planning authority has the power to issue a notice which allows it to direct the specified remedial actions considered necessary to stop the structure becoming endangered. Section 59(1) of the 2000 Act states:

> Where, in the opinion of the planning authority, it is necessary to do so in order to prevent a protected structure situated within its functional area from becoming, or continuing to be, endangered, the authority shall serve on each person who is the owner or occupier of the protected structure a notice-
>
> (a) specifying the works which the planning authority considers necessary in order to prevent the protected structure from becoming or continuing to be endangered, and
>
> (b) requiring the person on whom the notice is being served to carry out those works within a specified period of not less than 8 weeks from the date the notice comes into effect under s 62.[27]

If a protected structure is endangered, the planning authority can serve a notice on the owner or occupier, requiring the carrying out of any work that it considers necessary to protect the structure. The work must be done within 8 weeks of the date of service of the notice. The planning authority can also serve a notice to require the 'restoration of character' of the protected structure. This may include removing, changing, or replacing any parts of the structure specified in the notice.

---

[24] Planning and Development Act 2000, s 156(1)(a).

[25] An indictable offence is an offence that can be tried by judge and jury.

[26] Planning and Development Act 2000, s 156(2)(b).

[27] Planning and Development Act 2000, s 62, states that notice shall not have effect until 4 weeks from the date of service of such notice. This is subject to exceptions.

An owner or occupier can make written representations to the planning authority in relation to the terms of the notice. He or she may request more time or financial help in order to comply with the notice, and, in many cases, may be eligible for a conservation grant. The planning authority will take these representations into account when making its final decision. Owners and occupiers can, within two weeks of receipt of their last response from the planning authority, appeal to the District Court against the terms of the notice, if they are still not satisfied.[28]

If a person ignores a notice to prevent a structure from becoming endangered, the planning authority can take enforcement action. The planning authority can carry out the work itself and recover the cost of the work from the owner or the occupier.

The owner has four weeks from the date of service of the notice to make written representations to the planning authority. He or she may object to the remedial actions ordered by the planning authority, or may request necessary financial assistance to carry out the works.[29] If the planning authority decides to amend or vary the terms of the notice, the owner of the lands has the opportunity to appeal this to the District Court within two weeks.

Section 63 of the 2000 Act makes it an offence to fail to comply with a notice requiring works to be carried out on an endangered structure in accordance with the notice. If a notice of this nature is served on an individual, and he or she fails to comply with the notice, then they can be prosecuted in the District Court and, if convicted, may be liable to a fine not exceeding €5,000 or, at the discretion of the Court, to imprisonment for a term not exceeding six months or both.[30] If prosecuted in the Circuit Court and convicted, such person is liable to up to two years' imprisonment and/or a fine of €12,697,380.78.[31]

---

[28] Planning and Development Act 2000, s 62.
[29] Planning and Development Act 2000, s 59(3).
[30] Planning and Development Act 2000, s 156(1)(b).
[31] Planning and Development Act 2000, s 156(1)(a).

## Tree Preservation Order

It is sometimes common for a planning authority to issue orders protecting specified trees and forestry in the interests of amenity or the environment. Section 205 of the 2000 Act states:

(1) If it appears to the planning authority that it is expedient, in the interests of amenity or the environment, to make provision for the preservation of any tree, trees, group of trees or woodlands, it may, for that purpose and for stated reasons, make an order with respect to any such tree, trees, group of trees or woodlands as may be specified in the order.

(2) Without prejudice to the generality of subsection (1), an order under this section may—

(a) prohibit (subject to any conditions or exemptions for which provision may be made by the order) the cutting down, topping, lopping or wilful destruction of trees, and

(b) require the owner and occupier of the land affected by the order to enter into an agreement with the planning authority to ensure the proper management of any trees, group of trees or woodlands (including the replanting of trees), subject to the planning authority providing assistance, including financial assistance, towards such management as may be agreed.

These orders may include provisions preventing the cutting down, topping, lopping or wilful destruction of a tree or trees.[32] The breach of a preservation order is an offence punishable by a fine not exceeding €12,697,380.78 and/or up to two years' imprisonment on indictment,[33] or a maximum fine of €1,905.61 and/or up to six months' imprisonment on conviction in the District Court.[34]

It should be pointed out that a tree preservation order does not prevent the cutting down, topping or lopping of a tree in the following circumstances:

---

[32] A similar provision is available under the Forestry Act 2014, s 20, and it permits the imposition of preservation orders on any tree or trees, including exempted trees that are to be felled or otherwise removed. If an order is breached, a court can impose a class A fine or 6 months' imprisonment.

[33] Planning and Development Act 2000, s 156(1)(b).

[34] Planning and Development Act 2000, s 156(1)(a).

(i)   Where the tree is dead or dying;

(ii)  Where the tree has become dangerous;

(iii) Where it is necessary for the prevention or abatement of a nuisance or hazard; or

(iv)  Where it is in compliance with the provisions of any other enactment.[35]

In any event, it is important to understand that, in circumstances where there is no tree preservation order in place, this does not necessarily mean that a farmer can indiscriminately cut down trees. Under Irish law, a felling licence is required before a tree can be cut down.

### Felling Licences

Under Irish law, it is an offence to cut down a tree without a felling licence.[36] Section 17(6) of the Forestry Act 2014 states:

(6)   A person who—

(a) fells or otherwise removes one or more trees, or

(b) causes or permits one or more trees to be felled or otherwise removed,

without a licence, or in contravention of a condition of a licence, shall be guilty of an offence...

There are a number of exceptions to the rule, and s 19(1) of the 2014 Act stipulates that a felling licence is not necessary if the tree is, for example:

- in an urban area[37];
- within 30 metres of a building. Note that buildings built after the trees have been planted are excluded[38];
- less than 5 years of age and came about through natural regeneration and is removed from a field as part of the normal maintenance of agricultural land (but not where the tree is standing in a hedgerow)[39];

---

[35] Planning and Development Act 2000, s 205(11).

[36] For further information, see Department of Agriculture, Food and the Marine website, 'Felling' <www.agriculture.gov.ie/forestservice/treefelling/treefelling/>, Email <forestryinfo@agriculture.gov.ie>, or Telephone 1890 200 509 / 053 91 63400. For written enquiries, contact Felling Section, Forest Service, Department of Agriculture, Food and the Marine, Johnstown Castle, Wexford.

[37] Forestry Act 2014, s 19(1)(a).

[38] Forestry Act 2014, s 19(1)(b).

[39] Forestry Act 2014 , s 19(1)(h).

- uprooted in a nursery for the purpose of transplantation[40];
- outside of forest, if it is within 10 metres of a public road which, in the opinion of the owner (being an opinion formed on reasonable grounds) is dangerous to persons using the public road on account of its age or condition[41]; or
- the tree in question is an apple, pear, plum or damson species.[42]

## Penalty

Upon prosecution for unlicensed felling, on summary conviction, a person may be liable to a fine of €200 for every tree removed, or to imprisonment for up to six months, or both.[43] If convicted on indictment, the punishments are higher, with a maximum fine of €1 million or imprisonment for a term not exceeding five years, or both.[44]

# Commencement of a Prosecution

In most proceedings there is a time limitation within which proceedings must be initiated successfully. Most criminal offences prosecuted in the District Court must be initiated within 6 months of the date of the offence.

However, in the case of planning law, s 157 of the 2000 Act states that proceedings can be commenced within six months of the date on which there is evidence sufficient to justify the commencement of proceedings. Section 157 of the 2000 Act states:

(1) Subject to section 149, summary proceedings for an offence under this Act may be brought and prosecuted by a planning authority whether or not the offence is committed in the authority's functional area.

(2) Notwithstanding section 10(4) of the Petty Sessions (Ireland) Act, 1851, and subject to subsection (3) of this section, summary proceedings may be commenced—

    (a) at any time within 6 months from the date on which the offence was committed, or

    (b) at any time within 6 months from the date on which evidence sufficient, in the opinion of the person by whom the proceedings are

---

[40] Forestry Act 2014, s 19(1)(i).

[41] Forestry Act 2014, s 19(1)(m)(i).

[42] Forestry Act 2014, s 19(1)(o).

[43] Forestry Act 2014, s 17(6)(b)(i).

[44] Forestry Act 2014, s 17(6)(b)(ii).

initiated, to justify proceedings comes to that person's knowledge, whichever is the later.

(3) For the purposes of this section, a certificate signed by or on behalf of the person initiating the proceedings as to the date or dates on which evidence described in subsection (2)(b) came to his or her knowledge shall be evidence of the date or dates and in any legal proceedings a document purporting to be a certificate under this section and to be so signed shall be deemed to be so signed and shall be admitted as evidence without proof of the signature of the person purporting to sign the certificate, unless the contrary is shown.

Therefore, once the planning authority has become aware of circumstances justifying a prosecution arising out of a breach of the legislation, time starts running from the date of receipt of the relevant information.

## Enforcement Proceedings

Under the legislation, the planning authority is authorised to enforce planning control in circumstances where infringements arise. If it is reported that an individual is in breach of planning control legislation, the planning authority shall issue a warning letter to the owner or the occupier of the land where the development is being carried out. Section 152(4) of the 2000 Act sets out what a warning letter must contain. The following is a summary of same:

(a) A reference to the affected land and a statement that unauthorised development has come to the attention of the planning authority;
(b) Information on the making of submissions to the planning authority in respect of the development in question;
(c) A warning that an enforcement notice may issue;
(d) A statement that the planning authority may exercise its powers to enter land and inspect the unauthorised development;
(e) An outline of potential penalties; and
(f) An explanation that the recipient may incur the cost of enforcement proceedings.

Where there has been a breach of planning laws, the planning authority does not have the power to issue an enforcement notice without first having issued a warning letter. Before serving an enforcement notice, it is important that the planning authority has allowed the party affected to make representations to it, and that these representations are considered along with the original representations which caused the warning letter to issue. It should be noted that s 155 of the 2000 Act does permit the issuance of an enforcement notice without a prior warning letter in cases where urgent action is warranted.

Once a decision has been made by the planning authority, the decision, together with the reasons in support of that decision, must be entered into the planning register.[45]

## Enforcement Notice

The enforcement notice is important, and the contents of same must be considered in accordance with the statutory requirements. According to s 154(5) of the 2000 Act, an enforcement notice should contain the following:

- In the case of an unauthorised development, a direction that it must cease;
- Where planning permission is not being complied with, that the person to whom it is addressed must fully comply with the permission in question;
- That certain steps are to be taken within a specified period, including the removal, demolition, or alteration of any structure; the discontinuance of any use of land or the restoration of the land to its previous state before the unauthorised development began;
- That where these steps are not taken within the period stated:
  (i) the person will be guilty of an offence and that the planning authority may enter the land and do the work itself, with the cost being recoverable from the person in default;
  (ii) that other costs involved in taking the enforcement action can be recovered by the planning authority, for example, investigation, employee and consultancy costs.

It is mandatory that the notice complies with the prescribed form, and failure to do so will render the notice invalid. The most important elements of the notice are that it must clearly identify the category of breach that is being alleged and that it specifies both the steps required to remedy the breach and the specified time period within which the steps must be taken.

---

[45] Planning and Development Act 2000, s 153(4).

In *Dundalk Town Council v Lawlor*,[46] the planning authority served an enforcement notice specifying that the defendant cease all excavation site clearance works and return the site to its previous condition. The enforcement notice required the defendant to take the steps to return the site to its previous condition "within a period of immediately commencing on the date of the service of this notice". The planning authority subsequently sought to prosecute the defendant in the District Court for an alleged failure to comply with the enforcement notice. The District Court stated two questions to the High Court for consideration:

1. Whether the enforcement notice properly specified a period within which steps were to be taken; and
2. Whether the enforcement notice properly specified the steps to be taken.

O'Neil J considered the case and took the view that the answer to each question should be "no". The High Court stipulated that the enforcement notice was invalid, as it did not describe clearly the actions required and the specified period within which those actions were to be carried out. The court took the view that the enforcement notice must, with clarity and precision, set out the steps to be taken in a specified period. In that case, the defendant had removed top soil and stripped off sod. It was not readily clear from the notice whether the notice required that the topsoil be restored and the sod be restored, or merely the topsoil be reseeded.

### Defending Enforcement Proceedings

Failure to comply with an enforcement notice within the specified time can result in a criminal prosecution and the imposition of a penalty. If proceedings are prosecuted in the District Court, a person is liable to fine not exceeding €5,000 on conviction, or to imprisonment for a term not exceeding six months, or both.[47] A conviction on indictment can result in a fine not exceeding €12,697,380.78.[48]

---

[46] *Dundalk Town Council v Lawlor* [2005] IEHC 73.

[47] Planning and Development Act 2000, s 156(1)(b).

[48] Planning and Development Act 2000, s 156(1)(a).

In order for the prosecution to succeed, they must prove a number of matters by giving evidence in relation to the following:

1. the issue of a warning letter[49,50];
2. the decision taken as to whether or not an enforcement notice would issue[51];
3. the service of enforcement notice[52]; and
4. the non-compliance with enforcement notice.[53]

These steps must be followed in order for the prosecution to succeed in obtaining an enforcement order in respect of an offence involving the construction of an unlawful structure. It goes without saying that every offence is different, and the proofs necessary to secure a successful prosecution will vary from one offence to another.

It is a defence to an enforcement notice to establish that a person took all reasonable steps to comply with such a notice. Section 161(7) of the 2000 Act provides, "where an enforcement notice has been served under s 154, it shall be a defence to a prosecution under s 151 or s 154 if the defendant proves that he or she took all reasonable steps to secure compliance with the enforcement notice".

It is important to bear in mind that there is no defence available in circumstances where a person has applied for, or has been granted, permission for the retention of an unauthorised development.[54] Section 162(2) of the 2000 Act states the following:

(2) Notwithstanding subsection (1) of this section, it shall not be a defence to a prosecution under this Part if the defendant proves that he or she has applied for or has been granted permission under section 34(12)—
  (a) since the initiation of proceedings under this Part,

---

[49] Planning and Development Act 2000, s 155, permits the issuance of an enforcement notice without sending a warning letter where the urgency of the case warrants it.
[50] Planning and Development Act 2000, s 152(1).
[51] Planning and Development Act 2000, s 153(1).
[52] Planning and Development Act 2000, s 154(1).
[53] Planning and Development Act 2000, s 154(8).
[54] Planning and Development Act 2000, s 161(2).

(b)   since the date of the sending of a warning letter under section 152, or

(c)   since the date of service of an enforcement notice in a case of urgency in accordance with section 155.

(3)   No enforcement action under this Part (including an application under section 160) shall be stayed or withdrawn by reason of an [application for permission for retention of unauthorised development] under [section 34(12C)] or the grant of that permission.

## *Time*

The legislation places a seven-year limitation period on enforcement proceedings. Section 157(4)(a) of the 2000 Act states the following:

No warning letter or enforcement notice shall issue and no proceedings for an offence under this Part shall commence—

(i)   in respect of a development where no permission has been granted, after seven years from the date of the commencement of the development,

(ii)   in respect of a development for which permission has been granted under Part III, after seven years beginning on the expiration, as respects the permission authorising the development, of the appropriate period within the meaning of section 40 or, as the case may be, of the period as extended under section 42.

This means that an action cannot be taken in respect of an unauthorised development after a seven-year period has elapsed.[55] In relation to circumstances where permission has been granted, as set out above, the limitation period of seven years does not run until the expiration of the planning permission.[56]

In the case of quarrying operations and peat extractions, enforcement proceedings can be issued and commenced at any time to require unauthorised quarrying or peat extraction to cease.[57]

---

[55] Planning and Development Act, s 157(4)(a).

[56] Please note that the normal life of planning permission is 5 years under s 40 of the 2000 Act, unless it is extended under s 42 or s 42A of the Act.

[57] Planning and Development Act 2000, s 157(4)(a).

It should be noted that, irrespective of the time that has elapsed, enforcement action can still be taken where a person has failed to satisfy a planning condition concerning the use of land.[58]

## Appeal

Once a decision has been made by a planning authority, any affected party may appeal to An Bord Pleanála within 4 weeks of the decision being made.[59] An appeal can be lodged by the applicant who sought permission in the first instance, or by any person who made valid written submissions or observations in relation to the application for planning permission. Where a person other than the original applicant for permission is appealing the decision, he or she must include a copy of the planning authority's acknowledgement of receipt of the submission or observation.[60]

The law also allows a person who has an interest in land adjoining the land the subject of the planning application, to appeal, even if he or she did not make submissions or observations in the original planning application, in circumstances where the planning authority proposes to permit changes from that applied for, and where the imposition of these conditions will materially affect his or her enjoyment of the land or its value. Furthermore, it should be pointed out that the adjoining landowner must first apply to the board for permission to appeal the decision of the planning authority within four weeks of the decision, and must discharge the appropriate fee in respect of same.[61]

## Procedure

In order to properly lodge an appeal, the following steps should be followed[62]:

- The appeal must be in writing;
- It must state the name and address of the appellant or person making the referral, and of the person acting on his or her behalf;
- It must detail the subject matter of the appeal or referral;

---

[58] Planning and Development Act 2000, s 157(4)(b).
[59] Planning and Development Act 2000, s 37(1)(d).
[60] *MacMahon v An Bord Pleanála* [2010] IEHC 431.
[61] Planning and Development Act 2000, s 37.
[62] Planning and Development Act 2000, s 127(1).

- It must set out the full grounds of the appeal or referral and the reasons, considerations, and arguments on which they are based;
- If observations and submissions were made in relation to the original planning permission application, then the planning authority's acknowledgment of receipt of the submissions must be included;
- Enclose appropriate fees, if applicable; and
- Ensure the appeal is made within the specified period.

It should be noted that the law requires that the filing of an appeal be strictly in accordance with the legislation. Otherwise, such appeals will be deemed invalid.[63]

An appeal should be sent by prepaid registered post to An Bord Pleanála, or by leaving it with an employee of that office during office hours.[64] It is not sufficient to email and/or fax the appeal or to leave it at An Bord Pleanála's office outside office hours.[65] The requirements for a valid appeal are contained in the Planning Acts, and most of the requirements are mandatory, meaning that failure to comply will be fatal to the appeal.[66] An appeal can be dismissed for being late,[67] for not enclosing an acknowledgment of having made a submission to the planning authority,[68] for including the wrong appeal fee,[69] for not including the details of an agent,[70] where the appellant had an agent, and for delivering the appeal papers out of hours.[71] The foregoing makes it clear that an appeal must comply with the law to the fullest degree. It is always recommended that any person who wishes to appeal a planning decision should seek legal advice prior to filing the appeal with An Bord Pleanála.

## Costs

It is also very important to understand and be mindful of the potential cost implications of an appeal. An Bord Pleanála has a wide discretion, irrespective of the result, to award the costs of the board and the appellant in

---

[63] Planning and Development Act 2000, s 127(2)(a).
[64] Planning and Development Act 2000, s 127(5).
[65] Planning and Development Act 2000 s 127(2)(a).
[66] The requirements are set out in s 127(1) of the Planning and Development Act 2000.
[67] Planning and Development Act 2000, s 127(1)(g).
[68] Planning and Development Act 2000, s 127(1)(e).
[69] Planning and Development Act 2000, s 127(1)(f).
[70] Planning and Development Act 2000, s 127(1)(b).
[71] Planning and Development Act 2000, s 127(5)(b).

relation to an appeal or referral against the planning authority. If An Bord Pleanála is satisfied that there was no merit in an appeal against a decision of the planning authority, then it may award the costs of the board, the planning authority, and any other party, against the appellant.

## Judicial Review

Under Irish law, there is an important procedure, known as judicial review, available to any person who is aggrieved by the manner in which a decision of any public body or tribunal has been reached. The High Court has jurisdiction to supervise the decisions of lower courts, other tribunals, and a wide range of public bodies.[72] It is important to understand that judicial review proceedings are not concerned with the merits of a case or the arguments advanced at the hearing, but rather with the decision-making process. The High Court exercises a supervisory role by protecting against abuse of power by public authorities and ensuring that they act within the law. However, it is notable that the courts are reluctant to interfere with the decisions of specialist administrative bodies, such as planning authorities. The Courts will only step in where the decision made by a planning authority is unconstitutional or not in compliance with legislative requirements.[73]

In order to demonstrate the process involved in carrying out a judicial review, the basic steps involved are outlined below.

## Procedure

### Leave to Apply

As a preliminary step, this process requires an application to be made to the High Court, seeking permission to judicially review a decision of the planning authority in question in accordance with s 50 of the 2000 Act. The application must be made within 8 weeks from the date of the decision of the planning authority which it is intended to challenge.[74] Specialist legal advice should be sought to determine how the 8-week limitation applies under the section, in any given set of circumstances.

---

[72] Rules of the Superior Courts, Ord 84. As interpreted from http://www.citizensinformation.ie/en/environment/environmental_law/judicial_review_in_planning_and_environmental_matters.html.

[73] ibid.

[74] Planning and Development Act 2000, s 50(4)(a)(i).

## Substantial Interest and Grounds

The standard required for these type of judicial reviews is somewhat more stringent that an ordinary judicial review in other areas of law. In the case of judicial reviews of planning decisions, it is necessary for the applicant to show that he or she has a substantial interest[75] in the proceedings, and also that he or she has substantial grounds[76] for challenging the decision. There are a number of potential grounds for judicial review, and the list set out below is not an exhaustive one:

    (a)   It may be the case that the development is not unauthorised, as it comes within an established use or was within a class of exempted development;

    (b)   It may be that the development was immune from action as it came within the seven-year rule and, thus, no enforcement action should have been brought in the first place; or

    (c)   The steps taken on the enforcement notice went beyond what was necessary, or were disproportionate in all the circumstances.

## Administrative Process

The party applying for judicial review must have participated in the planning process, either as the applicant for the authorisation, or a prescribed body or other person who made submissions or observations in respect of the matter now being litigated.[77]

## Appropriate Remedy

Before seeking a judicial review of a decision of the planning authority, it is very important to consider whether a more appropriate remedy is available.[78] For example, whether it is more appropriate to appeal a decision of a planning authority to An Bord Pleanála, as opposed to taking judicial review proceedings. Where such an appeal could have been taken, leave to apply for judicial review will be refused.

## The Hearing of the Judicial Review

It must always be borne in mind that a judicial review is not concerned with the merits of the decision complained of. Rather, it focuses on the

---

[75] Planning and Development Act 2000, s 50(4).

[76] Planning and Development Act 2000, s 50(4)(b).

[77] Planning and Development Act 2000, s 50(4)c(i) and (ii).

[78] State (Abenglen Properties Ltd) v Dublin Corporation [1984] IR 381, 393.

decision-making process. The role of the court, in dealing with judicial review, is not to re-hear the matter and consider the arguments and evidence advanced. Instead, it looks at whether there has been compliance with the relevant statutory procedures, and satisfies itself that a basic standard of constitutional and natural justice has been applied.

Furthermore, a court will only interfere with a decision, where it can be shown that the decision reached is fundamentally at variance with common sense and reason, and is indefensible. These cases are extremely rare.

## Conclusion

It is important that farmers, like all other citizens, are fully aware of the importance of complying with the planning laws in any activity undertaken by them. They should seek appropriate advice from engineers and/ or architects prior to constructing any building or carrying out any works on their land. In some cases, it will also be necessary to seek legal advice. The planning laws have become much more restrictive and far-reaching in their impact on property owners with each passing year, making it very easy to fall foul of the provisions. The potential expense involved in defending proceedings brought by a planning authority, or in paying any penalty imposed by the court, and in rectifying a breach of the planning laws, could have devastating consequences for any farmer. The days when planning authorities took a relaxed approach to breaches of the planning laws are long gone. Farmers should be especially conscious of the existence of any protected structures, such as ring forts, on their land, and should familiarise themselves with their obligations in relation to those. In addition, farmers whose lands are affected by the Habitats Directives, Special Area of Conservation Orders, or any other similar restrictions, should be especially careful before undertaking any activity on their lands. The penalties for breaches can be enormous.

On a practical level, compliance with planning laws is essential in order to ensure that one's title is good and marketable. A farmer may easily find himself in a position where he cannot mortgage or sell his lands, due to a breach of planning permission in respect of any use of, or structure on, his lands. This inability to sell or mortgage can have serious consequences. It is, in reality, the primary reason to ensure compliance with the planning laws in everything a farmer does on his lands.

# CHAPTER THIRTEEN

# Employment Law

Work has long been, and will always remain, an integral part of life. It represents a significant part of a person's identity, self-worth and social affiliation in modern times. At the time of writing of this book, there is, thankfully, an improving economy, with more people gradually returning to the workplace. Historically, many farmers would never have had an employee working for him or her, but, with the expansion of farms, the popularity of collaborative farming, and farmers and their families striving for a better work/life balance, farmers taking on employees is becoming increasingly common. Most workers' lives are affected, often to a significant degree, by the laws dealing with work and the workplace. Employment law has become increasingly more complex in recent years, with more than thirty major pieces of employment legislation governing the area at the time of writing. Many of these were introduced in compliance with EU law. The need for employers to be aware of, and to ensure compliance with legislation is greater than ever before, as the level of employees' claims, as well as fines for breaches of employment law, is increasing each year. Long before the coming into effect of this vast array of employment legislation, the common law played a key role in the development of many employment law principles, and of the contract of employment.

The Workplace Relations Act 2015 (hereafter 'the 2015 Act') introduced significant reforms to the manner in which employment and equality disputes are dealt with. Previously, there were five separate bodies charged with addressing workplace related issues in Ireland, namely: the Labour Relations Commission; the Equality Tribunal; the Employment Appeals Tribunal (EAT); the Labour Court; and the National Employment Rights Authority (NERA). The 2015 Act has streamlined these entities, creating a single body which adjudicates on all employment and equality disputes at first instance, known as the Workplace Relations Commission ("WRC"), and a Labour Court, which hears all cases on appeal from the WRC. Decisions of the Labour Court may be appealed, on a point of law only, to the High Court. Cases in respect of gender-based equality may be instituted before the Circuit Court.[1]

It must be stated at the outset that the area of employment law is vast and dynamic. Of necessity, the treatment of employment law in this chapter is little more than a summary of the most important aspects of the topic. For the purposes of this book, this chapter focuses on some of the more relevant aspects of employment law from a farming perspective.[2] This chapter deals with thirteen key topics:

1. Distinguishing between an employee and an independent contractor;
2. Terms of employment;
3. Bullying in the workplace;
4. Employment equality;
5. Safety, health and welfare at work;
6. Dismissing an employee and fair procedures;
7. Minimum notice periods;
8. Working hours, Sunday work, public holidays, break periods, and annual leave;
9. Maternity leave;
10. Duty to keep records;
11. Duty to furnish payslips;
12. Rates of pay; and
13. Employing children and young people.

## Distinguishing between an Employee and an Independent Contractor

Before considering any aspect of the relevant law, it is essential to consider who, or what, is considered an employee by law.

At first glance, this might seem like a question that is easily answered, but that is not the case. It can, in fact, often be difficult to decide whether a person is an employee, or whether they are self-employed. A person who is self-employed is referred to as an independent contractor. The distinction is significant for many reasons. Surprisingly, there is no definition of 'employed', or 'self-employed', in employment law. A decision

---

[1] Employment Equality Act 1998, s 77(3).

[2] For further information, see Workplace Relations Commission <www.workplacerelations.ie> accessed 7 July 2016.

regarding a person's employment status is reached by looking at what he or she does, how it is done, and the terms and conditions under which he or she is engaged to carry out the work.

While, in most cases, it will be perfectly clear whether a person is an employee, this is not always so. An employed person works under a contract of employment. A self-employed person works under a contract for service, and hence falls outside of the "employee" categorisation. The importance of the distinction is that the self-employed person is not entitled to the rights conferred on the employee. This has far reaching consequences. For example, much of the existing employment legislation excludes from its coverage those who do not work under a contract of employment. An example of this is the Unfair Dismissals Acts 1997–2015 (hereafter 'the Unfair Dismissals Acts'), which are discussed later in the chapter. Most importantly, the tax and social insurance systems treat employees and people who are self-employed very differently.

To add to the complexity in this area, the process of identifying an "employee" varies, depending on the particular legislation in question. Virtually all employment legislation simply refers to an employee as someone who works under a "contract of employment"[3]. However, the definition of a "contract of employment" has been drafted differently in different pieces of legislation, such as the Terms of Employment (Information) Act 1994, the Payment of Wages Act 1991, and the National Minimum Wage Act 2000.

For this reason, it is not surprising that it has fallen to the courts to expand upon the concept. The courts have developed a number of tests to be used in deciding whether a contract of employment exists. However, as we will see, while these tests provide a useful and helpful framework, the decisions tend to turn on the specific facts and circumstances of the cases in question.

### Applicable Test

There is ample case law addressing the employee/contractor divide, as many "independent contractors" seek to take cases claiming unfair dismissal, or for breaches of other employment rights. These cases have

---

[3] Daly B and Doherty M, *Principles of Irish Employment Law* (Clarus Press, 2010) p 42.

resulted in the development of a number of key tests, which assist the court and the employer in determining whether someone is an employee. These tests include the following elements:

## Control

Control is an important element. Generally, an employee can be instructed as to which tasks to perform, and how to perform them.

In the case of *Roche v Kelly*,[4] the defendants had a contract with a farmer to build a barn and had employed the plaintiff to build it for a lump sum of £300. The defendants were to supply the construction materials and the plaintiff was to build the barn to their specifications. The defendants monitored the progress of the construction, but at no time did they tell the plaintiff how to do the job, nor did they supervise his working methods. The plaintiff had considerable general experience and specific expertise in building barns, and he had carried out similar jobs for the defendant in the past. Unfortunately, the plaintiff was injured during the construction of this barn, and one of the issues was whether he was an employee of the defendant, or an independent contractor. The Supreme Court found that the main factor in defining the relationship is the element of control that the employer can exercise over the employee.[5] In this instance, the court found that the plaintiff was not an employee, as the defendants did not have the right to interfere with the manner in which he carried out his obligations, and hence they did not exercise any control over him.

## Integration

The extent to which a person is integrated into an organisation is a significant factor. There must be a personal obligation on an employee to perform the work. An employee is generally obliged to carry out work personally. In contrast, an independent contractor may be able to substitute someone else to do the work.

In *Re Sunday Tribune*,[6] a freelance journalist who received commission in advance from a newspaper, where that newspaper had no obligation to

---

[4] *Roche v Kelly* [1969] IR 100.

[5] Frances Meenan, *Employment Law* (Round Hall, 2014) p 32, 2.15.

[6] *Re Sunday Tribune* [1984] IR 505.

publish her work, was considered to be an independent contractor.[7] By contrast a "staff" journalist, working 50 weeks per year for the newspaper, was an integral part of the newspaper, and therefore was considered to be an employee.[8] This case illustrates that the nature of the work itself is not always significant, as both journalists did the same substantive work (writing columns for the newspaper), but each nonetheless had a different employment status.[9]

## Independence

The worker's level of independence is important. Having a final say in how the business is run, risking his or her own money, being free to do other work in his or her spare time, and providing his or her own equipment, are key indicators of an independent contractor.

The case of *Minister for Agriculture and Food v Barry*[10] involved an appeal from the EAT to the High Court on a point of law. The respondents had worked as Temporary Veterinary Inspectors (TVIs) at a meat factory in County Cork. In order to become a TVI, each respondent had to apply for approval from the Department of Agriculture and Food. Once approval had been granted, each respondent had to apply, in writing, to the Department for inclusion in a TVI panel, from which they would be periodically selected to do work in particular meat plants, assisting the permanent Veterinary Inspector. When the plant closed down, the respondents claimed entitlements under the legislation on redundancy[11] and notice[12].

The EAT determined that the respondents had all been employed under contracts of service, and were therefore considered to be employees of the Department. The Department appealed to the High Court. Edwards J reviewed the case law, stating that it was unhelpful to speak of 'tests', such as the control test, the integration test, etc., because none of them are capable of resolving the issue. Rather, they are simply assistive in reaching

---

[7] [1984] IR 505, 510.

[8] ibid.

[9] Daly B and Doherty M, *Principles of Irish Employment Law* (Clarus Press, 2010) p 45.

[10] *Minister for Agriculture and Food v Barry* [2009] 1 IR 215.

[11] Redundancy Payments Acts 1967-2003 s 40.

[12] Minimum Notice and Terms of Employment Act 1973 – 2001, s 11(2).

a conclusion. Ultimately, Edwards J decided that no mutuality of obligation existed between the parties, and so the vets were not considered to be employees.

The judgment in this case is useful for its clarification that no one test can determine the issue. Instead, it asks that courts and tribunals consider a range of factors in coming to a conclusion. Thus, the facts of each case will determine whether the contract is of, or for, service. However, the intentions of the parties are important, and cannot be overlooked.

As is clear from the foregoing, the distinction between a self-employed person and an employee is not always clear. The finding of an employer-employee relationship, where both parties had previously regarded the worker as being self-employed, may create significant financial exposure for the employer.

## Terms of Employment

An employer is obliged to provide an employee with a statement, in writing, no later than two months after the commencement of employment,[13] containing certain information. A sample written statement of terms of employment can be found on the website on the Workplace Relations Commission.[14]

The terms and conditions must include:

- Full names of the employer and employee[15];
- Address of the employer[16];
- Place of work[17];
- Job title or nature of work[18];
- Date of commencement of the contract of employment[19];

---

[13] Terms of Employment (Information) Act 1994, s 3(1).
[14] Workplace Relations Commission, 'Sample Terms of Employment' <www.workplacerelations.ie/en/Publications_Forms/Sample_Terms_of_Employment.pdf> accessed 7 July 2016.
[15] Terms of Employment (Information) Act 1994, s 3(1)(a).
[16] Terms of Employment (Information) Act 1994, s 3(1)(b).
[17] Terms of Employment (Information) Act 1994, s 3(1)(c).
[18] Terms of Employment (Information) Act 1994, s 3(1)(d).
[19] Terms of Employment (Information) Act 1994, s 3(1)(e).

- Information in relation to a relevant registered employment agreement[20];
- Details of hours of work[21];
- Details of paid leave[22] – full-time workers are entitled to four working weeks paid annual leave per year[23]. Generally part-time workers are entitled to 8% of the hours worked in the leave year, subject to a maximum of four working weeks[24];
- Whether the pay is weekly, monthly or otherwise[25];
- Any terms and conditions relating to pension schemes[26];
- Any terms and conditions relating to incapacity for work due to illness or injury[27];
- Periods of notice or methods for determining periods of notice[28];
- The pay reference period for the purposes of the National Minimum Wage Act 2000[29];
- A statement that the employee has the right to ask the employer for a written statement of his/her average hourly rate of pay as provided for in the National Minimum Wage Act 2000[30]; and
- Details of any collective agreements that may affect the employee's terms of employment.[31]

In the case of temporary contracts, the expected duration, or, in the case of a fixed-term contract, the date on which the contract expires, must also be included.[32] It is important that the contract furnished by the employer is both signed and dated, and that the document provides sufficient evidence of the contractual terms.

---

[20] Terms of Employment (Information) Act 1994, s 3(1)(fa), as inserted by the Industrial Relations (Amendment) Act 2012, s 18(b).
[21] Terms of Employment (Information) Act 1994, s 3(1)(l).
[22] Terms of Employment (Information) Act 1994, s 3(1)(j).
[23] Organisation of Working Time Act 1997, s 19(1)(a).
[24] Organisation of Working Time Act 1997, s 19(1)(c).
[25] Terms of Employment (Information) Act 1994, s 3(1)(h).
[26] Terms of Employment (Information) Act 1994, s 3(1)(k)(ii).
[27] Terms of Employment (Information) Act 1994, s 3(1)(k)(i).
[28] Terms of Employment (Information) Act 1994, s 3(1)(l).
[29] Terms of Employment (Information) Act 1994, s 3(1)(g).
[30] Terms of Employment (Information) Act 1994, s 3(1)(ga).
[31] Terms of Employment (Information) Act 1994, s 3(1)(m).
[32] Terms of Employment (Information Act) 1994 Act, s 3(1)(f).

Section 5(1) of the Terms of Employment (Information Act) 1994 Act (here-after 'the 1994 Act') states that

> ... whenever a change is made or occurs in any of the particulars of the state-ment furnished by an employer ... the employer shall notify the employee in writing of the nature and date of the change as soon as may be thereafter, but not later than –
>
> (a) 1 month after the change takes effect, or
> (b) where the change is consequent on the employee being required to work out-side the State for a period of more than 1 month, the time of the employee's departure.

Section 7 of the 1994 Act provides that an employee may present a com-plaint to the WRC if an employer has breached the 1994 Act.[33] The deci-sion can be appealed to the Labour Court.[34] Section 7(2)(d) of the 1994 Act as amended by s 52 of the 2015 Act gives the WRC the power to order the employer to pay compensation that is just and equitable in the circumstances, but not exceeding 4 weeks' remuneration in respect of the employee's employment.

## Bullying in the Workplace

Bullying is an increasing problem in the workplace. Section 42 of the Industrial Relations Act 1990 provided for the creation of codes of prac-tice addressing particular industrial relations concerns. By virtue of this provision, the Labour Relations Commission introduced the Code of Practice Detailing Procedures for Addressing Bullying in the Workplace.[35] This Code defines "workplace bullying" as

> ... repeated inappropriate behaviour, direct or indirect, whether verbal, physical or otherwise, conducted by one or more persons against another or others, at the place of work and/or in the course of employment, which could reasonably be regarded as undermining the individual's right to

---

[33] Terms of Employment (Information) Act 1994, s 7(1) as amended by s 52 Workplace Relation Act 2015.

[34] Terms of Employment (Information) Act 1994, s 8(1) as amended by s 52 Workplace Relation Act 2015.

[35] Industrial Relations Act 1990 (Code of Practice Detailing Procedures for Addressing Bullying in The Workplace) (Declaration) Order 2002, SI No 17 of 2002.

dignity at work. An isolated incident of the behaviour described in this definition may be an affront to dignity at work but, as a once off incident, is not considered to be bullying.[36]

Each employer must take measures to ensure that employees are not subjected to verbal or physical bullying or harassment[37] from their supervisors, co-workers, or customers.[38] Every employer should ensure that any complaint is taken seriously and that it is dealt with in a manner that does not compound any issues experienced by the employee. Each employer should take active steps to discharge his or her own obligations and fulfill their duty of care. It is important that an employer establishes and maintains an appropriate policy in relation to bullying in the workplace,[39] and that a copy of the policy is provided to all employees.[40]

While this code does not impose any legal obligations, it is admissible in evidence and will be taken into account in any proceedings. The Code specifically recommends dealing with complaints promptly,[41] designating an impartial member of management to carry out investigations with a view to determining an appropriate course of action,[42] and allowing both parties to respond before any action is decided upon by management.[43]

Another relevant code of practice has been drawn up under the Safety, Health and Welfare at Work Act 2005. This is the Code of Practice for

---

[36] Workplace Relations Commission, 'Code of Practice Detailing Procedures for Addressing Bullying in The Workplace' (2006), section 2(5). <www.workplacerelations.ie/en/Publications_ Forms/Procedures_for_Addressing_Bullying_in_the_Workplace.pdf> accessed 7 July 2016.

[37] Health and Safety Authority 'Code of Practice for Employers and Employees on the Prevention and Resolution of Bullying at Work 2007', p 5.

[38] Health and Safety Authority 'Code of Practice for Employers and Employees on the Prevention and Resolution of Bullying at Work 2007' p 6.

[39] Health and Safety Authority 'Code of Practice for Employers and Employees on the Prevention and Resolution of Bullying at Work 2007' pp 9 and 10.

[40] Health and Safety Authority 'Code of Practice for Employers and Employees on the Prevention and Resolution of Bullying at Work 2007' p 11.

[41] Workplace Relations Commission, 'Code of Practice Detailing Procedures for Addressing Bullying in The Workplace' (2006), section 8(g).

[42] ibid, section 8(d).

[43] ibid, section 8(b).

Employers and Employees on the Prevention and Resolution of Bullying at Work. The Code recommends:

i.    Having in place a bullying-prevention policy, which adequately addresses the risks that have been assessed. The policy should be clear as to the manner in which it will be implemented. (Where bullying has been identified as a risk, this policy must be referenced or included in the Safety Statement)[44];

ii.   Providing appropriate training and development at all levels, but particularly for line manager roles[45];

iii.  Ensuring clarity of individual and department goals, roles and accountabilities[46]; and

iv.   Ensuring access to relevant competent and supportive structures, both internal and external.[47]

In the case of *O'Connor v Dairy Master*,[48] the claimant worked as a general operative and gave evidence that he could not recall ever receiving a copy of any documents on grievance procedures for bullying and harassment in the workplace. The claimant's main contention was that his supervisor subjected him to unwelcome and abusive language and treatment in relation to his work rate, his private life, and in relation to his medical condition. The respondent often assigned him less favourable tasks compared to those assigned to his co-workers, such as unblocking toilets and cleaning the septic tank. When these grievances were raised with the respondent, the claimant was told to go back to his work and forget about it. The claimant gave evidence that he had been undergoing medical treatment in relation to these workplace issues since 2009, eventually culminating in the claimant being prescribed medication and commencing a period of sick leave.

---

[44] Health and Safety Authority 'Code of Practice for Employers and Employees on the Prevention and Resolution of Bullying at Work 2007', p 9.

[45] Health and Safety Authority 'Code of Practice for Employers and Employees on the Prevention and Resolution of Bullying at Work 2007', p 12.

[46] Health and Safety Authority 'Code of Practice for Employers and Employees on the Prevention and Resolution of Bullying at Work 2007', p 12.

[47] For more information, see Health and Safety Authority Code of Practice for Employers and Employees on the Prevention and Resolution of Bullying at Work 2007.

[48] *O'Connor v Dairy Master* [UD351/2012].

The claimant's solicitor had written to the respondent asserting that bullying and harassment was the reason for the claimant's illness, and that if the respondent did not take steps to compensate the claimant, he would resign and claim constructive dismissal. The respondent simply denied that these issues had ever been raised, and advised that the claimant should contact his supervisor in relation to the matters.

The Tribunal accepted the claimant's argument that he had attempted to raise employment issues in the workplace and that there was no evidence that the claimant ever received a copy of the respondent's bullying and harassment policy. The Tribunal determined that it was reasonable for the claimant to resign, and allowed the claim for constructive dismissal, awarding the claimant €25,000.

If an employee feels that his or her complaint regarding bullying has not been dealt with properly by an employer, he or she may make a complaint under the Employment Equality Acts 1998 (hereafter called 'the Employment Equality Acts') to the WRC.[49]

## Employment Equality

The Employment Equality Acts place an obligation on all employers to prevent harassment in the workplace.[50]

Sexual harassment, and harassment on any of the following grounds, such as gender, civil status, family status, sexual orientation, religion, age, disability, race or membership of the Traveller community, are forms of discrimination in the context of conditions of employment.[51]

Harassment is defined as any form of unwanted conduct related to any of the discriminatory grounds, which has the purpose or effect of violating a person's dignity and creating an intimidating, hostile, degrading, humiliating or offensive environment for the person.[52]

---

[49] Employment Equality Act 1998, s 77(1).
[50] Employment Equality Act 1998, s 14A(7), as amended by the Equality Act 2004, s 8.
[51] Employment Equality Act 1998, s 6(2).
[52] Employment Equality Act 1998, s 14A(7), as amended by the Equality Act 2004, s 8.

Sexual harassment is defined as any form of unwanted verbal, non-verbal or physical conduct of a sexual nature which has the purpose or effect of violating a person's dignity and creating an intimidating, hostile, degrading, humiliating or offensive environment for the person.[53] Examples are unwanted physical contact, such as unnecessary touching, patting, pinching or brushing against another employee's body, whistling or making sexually suggestive gestures.[54]

It should be noted that the scope of the sexual harassment and harassment provisions extends beyond the workplace, for example, to conferences and training that occur outside the workplace. It may also extend to work-related social events.[55]

The Code of Practice on Sexual Harassment and Harassment at Work[56] offers practical guidance to employers and employees on how to prevent sexual and other harassment in the workplace, and how best to implement procedures to deal with it.[57] Bullying that is not linked to one of the discriminatory grounds is not covered by the Employment Equality Act.[58]

The Code of Practice on Sexual Harassment and Harassment at Work specifically states:

> Sexual harassment, and harassment on the eight other non-gender discriminatory grounds, pollute the working environment and can have a devastating effect on the health, confidence, morale and performance of those affected by it. The anxiety and stress produced by sexual harassment and harassment may lead to those subjected to it taking time off work due to sickness and stress, being less efficient at work or leaving their job to seek work elsewhere. Employees often suffer the adverse consequences of the harassment itself and, in addition, the short and long

---

[53] ibid.

[54] SI No 208 of 2012 – Employment Equality Act 1998 (Code of Practice) (Harassment) Order 2012 Part 3.

[55] Employment Equality Act 1998, s 14A(1) as amended by Equality Act 2004, s 8.

[56] Employment Equality Act 1998 (Code of Practice) (Harassment) Order 2012, SI No 208 of 2012.

[57] Equality Authority, 'Code of Practice on Sexual Harassment and Harassment at Work' <www.ihrec.ie/download/pdf/code_of_practice_on_sexual_harassment_and_harassment. pdf> accessed 7 July 2016.

[58] ibid Part 3, 'The Law and Employers' Responsibilities S8 EE Act'.

term damage to their employment prospects if they are forced to forego promotion or to change jobs. Sexual harassment and harassment may also have a damaging impact on employees not themselves the object of unwanted behaviour but who are witness to it or have a knowledge of the unwanted behaviour.

There are also adverse consequences arising from sexual harassment and harassment for employers. It has a direct impact on the profitability of the enterprise where staff take sick leave or resign their posts because of sexual harassment or other harassment. It can also have an impact on the economic efficiency of the enterprise where employees' productivity is reduced by having to work in a climate in which the individual's integrity is not respected.[59]

While this code of practice does not impose any legal obligations, it is admissible in evidence and will be taken into account in any proceedings.[60] The Code requires employers to act in a preventative and remedial way, and recommends:

1.   Having in place an up to date anti-harassment policy[61];
2.   Ensuring that it is communicated effectively to all staff, in their native language[62]; This is particularly relevant in relation to migrant workers;
3.   Holding regular training updates to ensure that management, in particular, understand how to implement the policy[63];
4.   When a complaint is made, carrying out the investigation promptly and confidentially[64]; and
5.   Following fair procedures at all times.[65]

## Safety, Health and Welfare at Work

Under the Safety, Health and Welfare at Work Act 2005 (hereafter 'the 2005 Act'), employers have a duty to ensure the safety, health and welfare of their employees in the workplace. Section 8 of the 2005 Act

---

[59]  ibid Part 1, 'Foreword'.
[60]  SI 208/2012 Employment Equality Act 1998 (Code of Practice)(Harassment) Order 2012.
[61]  ibid Part 4, 'Prevention'.
[62]  ibid Part 4, 'Preparing the Policy', and Part 4(7), 'Communication of Policy'.
[63]  ibid Part 4(9), 'Training'.
[64]  ibid Part 5, 'The Complaints Procedure'.
[65]  ibid Part 5, 'Investigation of the Complaint'.

states that an employer is required to "prevent any improper conduct or behaviour likely to put the safety, health and welfare of employees at risk".[66] This is dealt with in further detail in chapter 14.

## Dismissing an Employee and Fair Procedures

Section 2 of the Unfair Dismissals Act 1977 (hereafter 'the 1977 Act') confirms that an employee who is employed for a year or more, is entitled to claim unfair dismissal if he or she is dismissed, or constructively dismissed, should the conditions of work be made so difficult that the employee feels obliged to leave.

Section 6 of the `1977 Act states that the dismissal of an employee shall be deemed to be an unfair dismissal unless, having regard to all the circumstances, there were substantial grounds justifying the dismissal.

Section 6(2) of the 1977 Act states that the dismissal of an employee shall be deemed, for the purposes of this Act, to be an unfair dismissal if it results wholly or mainly from one or more of the following:

- Membership, or proposed membership, of a trade union, or engaging in trade union activities;
- Activities, whether within permitted times during work, or outside of working hours;
- Religious or political opinions;
- Legal proceedings against an employer where an employee is a party or a witness;
- Race, colour, sexual orientation, age or membership of the Traveller community;
- Pregnancy, giving birth or breastfeeding or any matters connected with pregnancy or birth;
- Availing of rights under legislation such as maternity leave, adoptive leave, carer's leave, parental or force majeure leave; or
- Unfair selection for redundancy.

The determination of the EAT in *Mannion v Naughton*[67] provides examples of the types of behaviour on the part of an employer which could provide

---

[66] Safety, Health and Welfare Act 2005, s 8(1)(b).
[67] *Mannion v Naughton* [UD749/2011].

grounds for a claim of constructive dismissal. In *Mannion*,[68] the claimant was a farm manager employed by the respondent, and, during a period of sick leave, an estate manager was recruited. On his return to work following his absence, the claimant asserted that his duties of employment were significantly diminished, in that he no longer had responsibility for the maintenance of the farm, the preparation of the budget, or the purchase and sale of cattle, all of which had been passed to the estate manager. In making a determination, the Tribunal concluded that, in reality, the 'control of the farm' had passed to the estate manager, and, accordingly, this constituted a fundamental breach of the employee's terms and conditions of employment, such that he was entitled to resign from his employment. The Tribunal awarded compensation of €40,000 pursuant to his claim under the Unfair Dismissals Acts.

Section 6(4) of the 1977 Act states that, in circumstances where an employer takes a decision to dismiss an employee, the dismissal must be justified on one or more of the following grounds:

- The capability, competence or qualifications of the employee[69];
- The redundancy of the employee[70];
- The fact that the continuation of the employment would contravene another statutory requirement[71]; or
- The conduct of the employee.[72]

In *O'Connor v Brewster*,[73] the claimant was employed as a night man at the respondent's stud farm, from 6 March 1989 until 12 May 1990, the date of his dismissal. The claimant's job was to monitor mares who were due to foal and to inform the stud groom when there were signs that foaling was imminent. The Tribunal accepted that the claimant was aware that failure to do so would endanger mares and foals, and possibly the respondent's business. The respondent had warned the claimant in relation to absence from work on a Sunday and his failure to alert the groomsman about a foaling. The Tribunal held that the claimant was aware of

---

[68] ibid.
[69] Unfair Dismissals Act 1977, s 6(4)(a).
[70] Unfair Dismissals Act 1977, s 6(4)(c).
[71] Unfair Dismissals Act 1977, s 6(4)(d).
[72] Unfair Dismissals Act 1977, s 6(4)(b).
[73] *O'Connor v Brewster* [UD435/90].

his job requirements and knew that the neglect of his duties would lead to termination of his employment. The claimant was warned that such neglect was unacceptable to the employer, and that it amounted to gross misconduct. The dismissal was upheld and the claimant's unfair dismissal claim was dismissed.

Should unfair dismissal be proven, the employer must do one of the following:

- Reinstate the person (i.e. with back-pay and continuity of service);
- Re-engage the person (this can happen without back pay or continuity of service); or
- Compensate the person.[74]

### Fair Procedures

Fair procedures must be followed in effecting the termination. This is an extremely contentious area, and one which employers should take great care in handling. If fair procedures are not followed in terminating an employee's employment, despite there being substantial grounds of dismissal, a termination of employment may still be deemed to be unfair.

A useful statement in relation to procedures that should be adopted by an employer prior to effecting a dismissal is to be found in *Gearon v Dunnes Stores Ltd*,[75] where the EAT held that fair procedures had not been followed, and concluded that:

> The right to defend herself, and have her arguments and submissions listened to and evaluated by the respondent in relation to the threat to her employment, is a right of the claimant and is not the gift of the respondent or this tribunal... the right is a fundamental one under natural justice and constitutional justice, it is not open to this tribunal to forgive its breach.

---

[74] Unfair Dismissals Act 1977, s 7.
[75] *Gearon v Dunnes Stores Ltd* [UD367/88].

It is important that, when any employee is facing disciplinary action, fair procedures are followed, including:

- Informing the employee of the complaint without delay[76];
- Carrying out an impartial investigation[77];
- Facilitating a fair hearing, which allows the employee make his or her counter arguments[78]; and
- Providing the employee with the opportunity to cross-examine witnesses as to facts which are essential to the establishment of charges against the employee.[79]

The question as to whether an employee should be allowed legal representation at a disciplinary hearing is relevant to any disciplinary hearing. In *Burns v Governor of Castlerea Prison & Anor*,[80] the Supreme Court held that it was undesirable to involve legal representation where a disciplinary process is in place unless, in all the circumstances, such was required by the principles of constitutional or natural justice.[81] The court stated that the following considerations should be taken into account in determining if such representation should be permitted[82]:

- The seriousness of the charge and of the potential penalty;
- Whether any points of law are likely to arise;
- The capacity of a particular disciplinee to present his or her own case;
- Procedural difficulties;
- The need for reasonable speed in making the adjudication, that being an important consideration; and
- The need for fairness as between the parties.

Section 7 of the 1977 Act as amended by s 80(1)(f) of the 2015 Act states that, where an employee is dismissed, and the dismissal is an unfair

---

[76] Industrial Relations Act 1946 (Code of Practice on Grievance and Disciplinary Procedures) SI No 146 of 2000, reg 4(6).
[77] ibid.
[78] ibid.
[79] ibid, reg 7.
[80] *Burns v Governor of Castlerea Prison & Anor* [2009] 3 IR 682.
[81] ibid.
[82] ibid, at 688.

dismissal, the employee shall be entitled to redress from the WRC, as it considers appropriate, having regard to all the circumstances.

Section 44 of the 2015 Act states that a party concerned may appeal to the Labour Court from a decision of the WRC in relation to a claim for redress under the Act, and the Labour Court shall hear the parties and any evidence relevant to the appeal tendered by them, and shall make a determination in relation to the appeal.

## Minimum Notice Periods

The Minimum Notice and Terms of Employment Act 1973 provides for the minimum notice periods for the termination of employment. The length of notice which employers must give to employees on termination depends on whether a contract of employment exists, and whether notice periods are provided for in that contract. In the event that a contract of employment does not exist, or the said contract of employment is silent as to notice periods, the length of the period of notice depends on the length of service.[83] Should an employer fail to provide the statutory notice period, he or she would be obliged to pay that employee for that period.

The notice periods are set out hereunder.

| Length of Service | Minimum Notice |
| --- | --- |
| 13 weeks to 2 years | 1 week |
| 2 years to 5 years | 2 weeks |
| 5 years to 10 years | 4 weeks |
| 10 years to 15 years | 6 weeks |
| More than 15 years | 8 weeks |

## Working Hours, Sunday Work, Public Holidays, Break Periods and Annual Leave

### Working Hours

Section 15 of the Organisation of Working Time Act 1997 (hereafter 'the 1997 Act') requires that an employer shall not permit an employee to work more than an average of 48 hours in each period of 7 days. In the agricultural

---

[83] Minimum Notice and Terms of Employment Act 1973, s 4.

sector, this refers to an average of 48 hours calculated over a period that does not exceed 6 months.[84] Such averaging cannot take into account periods of annual leave, periods of sick leave, or any absences from work due to maternity leave or adoptive leave.

Section 17 of the 1997 Act obliges an employer to notify an employee at least 24 hours before the first day or, as the case may be, the day, in each week that he or she proposes to require the employee to work, of the times at which the employee will normally be required to start and finish work on each day, or, as the case may be, the day or days concerned, of that week.[85]

## Sunday Work

Section 14 of the 1997 Act obliges an employer to compensate an employee for working on a Sunday by giving him or her a reasonable allowance, a reasonable pay increase or reasonable paid time off work.

## Public Holidays

An employer is obliged to give an additional day's pay, paid day off or annual leave in lieu, to an employee who works on a public holiday.[86]

## Break Periods

An employer has a duty to ensure that employees have certain break periods during the course of their work.

An employer is not obliged to pay an employee during those breaks.

Section 12 of the 1997 Act states that an employer shall not require an employee to work for a period of more than 4 hours and 30 minutes without allowing him or her a break of at least 15 minutes, and shall not require an employee to work for a period of more than 6 hours without allowing

---

[84] In the case of an employee employed in an activity referred to in Paragraph 2, point 2.1c (vi) of Article 17 of the Council Directive 93/104/EC. This includes the agricultural sector.

[85] This is on the basis that neither the contract of employment of the employee concerned nor any employment regulation order, registered employment agreement, or collective agreement that has effect in relation to the employee, specifies the normal or regular starting and finishing times of work of an employee.

[86] Organisation of Working Time Act 1977, s 21(1).

him or her a break of at least 30 minutes, which can include the first 15-minute break. However, in the context of farming, regulation 3(1) of the Organisation of Working Time (General Exemptions) Regulations 1998[87] provides an exemption to s 12 of the 1997 Act, whereby the employer is not obliged to comply with same, but must instead ensure that the employee has available to himself or herself a rest period or break, as the case may be, that, in all the circumstances, can reasonably be regarded as equivalent to the first-mentioned rest period or break[88], or if, for reasons that can be objectively justified, it is not possible for the employer to ensure that the employee has available to himself or herself such an equivalent rest period or break, otherwise make such arrangements as respects the employee's conditions of employment as will compensate the employee in consequence of this exemption[89]. There is a condition that the employee is wholly or mainly engaged in carrying on or performing the duties of the activity concerned.[90]

Regulation 5(1) states the following:

> An employer shall not require an employee to whom the exemption applies to work during a shift or other period of work (being a shift or other such period that is of more than 6 hours' duration) without allowing him or her a break of such duration as the employer determines.

It is important to note that all of the aforementioned section does not apply to a person who is employed by a relative[91] and is a member of that relative's household, and whose place of employment is a private dwelling house or a farm in or on which he or she and the relative reside.[92]

---

[87] Organisation of Working Time (General Exemptions) Regulations 1998, SI No 21 of 1998.

[88] Organisation of Working Time Act 1997, s 6(2)(a).

[89] Organisation of Working Time Act 1997, s 6(2)(b).

[90] Organisation of Working Time (General Exemptions) Regulations 1998, SI No 21 of 1998, Reg 3(2)(a)(i).

[91] Organisation of Working Time Act 1997, s 3(6), defines 'relative' in relation to a person, "as his or her spouse, father, mother, grandfather, grandmother, step-father, step-mother, son, daughter, grandson, grand-daughter, step-son, step-daughter, brother, sister, half-brother or half-sister".

[92] Organisation of Working Time Act 1997, s 3(2)(b).

## Annual Leave

Section 19(1) of the 1997 Act provides that an employee is entitled to annual leave equal to:

(a) 4 working weeks in a leave year in which he or she works at least 1,365 hours (unless it is a leave year in which he or she changes employment),

(b) one-third of a working week for each month in the leave year in which he or she works at least 117 hours, or

(c) 8% of the hours he or she works in a leave year (but subject to a maximum of 4 working weeks):

Provided that if more than one of the preceding paragraphs is applicable in the case concerned and the period of annual leave of the employee, determined in accordance with each of those paragraphs, is not identical, the annual leave to which the employee shall be entitled shall be equal to whichever of those periods is the greater. It should be noted that where an employee works longer than average hours he or she is entitled to a longer annual leave.

# Maternity Leave

Maternity leave is an entitlement of all female employees. It is irrelevant how long the employee has been working for the employer. An employee is entitled to 26 weeks' maternity leave[93] together with 16 weeks' additional unpaid maternity leave,[94] which begins immediately after the end of maternity leave.

The entitlement of an employee to be paid during maternity leave depends on the contract of employment. An employer is not obliged to pay an employee while on maternity leave[95].

An employee remains in employment during maternity leave and additional leave[96]. An employee is entitled to annual leave[97] and public holidays[98] in accordance with the 1997 Act or her contract of employment.

[93] Maternity Protection Act 1994 (Extension of Periods of Leave) Order 2006, SI No 51 of 2006, art 8.

[94] Maternity Protection Act 1994, s 14.

[95] Meenan, F, *Employment Law* (Round Hall 2014) p 669, 13-31.

[96] Maternity Protection Act 1994, s 22, as amended.

[97] Organisation of Working Time Act 1997, s 19.

[98] Organisation of Working Time Act 1997, s 21.

An employee on maternity leave is also entitled to the annual leave accumulated during the said period as if she were working during that period.

It should also be noted, as it is very relevant to a farming situation, that, due to the physical work involved, an employer may be obliged to move an employee to other work on health and safety grounds, as a result of a risk assessment. In the event that such a move cannot reasonably be required on duly substantiated grounds, the other work to which the employer proposes to move the employee is not suitable for her, or it is not technically or objectively feasible to move her, then the employee must be granted leave from her employment. This leave is not counted as maternity leave.[99]

Fathers in Ireland are entitled to two weeks paid paternity leave.[100] Any time off work is given solely at the discretion of the employer and is taken as annual leave.

## Duty to Keep Records

It is very important to keep a full employment file for each employee.

Section 25 of the 1997 Act states:

> An employer shall keep, at the premises or place where his or her employee works or, if the employee works at two or more premises or places, the premises or place from which the activities that the employee is employed to carry on are principally directed or controlled from, such records, in such form, if any, as may be prescribed, as will show whether the provisions of this Act are being complied with in relation to the employee and those records shall be retained by the employer for at least 3 years from the date of their making.

In addition, certain minimum information must be kept in the file, such as the name and address of each employee concerned, the tax reference number of that particular employee, and a brief statement of his or her duties as an employee, as well as a copy of the statement of terms provided to each

---

[99] Maternity Protection Act 1994, s 18(1).
[100] Paternity Leave and Benefit Act 2016, s 6(1).

employee, or any order or regulation made under that Act, that relates to him or her etc.[101]

Having an employment file in place can prove invaluable in the event of any subsequent litigation involving an employee. Not having written records in place may prove fatal to an employer's case.

## Duty to Furnish Payslips

Section 4(1) of the Payment of Wages Act 1991 obliges an employer to

> ... give or cause to be given to an employee a statement in writing specifying clearly the gross amount of the wages payable to the employee and the nature and amount of any deduction therefrom and the employer shall take such reasonable steps as are necessary to ensure that both the matter to which the statement relates and the statement are treated confidentially by the employer and his agents and by any other employees.

## Rates of Pay

The rate of pay is normally negotiated between the employer and employee. The National Minimum Wage Act 2000 (hereafter 'the 2000 Act') sets out the minimum wage to which most employees are entitled.[102]

Section 14 of the 2000 Act states that an employer is obliged to pay an employee over the age of 18 years at an hourly rate of pay that, on average, is not less than the national minimum hourly rate of pay, and an employee under the age of 18 years at an hourly rate of pay that on average is not less than 70% of the national minimum hourly rate of pay.

Agricultural workers are covered by the Joint Labour Committee for the agricultural sector. The Agricultural Workers Joint Labour Committee was established by s 4 of the Industrial Relations Act 1976, to regulate rates of pay and conditions of employment for the agricultural industry. It is important for a farmer to be aware of Employment Regulation Orders

---

[101] Organisation of Working Time (Records) (Prescribed Form and Exemptions) Regulations 2001, SI No 473 of 2001, reg 3.

[102] Since 1 January 2016, under the National Minimum Wage Order 2015, SI No 442 of 2015, art 2, the national minimum wage for an experienced adult employee is €9.15 per hour.

(EROs) in force concerning the agricultural sector, as these set a minimum wage for agricultural workers.[103] If the ERO sets an employee's rate of pay above the minimum wage then, in that instance, the ERO would prevail over the minimum wage as per the 2000 Act.

## Employing Children and Young People

The Protection of Young Persons (Employment) Act 1996 (hereafter 'the 1996 Act') was introduced for the purpose of implementing the Protection of Young Workers Directive,[104] which dealt with the protection of young people at work. A "young person" is defined as a person who has reached 16 years of age or the school-leaving age (whichever is higher), but is less than 18 years of age.[105] The legislation seeks to improve the safety and health of young persons at work. While the employment of children under 16 is generally prohibited, a child over 14 years may be permitted to do light work during the school holidays, as long as is it not harmful to their health, development, or schooling and the hours of work should not exceed 7 hours in any day or 35 hours in any week.[106]

An employer wishing to employ anyone under the age of 18 years must first require the production of his or her birth certificate.[107] Before employing a child under the age of 16 years, the written permission of the parents or guardians must be obtained.[108] It should be noted that the requirements of an employer to obtain details in respect of date of birth, the minimum hours, and the inclusion of time spent on vocational training as working time, does not apply in respect of the employment of close relatives.[109] The legislation provides time limits on the number of hours for which young people may work, prohibits night work, and outlines

---

[103] For further information, see Employment Regulation Order (Agricultural Workers Joint Labour Committee) 2010, SI No 164 of 2010.

[104] Council Directive 94/33/EC of 22 June 1994 on the protection of young people at work *OJ L216/12.*

[105] Protection of Young Persons (Employment) Act 1996, s 1.

[106] Protection of Young Persons (Employment) Act 1996, s 3(4).

[107] Protection of Young Persons (Employment) Act 1996, s 5(1)(a).

[108] Protection of Young Persons (Employment) Act 1996, s 5(1)(b).

[109] Protection of Young Persons (Employment of Close Relatives) Regulations 1997, SI No 2 of 1997.

rest periods.[110] Young people (over 16 and under 18) must not work more than 8 hours a day or 40 hours per week.

**Maximum weekly working hours for children under 16[111]**

| Age | 14 years | 15 years |
|---|---|---|
| School term time | 0 hours | 8 hours |
| Holidays | 35 hours | 35 hours |
| Work Experience | 40 hours | 40 hours |

**Time off and rest breaks for children under 16[112]**

| | |
|---|---|
| Half hour rest break | After 4 hours |
| Daily rest break | 14 consecutive hours off |
| Weekly rest break | 2 days off, to be consecutive as much as is practicable |

**Working hours, time off and rest breaks for young people aged 16 and 17[113]**

| | |
|---|---|
| Maximum Working Day | 8 hours |
| Maximum Working Week | 40 hours |
| Half hour rest break | After 4.5 hours |
| Daily rest break | 12 consecutive hours off |
| Weekly rest break | 2 days off, to be consecutive as is practicable |

## Conclusion

Employers often operate in an uncertain domestic and international economic environment, with considerable pressure on costs and overheads, including employment costs. In Ireland, as the average farm size steadily increases, the abolition of the milk quota, increased numbers of farmers entering into collaborative farming arrangements, and other factors, have

---

[110] Protection of Young Persons (Employment) Act 1996, s 6.

[111] Department of Enterprise, Trade and Employment, 'Guide to Protection of Young Persons (Employment) Act, 1996' para 2.1 <www.workplacerelations.ie/en/Publications_Forms/Guide_to_Protection_of_Young_Persons_Employment_Act.pdf> accessed 24 June 2016.

[112] ibid para 2.2.

[113] ibid para 2.3.

seen farmers expanding their workforce. This expansion brings with it the need to ensure that they are compliant with their obligations under what is now a very considerable body of employment legislation.

Before taking on any employee, a farmer, like any other employer, should familiarise him or herself with the main aspects of the legislation, as summarised in this chapter. The legislation should be complied with at all times. Where doubt arises, proper professional advice should be sought. Taking good advice and preventive action, combined with adopting and implementing fair and proper procedures, will help to reduce the potential for problems. Despite a farmer's best efforts, issues may nonetheless arise. For that reason, it is also critical that every employer puts in place a comprehensive employer's liability policy, ensuring that any claim arising can be met without fear of catastrophic financial and other consequences.

# CHAPTER FOURTEEN

# Health and Safety on the Farm

Farming remains the most dangerous occupation in Ireland, with farm deaths accounting for more than half of all workplace fatalities in 2010. In 2013, 16 people died on Irish farms. In 2014, that figure almost doubled to 30, with 55% of all work-related deaths categorised as farming fatalities. In 2015, 18 people died on Irish farms. A person is 8 times more likely to die whilst working on a farm in Ireland than in the general working population.[1]

Farms cannot be compared to any other work environment. Age and location are key factors in farm deaths in Ireland. Deaths in agriculture, unlike in many other sectors, often involve family members, including children and elderly persons. Age is a major contributing factor in farm accidents in Ireland (both fatal and non-fatal), with the average age of an Irish farmer currently standing at 57 years and increasing.

Farming is a rewarding, albeit a hazardous, occupation. A farmer has certain responsibilities to prevent accidents from happening, both on and off his or her farm.

Health and safety in Ireland is governed by a combination of common law (judge-made law) and statute. The main legislation providing for the health and safety of people in the workplace is the Safety, Health and Welfare at Work Act 1989, as amended by the Safety, Health and Welfare at Work Act 2005 (hereafter 'the 2005 Act').

At the outset, it should be noted that most farmers across the country are self-employed and even though reference is made to employers throughout

---

[1] Health and Safety Authority, 'Presentation to Oireachtas Joint Committee on Agriculture, Food and the Marine' (29 January 2015).

the 2005 Act, it is still applicable to the self-employed farmer. Section 7 of the 2005 Act states that:

> The relevant statutory provisions apply, where appropriate, to a self-employed person as they apply to an employer and as if that self-employed person was an employer and his or her own employee and references in the relevant statutory provisions to an employer shall be read as references to a self-employed person.

Furthermore, it should be noted that the 2005 Act applies, not only to employees (including fixed-term and temporary employees), but also to persons coming on to the farm, e.g. self-employed people in the course of their work, such as veterinarians, artificial insemination technicians, and milk lorry drivers.[2]

This chapter deals with an employer's obligations under the 2005 Act and under common law, the penalties for failure to comply with the legislation, and provides suggestions on how to maintain farm safety. Employment law is dealt with in greater detail in the Employment Law chapter. Occupiers' liability, which concerns the duty of care owed by those who occupy real property, through ownership or lease, to people who visit or trespass, is dealt with separately in the chapter on Occupiers' Liability.

## Risk Assessment

The 2005 Act places a legal duty on every person controlling a place of work to identify hazards at that place of work. "Place of work" is defined in s 2 of the 2005 Act as including "any, or any part of any, place (whether or not within or forming part of a building or structure), land or other location at, in, upon or near which, work is carried on whether occasionally or otherwise".

Section 19(1) of the 2005 Act states that:

> Every employer shall identify the hazards in the place of work under his or her control, assess the risks presented by those hazards and be in possession of a written assessment (to be known and referred to in this Act as a "risk assessment") of the risks to the safety, health and welfare at work of

---

[2] Safety, Health and Welfare at Work Act 2005, s 12.

his or her employees, including the safety, health and welfare of any single employee or group or groups of employees who may be exposed to any unusual or other risks under the relevant statutory provisions.

Interestingly, the 2005 Act does not define "hazards" or "risks". Commentary in the area suggests that a "hazard" refers to the potential to cause harm, which could be caused either by a machine or a chemical substance.[3] The term "risk" refers to the likelihood of the harm taking place and, of course, the number of persons at risk of exposure to the hazard.[4]

The risk assessment is an invaluable mechanism, which should provide a systematic and informed evaluation of the risks or dangers associated with tasks performed in the course of work. The case of *Miles v Parsons*[5] provides a useful example of the importance of risk assessment. In this case, a 14-year-old girl was employed by a newsagent to deliver newspapers on her bicycle. However, during the course of her duties, she was injured in a road traffic accident when a vehicle hit her as she was cycling across a busy road. The court took the view that the newsagents were 60% negligent due to the absence of a Risk Assessment Document. The court also found that the newsagents had failed to adequately assess the paper delivery route by taking into consideration the traffic conditions or the general safety implications of the paper round. The court further stated that the newsagents should have planned and prepared an order of delivery that effectively minimised the crossing of the road.

It should be noted that, in circumstances where there has been a significant change in the working environment or practices which relate to the risk assessment, s 19(3) of the 2005 Act stipulates that the assessment should be reviewed.

## Safety Statement

The Safety Statement is an important feature of the 2005 Act, as it requires that every employer put in place a statement in writing setting out how the safety, health and welfare of employees is to be secured.

---

[3] Health and Safety Authority, 'Hazard and Risk' <www.hsa.ie/eng/Topics/Hazards> accessed 6 June 2016.

[4] Geoffrey Shannon, *Health and Safety Law and Practice* (Round Hall 2007) 33.

[5] *Miles (M) v Parsons* (QBD, 10 February 2000).

Section 20(1) of the 2005 Act states:

> Every employer shall prepare, or cause to be prepared, a written statement
> (to be known and referred to in this Act as a "Safety Statement"), based on
> the identification of the hazards and the risk assessment carried out under
> *section 19*, specifying the manner in which the safety, health and welfare at
> work of his or her employees shall be secured and managed.

The Safety Statement is an integral element in ensuring the safe operation
of the workplace, assisting in the identification of hazards and highlighting
the protective and preventative measures put in place for the purpose of
safeguarding all workers.

A useful example is provided by the case of *Elmontem v Nethercross Ltd t/a
Roganstown Golf and Country Club and Usai*.[6] While this case does not deal
with a Safety Statement in an agricultural situation, it does highlight the
importance of having a Safety Statement in place. In this case, the second
named defendant worked for the first named defendant and, while at
his place of employment, assaulted the plaintiff, a co-worker at the first
named defendant's business.

In evidence, it was established that the general manager of the first named
defendant was aware, prior to hiring the second named defendant, that he
had been dismissed from his previous employment for assaulting another
employee.[7]

The court held that both defendants were jointly liable for failing to provide
a safe place of work, insofar as is reasonably practicable under the 2005
Act. The court pointed out that the first named defendant, the employer,
failed to take steps to protect against the danger of another assault in circumstances where the general manager of the first named defendant knew,
or ought to have known, that there was a real risk that the second named
defendant could become violent, given that they were aware of a previous assault, and, as a consequence, that it was reasonably foreseeable that
he could be a danger to other employees.[8] In the course of his judgment,

---

[6] *Elmontem v Nethercross Ltd t/a Roganstown Golf and Country Club and Usai* [2014] IEHC 91.
[7] ibid.
[8] ibid.

Herbert J made specific reference to the lack of a Safety Statement and, in particular, stated that the employer

> ... took no care to put in place measures to prevent a recurrence of such improper conduct or behaviour on the part of [the second defendant] likely to put the safety and health of other employees at risk. There was no evidence that [the first defendant] had a safety statement or a notified policy which identified conduct or behaviour in the workplace that would not be tolerated, conduct such as verbal abuse or physical violence of, or towards, other workers. There was no evidence that [the general manager] had notified and warned [the second defendant] in writing in clear and definite terms that physical violence towards any other employee would not be tolerated and would result in his being dismissed for gross misconduct.[9]

However, it is important to understand that, where a workplace has three or fewer employees, there are less stringent requirements concerning the maintenance of an up-to-date Safety Statement. Section 20(8) of the 2005 Act provides as follows:

> It shall be sufficient compliance with this section by an employer employing 3 or less employees to observe the terms of a code of practice, if any, relating to safety statements which applies to the class of employment covering the type of work activity carried on by the employer.

Essentially, this requirement obviates the need for compliance with the requirement to maintain an up-to-date Safety Statement and, instead, allows an alternative solution by observing the Code of Practice for Preventing Injury and Occupational Ill-Health in Agriculture.

## Codes of Practice

The Code of Practice for Preventing Injury and Occupational Ill-Health in Agriculture[10] (hereafter the 'Code of Practice'), came into effect in 2006 and incorporates a Risk Assessment Document and a Safe System of Work Plan.

---

[9] ibid.

[10] Health and Safety Authority, *Code of Practice for Preventing Injury and Occupational Ill-Health in Agriculture* (2006), as provided for by s 60 of the Safety, Health and Welfare at Work Act 2005.

Consequently, it is vital that farmers familiarise themselves with the Code of Practice, which will enable them to:

1. Identify potential hazards on the farm;
2. Assess the risk of each hazard occurring; and
3. Identify the measures that can be put in place to prevent an accident or reduce its impact.

This may be achieved by:

1. Eliminating the hazard; for example, by using artificial insemination instead of keeping a stock bull; and
2. Reducing the danger; for example, by erecting hazard warning signs and providing personal protective equipment, such as gloves, goggles etc.

The Code of Practice offers practical advice on the safe use of vehicles and machinery, safety when working with livestock, slurry storage, gas safety and the safe use of chemicals on the farm. Some examples of the practical advice offered in relation to a wide range of farming activities are as follows:

1. Ensure that the power take-off (PTO) can be turned on and off correctly, and that the PTO shield (U-guard) is kept in place at all times[11];
2. Do not leave the tractor seat while the engine is running[12];
3. Carry out as many activities as possible each time animals are put through the crush, such as hoof paring, checking of identification tags, and dosing[13];
4. Dehorning young calves with suitable equipment is a safer option than asking a vet to skull a mature animal[14];
5. Park on level ground where possible. Leave the vehicle in gear. If on a slope, use the reverse gear if facing downhill and low forward gear if facing uphill[15];
6. All bulls should be ringed when 10 months old, and the ring should be regularly examined[16];

---

[11] ibid 19.
[12] ibid.
[13] ibid 28.
[14] ibid.
[15] ibid 20.
[16] ibid 29.

7. When separating a bull from the herd, it is essential to have two adults on hand. This task is best accomplished using good cattle-handling facilities[17];

8. A person training young horses should have the necessary training and riding skills. Ensure that all tack is in safe condition. Wear approved riding gear, including skull cap, leather gloves and a back protector.[18]

The Safety Statement and Risk Assessment Document should be brought to the attention of all people who work on the farm. It should be noted that the common law duty of care owed by an employer to an employee will vary according to the employee's age, mental and physical capacity, and experience.

The Risk Assessment Document is a minimum legal requirement on all farms. In this document, a commitment is made to provide a safe place of work, to use safe systems of work, and, for all those using machinery, to provide the protective equipment, information, training and supervision necessary to minimise risk.

## Training

The 2005 Act places a strong emphasis on the requirement to provide training to employees. Section 10 of the 2005 Act obliges an employer to ensure that "employees receive, during time off from their work, where appropriate, and without loss of remuneration, adequate safety, health and welfare training, including, in particular, information and instructions relating to the specific task to be performed by the employee and the measures to be taken in an emergency" and training shall be provided to employees "on recruitment, in the event of the transfer of an employee or change of task assigned to an employee, on the introduction of new work equipment, systems of work or changes in existing work equipment or systems of work and on the introduction of new technology".

The Code of Practice states that training may be formal or informal. A person may undertake an appropriate health and safety course, or be shown the correct way of doing a job. A farmer should ensure that every person

---

[17] ibid.

[18] ibid 33.

on his or her farm has all the information and skills necessary to secure safety and health.

The Qualifications (Education and Training) Act 1999 established the National Qualifications Authority of Ireland. Teagasc, which was established in 1988, is a national body that provides training, amongst other services, to the agricultural sector. It offers further education and training courses in agriculture[19] and, in particular, courses on the Farm Safety Code of Practice.[20]

Basic training in first aid is extremely important in farming. Many organisations, such as St John Ambulance[21] and Irish Red Cross,[22] offer certified first-aid courses, which cover common injuries sustained in the workplace and elsewhere.

Children must be at least 14 years old, have attended a formal training course run by a competent training provider, and be under the supervision of a responsible adult before they are allowed to drive a tractor, and they must fully understand the purpose of all the controls and the consequences of improper use.[23] Courses are available to improve the safety skills of 14 to 16-year-olds in relation to driving a tractor.[24] Young adults over 16 years of age must, at a minimum, hold a learner permit before they can drive in a public place.

---

[19] Details of available courses can be found on the Teagasc website <www.teagasc.ie> or at any Teagasc office.

[20] Health and Safety Authority, *Farm Safety Code of Practice* (2006) 8 <www.hsa.ie/eng/Publications_and_Forms/Publications/Agriculture_and_Forestry/Code_of_Practice_-_Risk_Assessments.pdf> accessed 6 June 2016.

[21] St John Ambulance Ireland, 'Contact Us' <www.stjohn.ie/contact-us/> or phone (01) 668 8077.

[22] Irish Red Cross, email <courses@redcross.ie> or phone (01) 642 4679 / 1890 502 502.

[23] Health and Safety Authority, *Code of Practice on Preventing Accidents to Children and Young Persons in Agriculture* (2010) 8, as provided for by s 60 of the Safety, Health and Welfare at Work Act 2005 <www.hsa.ie/eng/Publications_and_Forms/Publications/Codes_of_Practice/Code_of_Practice_on_Preventing_Accidents_to_Children_and_Young_Persons_in_Agriculture.pdf> accessed 6 June 2016.

[24] FRS Training, 'Contact Us' <www.frstraining.com/contact.asp> or phone 1890 201 000.

The Code of Practice on Preventing Accidents to Children and Young Persons in Agriculture[25] states that

> … minors need training most when they start work to raise their capabilities and competence to a level where they can do the job safely. Minors will also need instruction and training on the hazards and risks on the farm and on the measures in place to protect their safety and health. Training should include an introduction to health and safety including first aid, fire and evacuation procedures.[26]

It also states that:

> Children under the age of 14 should be prohibited from riding on agricultural machines including agricultural trailers unless the risk assessment shows it to be safe to do so, with the following exception - Children between the ages of 7 and 16 may ride on a tractor provided the tractor is fitted with a properly designed and fitted passenger seat (with seat belts) inside a safety cab or frame.[27]

Health and safety law places a legal duty on employers to ensure the safety, health and welfare at work of their employees.

## Safe Place of Work

The 2005 Act states that an employer must provide a safe place of work.[28] Section 8(2)(c) of the 2005 Act states that an employer's duty extends in particular, as regards the place of work, to ensuring as far as is reasonably practicable:

(a) the design, provision and maintenance of it in a condition that is safe and without risk to health;

(b) the design, provision and maintenance of a safe means of access to and egress from it; and

(c) the design, provision and maintenance of plant and machinery or any other articles that are safe and without risk to health…

---

[25] Health and Safety Authority, *Code of Practice on Preventing Accidents to Children and Young Persons in Agriculture* (2010).

[26] ibid 8.

[27] ibid 9.

[28] s 8(2)(c) of the 2005 Act.

This applies to all areas of the farm. Proper safeguards, such as fencing a slurry pit or demolishing unstable structures, should be put in place to prevent injuries.

## Safe Use of Work Equipment

It is necessary for any farm business to ensure that work equipment is suitable for its purpose and is safe having regard to health and safety regulations.

The Safety, Health and Welfare at Work (General Application) Regulations 2007[29] (hereafter 'the 2007 Regulations') specifically deal with work equipment and machinery.

In considering the 2007 Regulations in terms of use of work equipment, a useful starting point is the definition of "work equipment" defined in regulation 2(1) of the 2007 Regulations as "any machinery, appliance, apparatus, tool or installation for use at work".

Regulation 27 of the 2007 Regulations further states that the "selection, installation and use of work equipment" relates to "any activity involving work equipment, including starting or stopping the equipment, its use, transport, repair, modification, maintenance and servicing and cleaning".

The foregoing definition is broad enough to encompass any activity and, thus, employers must bear this in mind in all work operations on the farm.

## Suitable Equipment

In the proper management of any farm business, safety must be incorporated at all levels. This includes ensuring that appropriate equipment is chosen for a task, having regard to the specific working conditions, characteristics and hazards that may be present in the place of work. Regulation 28(c) of the 2007 Regulations states that the employer must ensure that

> ...the necessary measures are taken so that the work equipment is installed and located and is suitable for the work to be carried out, or is properly adapted for that purpose, and may be used by employees without risk to their safety and health.

---

[29] Safety, Health and Welfare at Work (General Application) Regulations 2007, SI No 299 of 2007.

It is always advisable to have proper safeguards in place when using machinery, such as fitting a guard to a PTO shaft and providing helmets, goggles, protective gloves and earmuffs for use by workers.

## Information

It is vitally important for farm workers to be provided with adequate information in relation to the operation of equipment, and that all appropriate precautions should be taken. Regulation 29 of the 2007 Regulations specifically deals with this element and requires that:

(a) The necessary measures are taken so that employees have at their disposal adequate information and, where appropriate, written instructions on the work equipment, containing at least adequate safety and health information concerning:
   (i) the conditions of use of work equipment,
   (ii) foreseeable abnormal situations, and
   (iii) the conclusions to be drawn from experience, where appropriate, in using such work equipment, and
(b) Employees are made aware of safety and health risks relevant to them associated with work equipment located at or near their workstation or to any changes relating to that work equipment, even if they do not use the equipment.

This could be achieved by erecting warning notices near dangerous equipment, slurry pits, or other hazards, such as overhead power lines.

## Safe Employees

As noted above, an employer has a duty to ensure that all employees are properly trained.

Every person on a farm should have the requisite information and skills to secure health and safety. To this end, Teagasc and Agricultural Consultants provide short safety courses for farmers, at venues across the country.

The 2007 Regulations, specifically Part 6, require farmers to identify work that is suitable for children and work that is unsuitable, such as work that is beyond the physical or psychological capacity of the child or young person concerned, or work that involves harmful exposure to radiation.

Regulation 145 states the following:

> An employer shall not employ a child or young person at work where a risk assessment reveals that the work— (a) is beyond the physical or psychological capacity of the child or young person concerned, (b) involves harmful exposure to agents which are toxic, carcinogenic, cause heritable genetic damage, or harm to the unborn child or which in any other way chronically affects human health, (c) involves harmful exposure to radiation, (d) involves the risk of accidents which it may be assumed cannot be recognised or avoided by a child or young person owing to insufficient attention to safety or lack of experience or training, or (e) which presents a risk to health from exposure to extreme heat or cold or to noise or vibration.

## Insurance

A farmer should ensure that he or she has in place appropriate employers' and public liability insurance, which will provide him or her with cover for any legal liability he or she may attract, arising from an accidental bodily injury sustained by an employee or others and attributable, in whole or in part, to negligence on the part of the farm business.

## Duty to Report an Accident

When an accident does happen, it must be reported to the Health and Safety Authority. Regulation 59 of the Safety, Health and Welfare at Work (General Application) Regulations 1993[30] lists the circumstances in which an accident or incident is reportable to the Health and Safety Authority. These are as follows:

- Where there is a dangerous occurrence;
- Where the death of a worker occurs;
- Where there is an injury to an employee, after which he or she cannot perform his or her work for more than three days; and
- Where there is an injury to a visitor or member of the public for which medical treatment is required.

The Health and Safety Authority must also be notified of specified dangerous occurrences, for example, fires, explosions and chemical spillages.[31]

---

[30] Safety, Health and Welfare at Work (General Application) Regulations 1993, SI No 44 of 1993.
[31] Safety, Health and Welfare at Work Act 2005, s 2(1).

If a dangerous situation arises, work should stop immediately until the hazard or danger is controlled.

In the event of a fatal accident, the employer is obliged to immediately report the accident to the Health and Safety Authority.[32] The Gardaí should also be notified of all workplace accidents resulting in death. An injury may be reported online, using the "Report an Injury Online" facility on the Health and Safety Authority homepage and on several other pages of the Health and Safety Authority website. Accidents are also reportable by post, using an IR1 Form.[33]

## Duty to Inform

It is incumbent upon all employers to inform their employees on matters relating to employee health and safety.[34] Section 9(1)(b) of the 2005 Act stipulates that the information provided to employees should include information on:

(i)  the hazards to safety, health and welfare at work and the risks identified by the risk assessment;

(ii)  the protective and preventive measures to be taken concerning safety, health and welfare at work under the relevant statutory provisions in respect of the place of work and each specific task to be performed at the place of work; and

(iii)  the names of persons designated under s 11 [i.e. persons to contact in an emergency situation] and of safety representatives selected under s 25 [i.e. a person selected and appointed from amongst their number at their place of work], if any.

It is important to ensure that, in providing information of this nature to employees, it is done in a manner and in a language that is reasonably likely to be understood by them.

---

[32] Safety, Health and Welfare at Work (General Application) Regulations 1993, SI 44/1993, reg 59.

[33] An IR1 Form can be obtained from the Publications Section of the Health and Safety Authority online at <www.hsa.ie/eng/Publications_and_Forms/Forms/> or by telephoning 1890 289 389.

[34] Safety, Health and Welfare at Work Act 2005, s 9.

The Safety Statement[35] and Risk Assessment Document should be brought to the attention of all people who work on the farm and people who visit the farm in the course of their work, such as veterinarians and silage contractors. All people who work on the farm, including family members, must be made aware of the dangers on the farm. Dangers must also be brought to the attention of regular, casual and relief workers, contractors, and people supplying goods and services to the farm. People who have grown up on, and worked on farms, will be more than familiar with the dangers and risks inherent in farming, but one cannot assume that visitors to the farm are similarly aware.

## Criminal Prosecution

An inspector from the Health and Safety Authority may examine the Safety Statement or the Risk Assessment Document,[36] and may assess the implementation of the safety and health measures on the farm.[37]

An inspector has the authority to issue an improvement notice, pursuant to s 66(1) of the 2005 Act. This power permits the issuance of an improvement notice in circumstances where there is a breach of health and safety law that requires to be addressed. An improvement notice is a written notice served by the Health and Safety Authority on the person who has, or may reasonably be presumed to have, control over the work activity concerned. It sets out details of the contravention and directs the person to remedy the contravention by a date specified in the notice. It is an offence to contravene an improvement notice.[38]

Part 7 of the 2005 Act specifically deals with the offences and penalties associated with breaches of the 2005 Act. A number of the offences arise from failure to discharge duties under the Act. For example, s 77(2) (a) of the 2005 Act criminalises:

- Failure to discharge a duty by employers[39]; and
- Failure to discharge certain protective and preventative measures.[40]

---

[35] Safety, Health and Welfare at Work Act 2005, s 20(3).
[36] The power of an inspector to inspect information is provided for in the Safety, Health and Welfare at Work Act 2005, s 64(1)(d).
[37] Safety, Health and Welfare at Work Act 2005, s 64(1)(a).
[38] Safety, Health and Welfare at Work Act 2005, s 77(2)(k).
[39] Safety, Health and Welfare at Work Act 2005, pt 2, ch 1.
[40] Safety, Health and Welfare at Work Act 2005, s 18.

On summary conviction, a person can be fined up to €5,000 and/or be sentenced to 12 months' imprisonment.[41] On indictment (by judge and jury), a convicted person may face a fine of up to €3,000,000 and/or may be sentenced to 2 years' imprisonment.[42]

In a 2014 case taken by the Health and Safety Authority, an employer was successfully prosecuted when his employee was fatally electrocuted while picking up a damaged cable.[43] The defendant pleaded guilty to the following contraventions of health and safety law:

• Allowing the use of portable equipment in damp and confined locations[44];
• Failing to identify hazards, including the failure to assess the risks presented by those hazards, and failing to include this within a written assessment[45]; and
• Failing to prepare a written Safety Statement identifying the hazards and specifying the manner in which the safety, health and welfare at work of his employees should be secured and managed.[46]

Upon conviction, the court imposed a 12 month suspended sentence.

It should be noted that any failure to observe the relevant codes of practice may be admissible as evidence in criminal proceedings. Alternatively, where the codes of practice were followed and an accident occurred despite the precautions taken, the codes of practice may be relied upon by the farmer in defending criminal proceedings.

---

[41] Safety, Health and Welfare at Work Act 2005, s 78(2)(i), as amended by Chemicals (Amendment) Act 2010, s 12(f).
[42] Safety, Health and Welfare at Work Act 2005, s 78(2)(ii).
[43] Health and Safety Authority, Prosecutions 2014 – *Paul Dyer* <www.hsa.ie/eng/Topics/enforcement/Prosecutions/Prosecutions_2014/#dyer> accessed 6 June 2016.
[44] As set out in the Safety, Health and Welfare at Work Act 2005, s 77(2)(c), contrary to the Safety, Health and Welfare at Work (General Application) Regulations 2007, SI 299/2007, reg 81(4)(a)(iii).
[45] As set out in the Safety, Health and Welfare at Work Act 2005, s 77(2)(a), contrary to s 19(1) of the same Act.
[46] As set out in the Safety, Health and Welfare at Work Act 2005, s 77 (2)(a), contrary to s 20(1) of the same Act.

The best way to protect against potential personal injury claims and/ or criminal proceedings is to adhere to health and safety best practice. By doing so, one will not only reduce the risk of injury occurring, and the extent of any such injury, but will also reduce exposure to liability.

## Practical Suggestions on Farm Safety

Having set out the legal requirements and the potential repercussions for breach of health and safety law, it is appropriate to make some suggestions that may help to maintain farm safety:

- Always tell someone where you will be and for how long;
- Ensure your mobile phone is fully charged and with you at all times;
- Ensure that cattle crushes, cattle-handling units and holding pens are properly maintained;
- Bulls should have a ring and trailing chain attached;
- Always handle animals with caution, using appropriate handling facilities;
- Ensure that all animal handlers are competent and are provided with protective clothing and equipment for use in the course of their work;
- Provide staff with suitable breathing apparatus and ensure that it is worn. This is particularly important for those working with slurry pits, as these produce dangerous gases such as hydrogen sulphide and ammonia;
- While agitating slurry, it is very important to maintain high levels of ventilation. When planning, choose a windy day, evacuate all people and livestock from sheds, and open all doors and outlets;
- Always ensure that the PTO and the PTO shaft are properly covered, and that you disengage the PTO before you dismount the tractor;
- Allow only competent persons to drive tractors. Remember that children must be at least 14 years old, have received training, and be under the supervision of a responsible adult before they are allowed to drive a tractor. They must be 16 years of age and hold at least a learner permit before they can drive in a public place;[47]
- Provide training to ensure the safe operation of tractors and machinery and the safe completion of tasks;
- Check equipment and machinery before use;
- Take particular care when animals are initially released from buildings after being housed for a period of time;
- Ensure that safeguards are understood by all workers;

---

[47] Health and Safety Authority, *Code of Practice on Preventing Accidents to Children and Young Persons in Agriculture* (2010) 8.

- Do not erect fencing alongside overhead power lines;
- Do not rush jobs where safety might be put at risk. This is particularly important in potentially hazardous situations, such as on muddy ground, on ladders etc.;
- Use ladders properly. Ladders must always be solid and properly secured; and
- Plan work so as to ensure that it can be done safely.

## Conclusion

Identifying hazards and taking preventive and remedial action, combined with adopting safe behaviour, are proven ways of reducing the risk of farm accidents. Safety on the farm is of primary concern, something that is reflected in the onerous duties imposed on the farm owner by legislation and by common law.

Considering the risks to safety, health and welfare inherent in the farming enterprise, farmers should always be aware of the desirability, if not the necessity, of having executed a valid Will and an Enduring Power of Attorney.

# Index